Material Appearance Modeling: A Data-Coherent Approach

Yue Dong · Stephen Lin · Baining Guo

Material Appearance Modeling: A Data-Coherent Approach

Springer

Yue Dong
Stephen Lin
Baining Guo
Microsoft Research Asia
Beijing, China

ISBN 978-3-642-35776-3 ISBN 978-3-642-35777-0 (eBook)
DOI 10.1007/978-3-642-35777-0
Springer Heidelberg New York Dordrecht London

Library of Congress Control Number: 2013938953

ACM Computing Classification (1998): I.3

Printed on acid-free paper

Springer is part of Springer Science+Business Media (www.springer.com)

Preface

One of the most prominent goals of computer graphics is to generate images that look as real as photographs. Realistic computer graphics imagery has however proven to be quite challenging to produce, since the appearance of materials arises from complicated physical processes that are difficult to analytically model and simulate, and image-based modeling of real material samples is often impractical due to the high-dimensional space of appearance data that needs to be acquired.

This book presents a general framework based on the inherent coherency in the appearance data of materials to make image-based appearance modeling more tractable. We observe that this coherence manifests itself as low-dimensional structure in the appearance data, and by identifying this structure we can take advantage of it to simplify the major processes in the appearance modeling pipeline. This framework consists of two key components, namely the coherence structure and the accompanying reconstruction method to fully recover the low-dimensional appearance data from sparse measurements. Our investigation of appearance coherency has led to three major forms of low-dimensional coherence structure and three types of coherency-based reconstruction upon which our framework is built.

This coherence-based approach can be comprehensively applied to all the major elements of image-based appearance modeling, from data acquisition of real material samples to user-assisted modeling from a photograph, from synthesis of volumes to editing of material properties, and from efficient rendering algorithms to physical fabrication of objects. In this book we present several techniques built on this coherency framework to handle various appearance modeling tasks both for surface reflections and subsurface scattering, the two primary physical components that generate material appearance. We believe that coherency-based appearance modeling will make it easier and more feasible for practitioners to bring computer graphics imagery to life.

Beijing, China

Yue Dong
Stephen Lin
Baining Guo

Contents

Chapter 1
Introduction

It has long been a goal of computer graphics to synthesize imagery indistinguishable in appearance from the real world. With high realism in computer graphics, created objects and scenes can come to life, providing viewers with compelling visual experiences in a variety of media, including simulators, movies and video games. A high level of realism however has been challenging to achieve, due to complex factors that determine the appearance of objects and scenes.

In images, the appearance of an object is formed from two components. One is shape, for which there exists various methods for accurate 3D measurement, including systems such as stereo cameras and laser scanners. The other is reflectance, which describes the way an object's materials appear under different viewing and illumination conditions. Different materials can have vastly different reflectance properties, depending on how they interact with light. Some materials, such as wax, are characterized by light penetration and extensive scattering within their volumes, which leads to a soft and smooth appearance from the emergent radiance. Others such as polished metals have a relatively hard appearance because of highly directional mirror-like reflections of light off the material surface. Yet others exhibit different visual effects, such as the retro-reflection of street signs where the illumination of car headlights is largely reflected back in the direction from which it came, or the transparency of apple juice, through which light passes with little interaction at all. Reflectance is the source of a material's intrinsic visual appearance, and modeling of this phenomena is the focus of this book.

For realistic modeling of appearance, detailed reflectance data is essential, as illustrated in Fig. 1.1. Often only slight differences in reflectance distinguish the appearance of one material from another, so even subtle reflectance features need to be accounted for, and done so with high accuracy, to make a material look convincing. The reflectance of a material encompasses not only the appearance of a single point, but also the spatial variations over the surface and within the material volume. These spatial variations may simply be changes in color, such as on a magazine cover, or they may include complete changes in optical properties, such as glitter in nail polish. The need for highly detailed appearance models has been magnified by recent increases in image display resolution, from VGA to XVGA, and

Y. Dong et al., *Material Appearance Modeling: A Data-Coherent Approach*,
DOI 10.1007/978-3-642-35777-0_1,

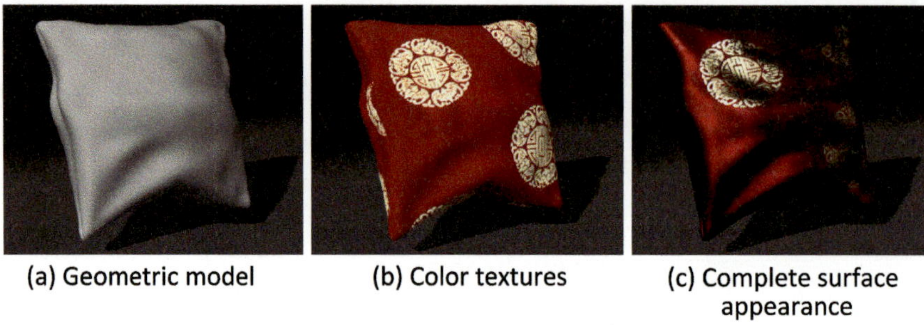

Fig. 1.1 Reflectance detail in appearance modeling. For this example of a silk pillow, just a geometric model without further appearance information conveys only its basic shape and diffuse shading. Adding color textures to the geometry brings more realism to the pillow, but it still lacks the look and feel of silk. With a more comprehensive model of surface appearance, the pillow exhibits the natural reflectance properties of silk

then to full HD (high definition). With higher resolutions come greater visibility of fine-scale surface features and appearance characteristics, making high fidelity appearance modeling even more essential for rendered objects and scenes to appear real.

Detailed modeling of material appearance, however, is challenging because of the numerous material and physical factors on which it depends. The complex interactions of light and material that give rise to appearance may span a variety of reflectance mechanisms, and how they unfold depends upon the optical properties of the material as well as the physical nature of the interactions themselves. Simple analytical models have been developed for the physical processes that yield material appearance, but they generally provide only a rough approximation of the observed behavior and lack the power to preserve subtleties that characterize a material. To accurately reproduce material appearance in computer graphics imagery, detailed appearance properties need to be directly and precisely derived from real material samples.

Modeling material appearance from a real sample is unfortunately a painstaking task. This is because the appearance of a material depends not only on the intrinsic optical properties of the material itself, but also on various extrinsic factors such as the shape of its volume, lighting conditions and viewpoint. Appearance variations over the surface and within the 3D volume, due to different constituent elements with spatially varying distributions, need to be accounted for and modeled as well. All of these variables influence in different ways how a material looks, and it is hard in practice to capture and model the tremendous amount of data on the different appearances that a material can take. As a result, computer graphics practitioners typically avoid appearance modeling from real samples, and instead rely on artistic skill to generate graphics content. While excellent renderings have been produced in this manner, it is rare for such imagery to appear just like the real thing.

In this book, we present a general framework for modeling and rendering the appearance of materials from real images. This framework is based on the coherent structure that naturally exists in some form in appearance data, which we exploit to simplify the appearance modeling problem. Before introducing the underlying philosophy that guides this work, we first review in Sect. 1.1 some basic background on appearance modeling that is needed for understanding the contents of this book. Readers with prior knowledge of this material may wish to skip forward to Sect. 1.2 where we describe our approach to appearance modeling. The chapter concludes in Sect. 1.3 with an overview of the book.

1.1 Background

Our review of background knowledge begins with basic principles of light interaction with materials and how they contribute to object appearance. A taxonomy of the different types of interaction models, referred to as reflectance functions, is then presented, with specific attention to the commonly used representations that will be focused on in this book. This is followed by a brief description of the general pipeline for appearance modeling and rendering, which provides further context for the methods we will present.

1.1.1 Fundamentals of Light Interaction with Materials

The appearance of a material or object arises from how it scatters light that arrives from the surrounding environment. The scattering of light at a given point in a material is determined by its geometric structure and optical properties, and is referred to as reflectance.

Reflectance depends on various forms of physical interaction between material and light. When a light ray reaches a surface, some portion of it may be reflected at the air-material interface, which is referred to as specular reflection, while the rest of the light penetrates the surface where it may undergo further interaction with the material. This component of light, when eventually emitted out of the material, is called diffuse reflection.

The amount of incident light that reflects diffusely or specularly is determined by the Fresnel reflection formulas derived from Maxwell's equations for electromagnetic waves. Specifically, the ratio of specularly reflected light I_r to the incoming lighting I_i is given by the following equation:

$$\frac{I_r}{I_i} = \frac{1}{2}\left[\left(\frac{n_a \cos\theta_i - n_m \cos\theta_t}{n_a \cos\theta_i + n_m \cos\theta_t}\right)^2 + \left(\frac{n_a \cos\theta_t - n_m \cos\theta_i}{n_a \cos\theta_t + n_m \cos\theta_i}\right)\right] \tag{1.1}$$

where n_a and n_m denote the refractive index of air and the material, and θ_i and θ_t are the reflection and refraction angles modeled by Snell's law:

$$\frac{\sin\theta_i}{\sin\theta_t} = \frac{n_a}{n_m}. \tag{1.2}$$

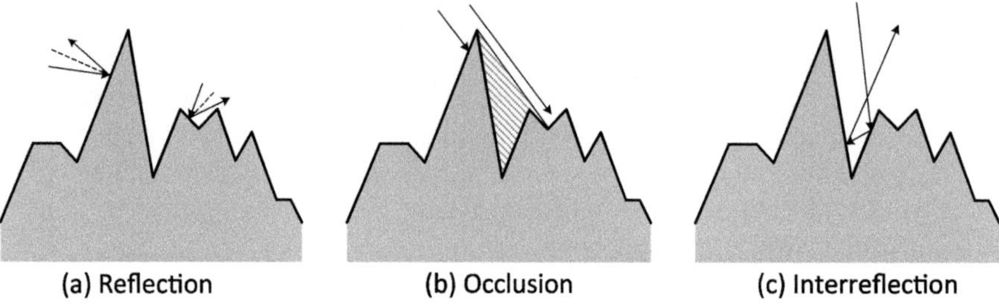

Fig. 1.2 Different microfacet interactions at a microscopic scale

The relative amounts of specular and diffuse reflection can vary significantly among different materials, particularly between metals such as copper and dielectrics (non-conductors) such as glass, and is a major factor in material appearance.

Light that specularly reflects may encounter further interaction with the surface in the form of additional specular reflections and surface penetrations. Multiple reflections from a surface are referred to as interreflections, which can occur not only for specular reflections but for diffuse reflections as well. Even for an apparently convex object, interreflections may occur within micro-scale surface concavities that are a characteristic of many rough materials.

At a micro-scale level, a material surface is composed of microscopic planar facets, or *microfacets*, from which specular reflections are considered to follow the mirror reflection law [1], where the direction of incoming light and outgoing reflected light have equal and opposite angles with respect to the microfacet surface normal. At the macro-level at which we view an object, the reflectance is the sum of light interactions among the microfacets. Several microfacet interactions are illustrated in Fig. 1.2, which shows different reflection directions and energy due to different microfacet normal directions. Microfacets may mask and cast shadows onto each other, in addition to producing interreflections of light. What we see as surface reflectance is an aggregation of all these effects mixed together in a local region.

For light that penetrates into the object volume, a significant amount of interaction with the material medium generally occurs, and is termed as subsurface scattering. In subsurface scattering, light strikes particles within the material and disperses in various directions according to a scattering distribution function. The dispersed rays subsequently interact with other particles in the medium, and eventually the light emerges from the object as diffuse reflection. This diffuse component may leave the object from points other than the surface point at which it entered the material volume, and for translucent or transparent materials, some or all of the light may emerge from opposite surfaces of the object without interacting with the material, in a process referred to as light transmission.

Based on the number of scattering events for a light ray beneath the surface, the subsurface scattering can be further classified into single scattering or multiple scattering. In single scattering, only one interaction of light with the material occurs within the object. This interaction determines the direction of the light path, and the material properties along the path determine the amount of light attenuation due to absorption by the material. In multiple scattering, light interacts more than once in the material volume before exiting through the object surface. Due to its relative complexity, the effects of multiple scattering are harder to compute.

Since the appearance from subsurface scattering is an integration of large number of scattered light paths, statistical models are often applied. At an interaction point, the probability of its scattering in a given direction can be modeled by a phase function $p(\omega, \omega')$. Based on the phase function, the light transport process for subsurface scattering can be formulated as the radiative transport equation (RTE) [2]:

$$\omega \cdot \nabla \phi_d(x, \omega) + \sigma_t \phi_d(x, \omega) = \frac{\sigma_s}{4\pi} \int_{4\pi} p(\omega, \omega') \phi_d(x, \omega) \mathrm{d}\omega' + \phi_i(x, \omega) \tag{1.3}$$

where the extinction coefficient σ_t and scattering coefficient σ_s are optical properties of the material. ϕ_i is the reduced incident intensity that measures the distribution of incoming light within the object, while the distribution of scattered light is represented by the diffuse intensity ϕ_d. The RTE is a differential equation that considers the distributions of light at all spatial positions and angular directions, and in its general form the RTE does not have an analytical solution. The substantial computation required to solve the RTE directly necessitates a simplified representation for subsurface scattering effects for efficient modeling of subsurface scattering appearance in computer graphics.

For many objects and materials, the optical properties and surface structure that determine the scattering of light are not uniform over a surface or throughout a volume. The spatial and volumetric variations of reflectance and surface geometry, such as the grain pattern in wood and the roughness of cement, are commonly referred to as texture. The detailed material features provided by textures can significantly enrich the appearance of an object. In this book, we primarily consider textures that are statistical in nature, as these forms of textures frequently occur in both natural and man-made scenes, and facilitate efficient use of computational resources. In particular, we take an approach to texturing based on image samples, which can take advantage of the inherent realism of actual images.

1.1.2 Taxonomy of Light Scattering Functions

Rather than simulate intricate and computationally expensive low-level scattering interactions, a vast majority of rendering algorithms employ an abstraction of these physical processes in the form of light scattering functions that relate incoming light to outgoing light from a surface. A scattering function can be measured for a given object or precomputed from a given scattering model, and provides all the information necessary to generate a material's appearance in a given illumination environment. Convincing appearance can be obtained with this simplification, with a significant reduction in rendering costs.

Scattering functions may be represented in different forms. Most basically, light scattering physically measured from objects is listed in a table, whose entries enumerate a range of lighting and viewing conditions. More compactly, scattering functions have been represented in terms of basis functions such as spherical harmonics, wavelets, and Zernike polynomials. Most typically, scattering is modeled by parametric functions, whose simplicity allows for rapid evaluation.

Because of differences in optical and geometric properties among various materials, varying degrees of approximation accuracy are achieved by different parametric scattering functions for different objects. For instance, the Lambertian reflectance function, in which the intensity of reflected light towards all directions is modeled as being proportional to the inner product of the light direction and surface normal, is effective in modeling the strongly diffuse light scattering of matte materials, but is inadequate for representing the highly directional scattering of light by metallic objects. Due to the diversity of material properties, different scattering functions have been proposed for different target materials. For many materials, particularly organic substances such as human skin and tree bark, the scattering properties are complex and not entirely understood, and consequently much room exists for further development of parametric scattering functions.

A comprehensive model of scattering can be described by a 12D function parameterized by the surface location (x, y), light direction (θ, ϕ), time t and wavelength λ of light incident on a surface and outgoing from the surface: $(x, y, \theta, \phi, \lambda, t)_{in} \rightarrow (x, y, \theta, \phi, \lambda, t)_{out}$. The amount of light transmitted with respect to these twelve parameters defines a model for reproducing the appearance of a material. However, a 12D function is infeasible both to measure, store or process. Because of this, computer graphics applications utilize low-order approximations that disregard certain parameters.

The most commonly-used reductions of the 12D general scattering function are organized in Fig. 1.3. A few simplifications to the general function are employed almost universally in rendering methods. These include the assumption that scattering properties do not change over time and reflections occur instantaneously, which removes the dependence on time. It is also assumed that scattering is wavelength independent or discretized into red, green and blue bands such that the outgoing light in a wavelength band results from scattering of only this band of incoming light. Disregarding wavelength in addition to time results in an 8D function, commonly called the bidirectional scattering-surface reflectance distribution function (BSSRDF). The BSSRDF is a significant appearance representation in computer graphics, since it fully accounts for the optical features of heterogeneous translucent materials as well as opaque materials with spatial variations in appearance.

Different simplifications of the 8D function have been utilized, most commonly that light entering a material exits from the same point. This assumption disregards light transport due to internal light scattering in the material. With $(x, y)_{in} = (x, y)_{out}$, we are left with a 6D function that is referred to either as a bidirectional texture function (BTF) or a spatially-varying bidirectional reflectance distribution function (SVBRDF). Although BTFs and SVBRDFs essentially represent the same scattering function, a difference in emphasis is placed in the scattering process. For

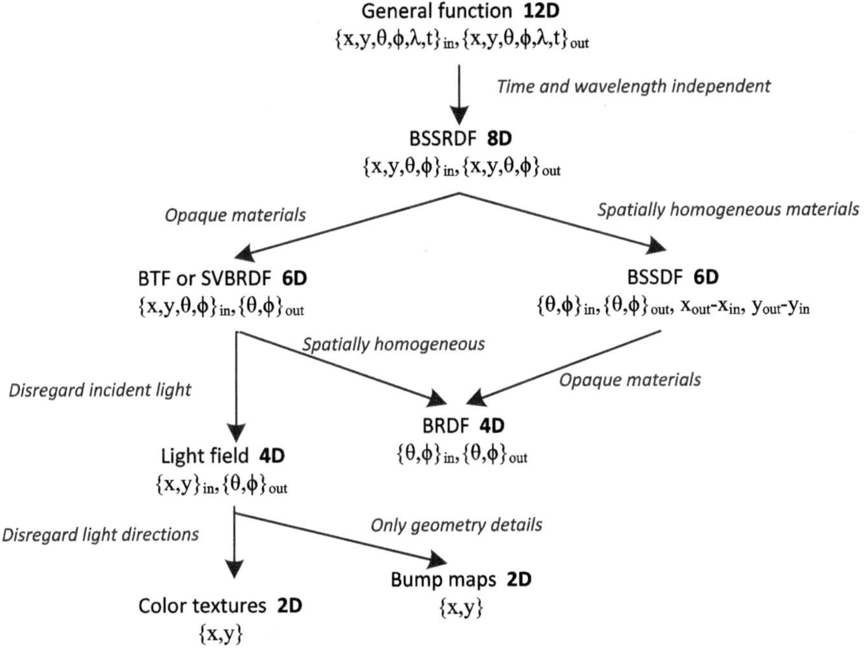

Fig. 1.3 Taxonomy of reflectance functions derived as reductions of the 12D general scattering function

a BTF, changes in scattering with respect to position (x, y) are attributed mainly to 3D surface geometry and the shadowing, masking and interreflections that they produce. On the other hand, the spatial dependence of an SVBRDF is focused primarily on variations in the optical properties of a surface.

Another reduction of the 8D function ignores the effect of absolute position on scattering. This 6D function, referred to as the bidirectional subsurface scattering distribution function (BSSDF) depends only upon relative surface positions of incoming and outgoing light $(x_{out} - x_{in}, y_{out} - y_{in})$, such that scattering characteristics do not vary over a surface. Accounting for light transport within a material is particularly important for translucent objects such as milk, human skin, and marble, for which subsurface scattering is a significant component of their overall appearance.

A 4D bidirectional reflectance distribution function (BRDF) can be considered as a BSSDF without internal light transport, or a BTF or SVBRDF that does not vary spatially. It depends only on incident and outgoing light directions, and is the most common form of scattering function used in computer graphics. BRDFs may be further simplified, for example, to consider relative elevation angles $\phi_{out} - \phi_{in}$ instead of absolute angles, or to measure reflections only on the incident plane defined by the incident light ray and its projection onto the surface.

From the 6D BTF or SVBRDF function, another simplification to 4D light fields and related structures disregards the direction of incident light and is usually employed in conjunction with image-based representations of object appearance. By further excluding the dependence on viewing direction, we are left with a 2D texture map or bump map, which records spatial variations of surface color or surface normal orientation, respectively. These 2D functions do not explicitly represent light scattering, but instead provide appearance attributes that are typically used in conjunction with BRDFs in rendering.

In practice, simpler lower-dimensional scattering functions have been favored for their greater computational efficiency, even with some noticeable reduction in accuracy. However, recent increases in computation power have led to considerable interest in more detailed modeling and rendering of texture and appearance. With this burgeoning attention, much effort has recently been focused on developing more accurate characterizations of light scattering processes and efficiently incorporating these more complex scattering features into rendering techniques to elevate the reality of computer graphics. In this book, we focus primarily on the BSSRDF and SVBRDF, since they fully represent a broad range of real-world materials ranging from heterogeneous translucent volumes to opaque surfaces with rich spatial and angular reflectance details.

1.1.3 Modeling and Rendering Pipeline of Material Appearance

The appearance data of materials in computer graphics flows through a modeling and rendering pipeline that consists of various processing components addressed in this book. The different pipeline components are briefly described in the following.

Realistic material modeling often begins with an *appearance acquisition* stage. In this stage, direct measurements are recorded of how light is reflected from or transported within a given material sample. Typically this involves sampling of all visible points on the object surface and numerous viewing and lighting angles. Measuring data from real materials is an important step towards high fidelity appearance, but full sampling of high dimensional reflectance functions requires a tremendous amount of data storage. Furthermore, capturing processes tend to be long and tedious. While some recently proposed acquisition methods recover reflectance functions of certain forms without full sampling, efficient capture of high-quality appearance data remains a challenging task.

An alternative to appearance acquisition is the use of *appearance modeling* tools, with which high quality appearance data can be produced from very little image data with the help of user interaction. This interaction generally requires the user to provide information about surface points in an image, such as surface normal orientations and reflectance model parameters. From just a small amount of appearance data obtained through either acquisition or modeling, *appearance synthesis* algorithms can be used to generate additional novel appearance data with similar characteristics. Modeling and synthesis, though producing appearance data that is just a perceptual match to real materials, are generally more time efficient than appearance acquisition, and are thus important components in the general appearance modeling and rendering pipeline. Data obtained through acquisition, modeling and/or synthesis may also be processed by *appearance editing*, to modify the appearance data to suit the user's requirements or preferences. Editing is of particular importance when one wants to produce an appearance that does not match a material available for appearance acquisition, or if one wishes to change the visual features of an existing material for artistic purposes.

After obtaining the appearance data, the appearance pipeline ends with a process of *appearance rendering* of the material as objects and surfaces. Typically, objects are rendered in a display system such as a computer or television monitor. Alternatively, an object could be fabricated from physical materials such as with a 3D printer. The goal of *appearance fabrication* is to automatically produce materials with a desired material appearance from a limited number of manufacturing base materials. Appearance fabrication is a relatively new concept in the computer graphics field, and it closes the loop of the appearance pipeline by bringing the acquired material model back to the physical world. Within this book, all parts of the appearance pipeline will be discussed with respect to the central theme of appearance coherency.

1.2 Data Coherence for Appearance Modeling

The different appearances of a real-world material under different lighting and viewing conditions, though complicated and widely varying, are far from random. A material exhibits commonalities and patterns that characterize its appearance, such as the soft translucency and flowing veins in marble, or the configurations of green patina on exposed areas of weathered bronze. Aside from its distinctive aspects, a material's appearance under different viewing conditions must also exhibit some form of physical consistency, as its optical properties and volumetric composition remain unchanged. The work in this book is built upon the inherent coherency in the appearance data of real materials, and we take advantage of this property to overcome practical difficulties in appearance modeling.

1.2.1 Data Coherence

The key observation on this coherence is that it manifests itself as low-dimensional structure in the appearance data. Various forms of low-dimensional structure may potentially exist. One common type of coherency is the repetition of material attributes over a surface, as shown by the silk pillow in Fig. 1.4 where many points share the same intrinsic color, material composition and fine-scale geometry. Generally this repetition results from a limited number of material elements that comprise a material sample, and we refer to this type of coherence as *material attribute repetition*. By contrast, other kinds of repeated patterns may not be suitable for appearance

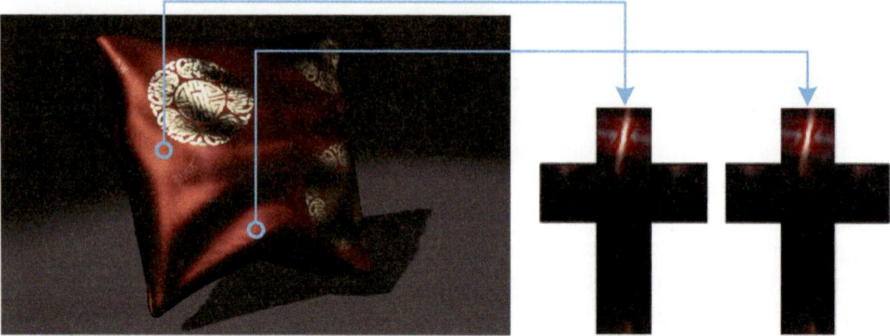

Fig. 1.4 Repetition in material reflectance. Though different points on the fabric may not appear exactly the same, they share commonalities in color, material composition and geometric thread structure that lead to strong consistencies in their reflectance and appearance properties. In addition, the color patterns in many local regions are a close match to others on the surface

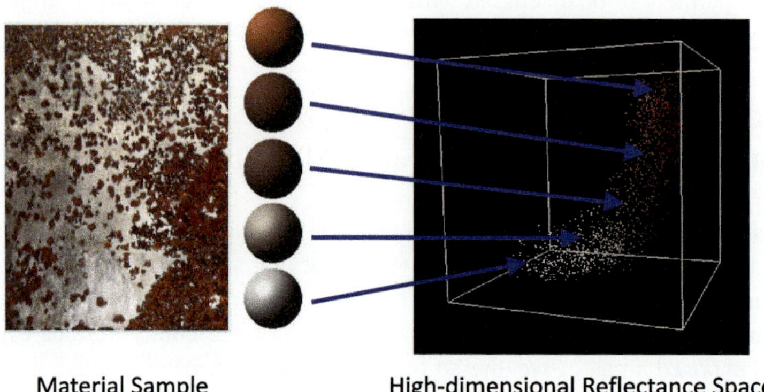

Fig. 1.5 Low-dimensional manifold structure of surface reflectance variations in the high-dimensional reflectance space. A 3D slice of the space is shown for viewing purposes [3]. © Association of Computing Machinery

modeling. Taking measured RGB values as an example, the same material may produce different RGB values over its surface due to variations in surface orientations as exhibited in Fig. 1.4. Likewise, the same observed RGB values do not necessarily result from the same material attributes. Repetition in material attributes is intrinsically tied both to appearance and to the small set of elements in a material, so it is this form of repetitive coherence that is important for appearance modeling.

A material volume might be characterized not by a small set of discrete element types, but instead by continuous transitions across different elements or different local geometric properties. This leads to a coherence of appearance in which the measured appearance data resides in a smooth low-dimensional linear subspace. We refer to such low-dimensional structure as *appearance subspace* coherency. An example of this kind of coherency is shown in the rusting iron of Fig. 1.5. Its gradual variations in appearance over the surface span a broad swath of the high-dimensional

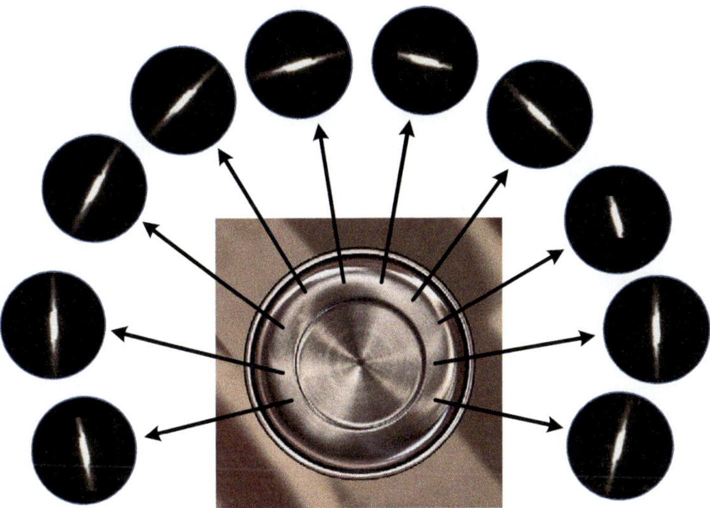

Fig. 1.6 Low-dimensional coherence in reflectance. Points on the metal plate have very similar reflectance properties, and differ by a rotational transformation due to the different orientations of the brushed grooves

reflectance space, but lie on a low-dimensional manifold in which the reflectance of a point can be well approximated as a linear combination of neighboring points. A special case of this occurs when appearance coherency takes the form of low-dimensional transformations. The brushed metal plate of Fig. 1.6 provides such an example, where the reflectance of surface points are well represented by 1D rotations of each other.

These two forms of low-dimensional coherency in appearance data may exist not only from point to point, but also among local areas. At a local level of appearance, coherence often can be described statistically, with accurate representations of appearance variations by Markov random fields [4] or filter bank responses [5]. Also for many material surfaces, the number of perceptually distinct local elements may be small, such that a surface could be represented by a small vocabulary of repeated prototypes, called textons [6].

The aforementioned types of coherence for surface appearance may furthermore present itself within material volumes, with similar consistencies and relationships among volumetric elements (voxels) or local sub-volumes. Coherence may also exist among light paths and scattering profiles within a volume, from which the appearance of transparent and translucent objects are determined.

The low-dimensional structure of appearance data may lead to coherence not only within a given appearance attribute or part of the appearance data, but also to correlations among different components of the data. In particular, similarities (or differences) in one part of the appearance data can indicate similarities (or differences) in other parts. Such coherence can neither be modeled by linear subspaces nor by spatial repetitions, and we refer to such correlation based coherence as *inter-*

attribute correlation. This type of coherence between attributes exists in the rusting iron of Fig. 1.5, where surface points of the same color have the same reflectance properties as well.

Coherency is a property that permeates nature, and in some aspect of a material's appearance, coherency of some form generally exists. In our framework for coherency based modeling, we first identify the primary type of coherence and the aspects of the appearance data to which it applies. If different forms of coherence are present together in the data, we seek that with the strongest coherence as it typically leads to greater gains in appearance modeling.

1.2.2 Coherence-Based Reconstruction

With coherency we have relationships within the appearance data that can be used to simplify the various aspects of the modeling process. Taking material attribute repetition as an example, it can be seen that repetitive patterns in appearance data allow the data to be represented more concisely, such as with a small set of basic elements. This type of coherency can significantly reduce the acquisition burden, by allowing appearance information at a point to be inferred from observations of other similar elements on the material surface. Also, appearance editing can be expedited by propagating modifications of an element to others that are similar, and rendering can be made faster with relatively small memory footprints and frequent reuse of appearance computation for multiple points.

To make appearance modeling from real samples practical, we take advantage of the identified coherence to fully reconstruct the appearance data from only sparse measurements. Reconstruction from sparse data, however, presents a challenging problem that differs according to the type of coherence and the modeling task. In contrast to data decompression, in which the decoding algorithm is known based on the encoding performed on the full data set, our case of appearance modeling from sparse measurements needs to uncover how the coherence can be utilized to recover unmeasured data.

We have found through our investigations that coherence-based reconstruction methods typically fall into three categories. Since coherence exists as low-dimensional structure in the appearance data, a natural approach is to reconstruct unmeasured appearance data by *linear combinations* of measured data. For appropriate linear combinations of measured data to be determined, the low-dimensional structure within the high-dimensional appearance space needs to be obtained, along with some partial appearance data for each surface point. Often this type of reconstruction employs mathematical tools such as the Nyström method or compressive sensing.

Some scenarios employ a low-dimensional appearance structure based on a complex scattering model and a small set of material attributes. In such cases, the attributes may be reconstructed by *direct optimization*, in which the optical properties that best fit the measured appearance are solved. The coherency properties that exist

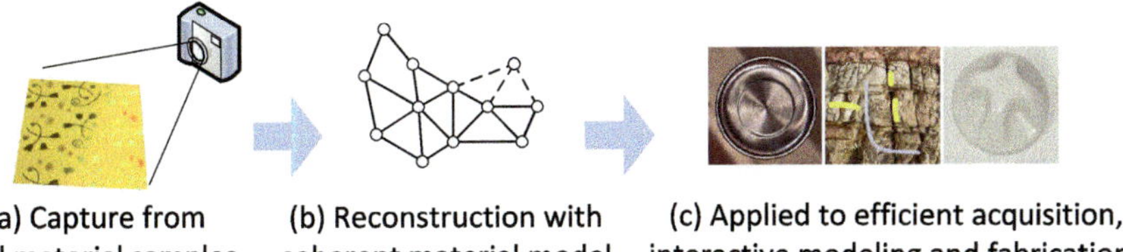

Fig. 1.7 Pipeline of coherence-based appearance modeling. From measured data of a real material sample, a coherent material model is reconstructed. The coherent model then can be applied for efficient appearance acquisition, interactive modeling and appearance fabrication

among the different attributes need to be found, and this coherence is then formulated together with the scattering model into a solvable optimization problem to reconstruct unmeasured data.

A third form of coherence-based reconstruction is to employ *subspace search*, in which the reconstructed data is found within a material-specific subspace. Constraining appearance to a low-dimensional subspace reduces the solution space considerably, leading to greater efficiency and robustness while potentially also reducing the measurement that is needed. Since subspace constraints may rule out possible solutions, it is essential to use the correct subspace. If the subspace is built by sampling, mechanisms are needed to uniformly and completely sample the subspace. During reconstruction, the subspace needs to be efficiently and comprehensively searched while rejecting solutions that do not obey the identified coherence.

1.2.3 A General Framework for Coherence-Based Appearance Modeling

Based on the preceding analysis of data coherence and reconstruction, we present a general framework for coherence-based appearance modeling. The framework consists of two major, mutually dependent components: the data coherence model and the accompanying reconstruction method. An appropriate coherence model is needed to determine the low-dimensional structure of the appearance data, since the reconstruction cost in the high-dimensional appearance space is prohibitively high. On the other hand, though a low-dimensional structure may fully describe the appearance data and its coherence, an efficient method is needed to reconstruct it from sparse measurements, so that appearance modeling can benefit from it. In this book, we follow this general framework to find an appropriate coherence model and develop a suitable reconstruction algorithm to efficiently model high quality appearance data, as illustrated in Fig. 1.7.

In summary, this book presents the use of coherence in the form of low-dimensional structure to make acquisition, modeling and rendering from real material samples considerably more efficient and practical. Our general framework involves identifying in the appearance data its underlying coherence—*material at-*

tribute repetition, *appearance subspace*, or *inter-attribute correlation*—and then capitalizing on this coherence to reconstruct the appearance data from sparse samples using *direct optimization*, *linear combinations*, or *subspace search*. We apply this approach over a full range of appearance modeling tasks, while purposely employing hardware constructed almost entirely from off-the-shelf components, to make these techniques accessible to non-expert practitioners.

1.3 Overview

In this book, we employ our comprehensive framework for coherency-based appearance modeling to all the major components of the appearance modeling pipeline, including acquisition, user-assisted modeling, editing, synthesis, rendering and fabrication. These methods are organized into three sections. The first two respectively address the two principal mechanisms of reflectance: surface reflections and subsurface scattering. The third part focuses on a new appearance-based application in computer graphics, namely the fabrication of materials with a desired translucent appearance.

1.3.1 Acquisition and Modeling of Opaque Surfaces

Surface appearance is often represented by a *Spatially-Varying Bi-Directional Reflectance Distribution Function* (SVBRDF), which models reflected light with respect to surface point position, lighting direction, and viewing direction. It is one of the most commonly used models in computer graphics, as it can fully represent the appearance of opaque materials in which light does not penetrate the surface.

In Chaps. 3 and 4, we propose practical methods to acquire SVBRDFs from real objects and materials by taking advantage of appearance coherency. Chapter 3 presents a method called *manifold bootstrapping* for high quality reflectance capture from a real material sample [7]. An SVBRDF consists of a considerable amount of reflectance data that can make its acquisition a long and tedious process. Based on *appearance subspace* coherency in which the reflectance of a material's surface points forms a low-dimensional manifold in the high-dimensional reflectance space, we develop an efficient acquisition scheme that obtains a high resolution SVBRDF from just sparsely measured data. This scheme reconstructs the SVBRDF manifold by decomposing reflectance measurement into two phases. The first measures reflectance at a high angular resolution, but only for sparse samples over the material surface, while the second acquires low angular resolution samples densely over the surface. Using a *linear combination* reconstruction scheme, we show that from this limited data, measured with a novel and simple capturing technique, the rest of the SVBRDF can be inferred according to the coherency that exists.

Besides direct acquisition of an SVBRDF from a real material sample, an SVBRDF may alternatively be obtained using just a single image of a material surface together with additional input from the user. This approach is presented in

Chap. 4, where the user provides simple annotations that indicate global reflectance and shading information [8]. This data is propagated over the surface in a manner guided by *inter-attribute correlation* coherence in the material, and this is used jointly with some image analysis to decompose the image by *direct optimization* into different appearance components and fine-scale geometry, from which the SVBRDF is reconstructed. Convincing results are generated with this technique from minimal data and just minutes of interaction, in contrast to the hour or more needed to obtain similar results using professional editing software.

1.3.2 Modeling and Rendering of Subsurface Light Transport

Besides surface reflections, the transport of light beneath the material surface has a significant effect on the appearance of many objects and materials. The appearance of translucent volumes, within which light can penetrate and scatter, is frequently modeled by the *Bi-Directional Surface Scattering Reflectance Distribution Function* (BSSRDF), which represents the appearance of a surface point with respect to light that enters the volume from other points. In Chap. 6, the problem of modeling and analyzing such light transport within a material volume is addressed. The nonlinear consistencies in light transport are transformed by kernel mapping into a form with *appearance subspace* coherence. This coherence is exploited to reconstruct the subsurface scattering of light within an object from a relatively small number of images [9] by a *linear combination* based scheme. These images are acquired using an adaptive scheme that minimizes the number needed for reconstruction. With this technique, the appearance of an object can be regenerated under a variety of lighting conditions different from those recorded in the images.

Often one wants to edit the appearance of a captured material. In such cases, the surface-based BSSRDF described in Chap. 6 provides an unsuitable representation, since there is no intuitive way to modify it to fit different material properties or shapes. In Chap. 7, we present a system based on a volume-based representation that allows for capturing, editing and rendering of translucent materials [10]. This solution is built on the diffusion equation, which describes the scattering of light in optically dense media. With this equation and a volumetric model, our method solves for a material volume whose appearance is consistent with a sparse number of image observations. For sparse image data, many material volume solutions can possibly fit the measured observations. To deal with this ambiguity, we take advantage of the *material attribute repetition* coherency that exists within the volumes of natural materials, and use this as a reconstruction constraint in a *direct optimization* scheme to solve for the material volume. Such solutions are shown to yield accurate renderings with novel lighting conditions and viewpoints. In addition, the captured volumetric model can be easily edited and rendered in real time on the GPU.

For translucent objects with texture-like material distributions, we present in Chap. 8 an algorithm to generate high-resolution material volumes from a small 2D slice [11]. With this limited data, we capitalize on the *material attribute repetition*

Table 1.1 Within the coherency-based appearance modeling framework, the coherency and reconstruction employed in each chapter

	Material attribute repetition	Appearance subspace	Inter-attribute correlation
Linear combinations	/	Chaps. 3 and 6	/
Direct optimization	Chap. 7	/	Chap. 4
Subspace search	Chap. 8	/	Chap. 10

coherence of textures for material modeling, and utilize *subspace search* to synthesize full objects. This approach, together with the volumetric model for translucent rendering, is fast enough to enable interactive texture design and real-time synthesis when cutting or breaking translucent objects, which greatly facilitates modeling of translucent materials.

1.3.3 Material Fabrication

From an acquired model of material appearance, efficient techniques for recreating objects are needed to ultimately view them. While most methods aim for rapid display on monitors, we present in Chap. 10 a novel solution for fabricating actual materials with desired subsurface scattering effects [12]. Given the optical properties of material elements used in a manufacturing system, such as a 3D printer, a volumetric arrangement of these elements that reproduces the appearance of a given translucent material is solved. The solution is obtained both efficiently and stably by accounting for *inter-attribute correlation* coherence between scattering profiles and element arrangements. The reconstruction technique in this method is based on *subspace search.*

Within the coherency-based appearance modeling framework, an overview of the coherency and reconstruction utilized in each chapter is shown in Table 1.1. This book concludes in Chap. 11 with a summary of its contributions and a discussion of potential future work in coherency-based appearance modeling.

References

1. Ashikmin, M., Premože, S., Shirley, P.: A microfacet-based brdf generator. In: Proceedings of the 27th Annual Conference on Computer Graphics and Interactive Techniques, SIGGRAPH '00, pp. 65–74. ACM/Addison-Wesley, New York (2000)
2. Ishimaru, A.: Wave Propagation and Scattering in Random Media. IEEE Press Series on Electromagnetic Wave Theory (1999)
3. Wang, J., Tong, X., Lin, S., Pan, M., Wang, C., Bao, H., Guo, B., Shum, H.-Y.: Appearance manifolds for modeling time-variant appearance of materials. ACM Trans. Graph. **25**(3), 754–761 (2006)

4. Zhu, S.-C., Wu, Y., Mumford, D.: Filters, random fields and maximum entropy (frame): towards a unified theory for texture modeling. Int. J. Comput. Vis. **27**(2), 107–126 (1998)
5. Malik, J., Perona, P.: Preattentive texture discrimination with early vision mechanisms. J. Opt. Soc. Am. A **7**(5), 923–932 (1990)
6. Leung, T., Malik, J.: Representing and recognizing the visual appearance of materials using three-dimensional textons. Int. J. Comput. Vis. **43**(1), 29–44 (2001)
7. Dong, Y., Wang, J., Tong, X., Snyder, J., Lan, Y., Ben-Ezra, M., Guo, B.: Manifold bootstrapping for svbrdf capture. ACM Trans. Graph. **29**(4) (2010)
8. Dong, Y., Tong, X., Pellacini, F., Guo, B.: Appgen: interactive material modeling from a single image. ACM Trans. Graph. **30**(5) (2011)
9. Wang, J., Dong, Y., Tong, X., Lin, Z., Guo, B.: Kernel Nyström method for light transport. ACM Trans. Graph. **28**(3), 29 (2009)
10. Wang, J., Zhao, S., Tong, X., Lin, S., Lin, Z., Dong, Y., Guo, B., Shum, H.-Y.: Modeling and rendering of heterogeneous translucent materials using the diffusion equation. ACM Trans. Graph. **27**, 9 (2008)
11. Dong, Y., Lefebvre, S., Tong, X., Drettakis, G.: Lazy solid texture synthesis. Comput. Graph. Forum **27**(4), 1165 (2008)
12. Dong, Y., Wang, J., Pellacini, F., Tong, X., Guo, B.: Fabricating spatially-varying subsurface scattering. ACM Trans. Graph. **29**(4) (2010)

Part I
Acquisition and Modeling of Opaque Surfaces

Many materials have optical properties which make them opaque. Within such volumes, light penetration and subsurface scattering can be considered to be negligible. The appearance of opaque materials depends primarily on reflections from the surface. Though such materials may be optically less complex than other materials in certain ways, they nevertheless can exhibit rich and detailed reflectance variations. Modeling and acquisition of these appearance details is essential for producing realistic computer graphics imagery with opaque objects.

Surface appearance is influenced by several physical factors. Besides the optical properties at each surface point, the appearance of opaque surfaces depends also on local geometric features and surface orientations at the micro-structure level. These different factors can combine to produce various surface appearance properties, ranging from diffuse to glossy, from smooth to rough, and from patterned to random.

As described in Chap. 1, the spatially varying reflectance of surfaces can be represented by the six-dimensional spatially varying bidirectional reflectance distribution function (SVBRDF) $f(x, i, o)$ [1], which describes the proportion of radiance that is reflected towards a given viewing direction with respect to surface point position and lighting direction. Surface positions are defined in the spatial domain, while lighting and viewing directions are expressed in the angular domain. Since the SVBRDF can fully represent the appearance of opaque materials, it is one of the most commonly used reflectance models in computer graphics.

There are two approaches to SVBRDF acquisition and modeling in computer graphics. The first of these is to capture the SVBRDF data directly by measuring them from real material samples. This provides high realism as the created model is built from actual material appearance. It also leads to considerable technical challenges, because material capture often requires large and expensive hardware, as well as hours of measurement and processing. These issues greatly limit the use of direct SVBRDF capture in computer graphics applications.

A second approach which is employed for the vast majority of CG materials is to manually model surface appearance using color textures and analytic reflectance models. For this, a design artist typically starts from a single texture image (e.g.

a cataloged texture or a photograph of a material sample under specific lighting conditions) which is used as a guide for assigning parameter values of an analytic reflectance model together with a bump map of local geometric variations. For many materials, this process takes hours to perform, with the use of image manipulation programs (e.g. Photoshop), inverse shading tools (e.g. CrazyBump), and 3D shading network software (e.g. Maya). Not only is this process cumbersome, but it often does not lead to the highest quality material models, since it is difficult to derive detailed reflectance and normal maps from a texture image.

The complexity of direct capture and the difficulty of manual modeling are the two principal roadblocks in surface appearance modeling. In this section, we address each of these problems in a manner that capitalizes on material coherency to enable efficient reflectance capture and easy interactive material modeling. After an overview of related work in Chap. 2, we present in Chap. 3 a technique called manifold bootstrapping [2], which obtains high-resolution reflectance from sparse captured data using *appearance subspace* coherence and data reconstruction by *linear combinations*. For instances when physical acquisition is impractical, we propose AppGen [3] in Chap. 4, a system that significantly accelerates the manual appearance modeling process. AppGen takes advantage of *inter-attribute correlation* coherence in the appearance data and uses *direct optimization* for reconstruction. With these methods, we can efficiently obtain high quality SVBRDFs that faithfully represent the actual reflectance features of real-world materials.

References

1. Nicodemus, F.E., Richmond, J.C., Hsia, J.J., Ginsberg, I.W., Limperis, T.: Geometric Considerations and Nomenclature for Reflectance. Monograph, vol. 161, pp. 1–67. Natl. Bur. of Standards, Washington (1977)
2. Dong, Y., Wang, J., Tong, X., Snyder, J., Lan, Y., Ben-Ezra, M., Guo, B.: Manifold bootstrapping for SVBRDF capture. ACM Trans. Graph. **29**(4) (2010)
3. Dong, Y., Tong, X., Pellacini, F., Guo, B.: AppGen: interactive material modeling from a single image. ACM Trans. Graph. **30**(5) (2011)

Chapter 2
Surface Reflectance Overview

To provide some context for our work on acquisition and modeling of opaque surfaces, we present in this chapter a brief introduction of related methods. We first discuss various approaches for acquisition of a material's surface reflectance, and then describe interactive techniques for material modeling and editing.

2.1 Surface Reflectance Acquisition

2.1.1 Direct Measurement

The most direct method of acquiring surface reflectance is to densely measure the values of a reflectance function from a real material sample. This brute-force approach has been used to obtain SVBRDFs [1–3], BTFs [4, 5], and reflectance fields [6]. Dense measurements are acquired both in the angular domain of view and light directions and in the spatial domain over points on the surface. Special rigs called gonioreflectometers are needed for this capture process, and the acquired 6D datasets are of enormous size and require hours to collect and process. A compact kaleidoscope-based device was developed by Han et al. [7] for quickly measuring BTFs. This device can also be used for SVBRDF acquisition, but only with a low angular resolution.

For the case of homogeneous materials, significant time can be saved in the acquisition process by using convex or spherical objects [8, 9]. Such objects display a broad range of surface normal orientations for the given material. An image of the object therefore provides numerous BRDF measurements over the points on the surface, and substantially reduces the number of images that need to be captured to densely sample a 4D BRDF. A few devices [10, 11] have also been proposed for fast BRDF measurement, using specially designed optics and sensors that expedite the measurement process. These approaches, while efficient for homogeneous materials, cannot be applied to materials with spatial variations.

Y. Dong et al., *Material Appearance Modeling: A Data-Coherent Approach*,
DOI 10.1007/978-3-642-35777-0_2,

To expedite data capture for materials with spatially varying surface reflectance, several techniques employ parametric reflectance models. In [12, 13], a simple parametric model is fit to the BRDF measurements at each surface point using data taken from a sparse set of view and light directions. Though this approach is considerably more efficient than brute-force acquisition, existing research shows that simple parametric models lack the power to accurately capture the appearance of real materials [14].

Another approach is to use data-driven non-parametric models to represent surface reflectance [15], in which reflectance data is modeled more concisely in a space of possible material reflectances using dimensionality reduction tools. By exploiting data coherence in both the angular and spatial domains, data-driven nonparametric models can well reproduce the complex reflectance features of real-world materials with a manageable amount of reflectance modeling.

2.1.2 Angular Coherence

The acquisition of surface reflectance is often simplified by taking advantage of its angular coherence. This angular coherence is represented in the microfacet theory of reflectance, in which real-world surface reflectance is modeled as a result of perfect mirror reflections by many micro-scale surface facets. Only those facets with the appropriate orientation according to the lighting and viewing direction and with visibility toward both the light and viewpoint can contribute to the final surface reflectance. The reflected energy can be calculated by counting the number of microfacets that can reflect light under the given lighting condition towards the viewing direction. In determining the final reflectance, what matters is only the angular distribution of the microfacets, rather than their spatial distribution.

Microfacet theory was first used with parametric orientation distribution functions, such as a Gaussian or Beckmann distribution, or a sum of these [16–18]. Based on those pioneering works, Ashikhmin et al. [19] introduced a method to compute surface reflectance from non-parametric microfacet normal distributions.

A non-parametric microfacet normal distribution function provides more versatility for representing surface reflectance, and can reproduce the reflectance of a wide range of real-world materials. Moreover, a normal distribution function is only a 2D function instead of the 4D function of a general BRDF. This greatly reduces the data that is required to capture.

Besides the microfacet model, other non-parametric models have also been proposed to exploit the angular consistency of surface reflectance. Romeiro et al. [20] proposed a bivariate BRDF model specific to isotropic BRDFs, which are 3D functions instead of 4D because of symmetry in the reflected light distribution. With their assumptions that surface reflectance tends to be unchanged under certain rotations, 3D isotropic BRDFs can be reduced into a 2D tabulated form.

2.1.3 Spatial Coherence

Spatial coherence can be utilized in addition to angular coherence to simplify acquisition even for surfaces with spatially varying reflectance. Reflectance measurements for a given pixel can be "borrowed" from other pixels that have the same reflectance and different orientation. Lensch et al. [21] first studied this with known surface geometry as input. BRDFs from different surface points are grouped into small sets, with each set fit using a Lafortune model [22] basis. The reflectance at each point is then represented as a linear combination over this basis. Taking this a step further with unknown geometry, Goldman et al. [23] use the same linear combination approach but with an isotropic Ward model as the BRDF basis. To reconstruct both an object's shape and its SVBRDF from sparse measurements, they iteratively solve the normal map and the reflectance by fixing the current SVBRDF or normal, respectively. By combining the angular reflectance data from multiple pixels, the number of samples needed to measure a given pixel can be significantly reduced.

Following a similar spatial linear combination model, Zickler et al. [24] represented the SVBRDF using six-dimensional radial basis functions. By assuming isotropic reflectance that varies smoothly over space, BRDF fitting at each point can be done with sparse reflectance data by using information from neighboring points. Later, Alldrin et al. [25] extended the linear combination idea using an isotropic bivariate function as the BRDF basis. With more measured data, realistic results can be reproduced with their non-parametric BRDF model.

When measuring anisotropic data, differences in the tangent direction of pixels can be used in a manner similar to surface normal variations. Samples measured with different tangent directions due to the anisotropy can be merged together to reduce the acquisition cost. In Wang et al. [26], this is done by modeling anisotropic surface reflectance from data captured from a single view and dense lighting directions. Reconstruction involves merging data from surface points having consistent reflectance properties with respect to microfacet normal distributions, and requires dense measurements over both space and lighting directions.

A different approach to using spatial coherence is to measure a set of representative BRDFs from a small number of points and then use them to represent other points with similar appearance. This was done for large outdoor scenes by Debevec et al. [27]. They measure representative BRDFs from small regions of the scene using controlled lighting, as well as images of the entire scene under natural lighting. At each scene point, the Lambertian color is recovered and its BRDF is modeled as a linear combination of two representative BRDFs whose diffuse colors are most similar to that of the point. This approach works well for the targeted application, but fails in general when surface points have similar diffuse colors but different specular reflectance. In many cases, a representative BRDF or combination of such BRDFs cannot be accurately inferred for a pixel from a small number of samples. This is addressed by Dong et al. [28] with a bootstrapping technique that efficiently captures high-resolution microfacet BRDFs sparsely over a surface with a hand-held device, and then densely acquires reflectance measurements with low angular resolution.

High-quality SVBRDFs with complex reflectance effects including anisotropic and normal variations can be well reconstructed with sparse measurements in this way.

A related technique utilizes a database of BRDFs to serve as representatives. Matusik et al. [29] modeled an isotropic BRDF as a linear combination of 100 BRDFs chosen from an existing data set. This reconstruction is obtained through a projection of about 800 measurements. Similarly, [30] represented the reflectance of human skin as a linear combination of a set of isotropic BRDFs manually selected from an existing database. Weights for each surface point are computed via non-negative matrix factorization (NMF), based on data that is densely acquired from 15 views and 300 light directions. A potential drawback of using existing data sets in comparison to directly measured BRDFs as in [28] is that the given material may not be well approximated by the predefined data.

2.2 Interactive Modeling and Editing

An alternative to direct acquisition of material reflectance models is for the user to interactively provide information within a single input image to recover the geometry and reflectance of objects. Oh et al. [31] developed a set of tools for interactively modeling the depth layers in a single image. The tools included a filter to extract the shading component in uniformly textured areas. Their method is designed for modeling the geometry of a scene or character but not materials with the rich texture and geometric details we are interested in.

Several interactive methods have been developed for modeling a bump map of structured textures [32], displacement map of tree barks [33], and stochastic/procedural volumetric textures [34] from single image input. All these methods are designed for specific kinds of textures and cannot easily be extended to model others. In industry, CrazyBump [35] is widely used by artists to generate bump maps from single images. For most texture inputs, it simply takes the image intensity as the shading map. Since image intensity is also influenced by the albedo variations of the underlying material, much manual work is needed to refine the results.

User interaction has also been employed for editing materials in a photograph to alter its appearance. Fattal et al. [36] compute a multi-scale decomposition of images under varying lighting conditions and enhance the shape and surface details of objects by manipulating its details in each scale. Fang and Hart [37] and Zelinka et al. [38] decorate an object in a photograph with synthesized texture, in which the object normals recovered via shape from shading are used to guide texture synthesis. Both methods assume the object geometry to be smooth and ignore intensity variations caused by albedo. Khan et al. [39] infer the shape and surrounding lighting of an object in a photograph and render its appearance with altered material. This method does not recover object reflectance and simply maps smoothed pixel intensities to depth. Xue et al. [40] model the reflectance of weathered surface points in a photograph as a manifold and use it for editing the weathering effects in the image. All these methods only recover partial material information for editing object appearance under the view and lighting of the original image. New viewing and lighting conditions cannot be rendered in this way.

References

1. Dana, K.J., Nayar, S.K., van Ginneken, B., Koenderink, J.J.: Reflectance and texture of real-world surfaces. ACM Trans. Graph. **18**(1), 1–34 (1999)
2. McAllister, D.K., Lastra, A.A., Heidrich, W.: Efficient rendering of spatial bi-directional reflectance distribution functions. In: The 17th Eurographics/SIGGRAPH Workshop on Graphics Hardware (EGGH-02), pp. 79–88. ACM, New York (2002)
3. Lawrence, J., Ben-Artzi, A., DeCoro, C., Matusik, W., Pfister, H., Ramamoorthi, R., Rusinkiewicz, S.: Inverse shade trees for non-parametric material representation and editing. ACM Trans. Graph. **25**(3) (2006)
4. Dana, K.J.: BRDF/BTF measurement device. In: Eighth IEEE International Conference on Computer Vision (ICCV), July 2001, vol. 2, pp. 460–466 (2001)
5. Muller, G., Meseth, J., Sattler, M., Sarlette, R., Klein, R.: Acquisition, synthesis, and rendering of bidirectional texture functions. Comput. Graph. Forum **24**(1), 83–109 (2005)
6. Garg, G., Talvala, E.-V., Levoy, M., Lensch, H.P.A.: Symmetric photography: exploiting data-sparseness in reflectance fields. In: Eurographics Workshop/Symposium on Rendering, Nicosia, Cyprus, pp. 251–262. Eurographics Association, Geneva (2006)
7. Han, J.Y., Perlin, K.: Measuring bidirectional texture reflectance with a kaleidoscope. ACM Trans. Graph. **22**(3), 741–748 (2003)
8. Marschner, S., Westin, S., Lafortune, E., Torrance, K., Greenberg, D.: Image-based BRDF measurement including human skin. In: 10th Eurographics Rendering Workshop (1999)
9. Lu, R., Koenderink, J.J., Kappers, A.M.L.: Optical properties bidirectional reflectance distribution functions of velvet. Appl. Opt. **37**(25), 5974–5984 (1998)
10. Mukaigawa, Y., Sumino, K., Yagi, Y.: High-speed measurement of BRDF using an ellipsoidal mirror and a projector. In: Computer Vision and Pattern Recognition, June 2007, pp. 1–8 (2007)
11. Moshe, B.-E., Wang, J., Bennett, W., Li, X., Ma, L.: An LED-only BRDF measurement device. In: Computer Vision and Pattern Recognition, June 2008, pp. 1–8 (2008)
12. Debevec, P., Hawkins, T., Tchou, C., Duiker, H.-P., Sarokin, W., Sagar, M.: Acquiring the reflectance field of a human face. In: Proc. SIGGRAPH 2000, pp. 145–156 (2000)
13. Gardner, A., Tchou, C., Hawkins, T., Debevec, P.: Linear light source reflectometry. ACM Trans. Graph. **22**(3), 749–758 (2003)
14. Ngan, A., Durand, F., Matusik, W.: Experimental analysis of BRDF models. In: Eurographics Symposium on Rendering (2005)
15. Matusik, W., Pfister, H., Brand, M., McMillan, L.: A data-driven reflectance model. ACM Trans. Graph. **22**(3), 759–769 (2003)
16. Torrance, K.E., Sparrow, E.M.: Theory for off-specular reflection from roughened surfaces. J. Opt. Soc. Am. **57**(9), 1105–1112 (1967)
17. Blinn, J.F.: Models of light reflection for computer synthesized pictures. SIGGRAPH Comput. Graph. **11**(2), 192–198 (1977)
18. Cook, R.L., Torrance, K.E.: A reflectance model for computer graphics. ACM Trans. Graph. **1**(1), 7–24 (1982)
19. Ashikhmin, M., Premoze, S., Shirley, P.: A microfacet-based BRDF generator. In: Siggraph 2000, Computer Graphics Proceedings, pp. 65–74. ACM/Addison-Wesley Longman, New York (2000)
20. Romeiro, F., Vasilyev, Y., Zickler, T.: Passive reflectometry. In: Proceedings of the 10th European Conference on Computer Vision: Part IV, ECCV '08, pp. 859–872. Springer, Berlin (2008)

21. Lensch, H.P.A., Kautz, J., Goesele, M., Heidrich, W., Seidel, H.-P.: Image-based reconstruction of spatial appearance and geometric detail. ACM Trans. Graph. **22**(2), 234–257 (2003)
22. Lafortune, E.P.F., Foo, S.-C., Torrance, K.E., Greenberg, D.P.: Non-linear approximation of reflectance functions. In: The 24th Annual Conference on Computer Graphics and Interactive Techniques, pp. 117–126. ACM/Addison-Wesley, New York (1997)
23. Goldman, D.B., Curless, B., Hertzmann, A., Seitz, S.M.: Shape and spatially-varying BRDFs from photometric stereo. In: International Conference on Computer Vision, pp. 341–348 (2005)
24. Zickler, T., Enrique, S., Ramamoorthi, R., Belhumeur, P.: Reflectance sharing: image-based rendering from a sparse set of images. In: Bala, K., Dutré, P. (eds.) Eurographics Symposium on Rendering, Konstanz, Germany pp. 253–264. Eurographics Association, Geneva (2005)
25. Alldrin, N., Zickler, T.E., Kriegman, D.: Photometric stereo with non-parametric and spatially-varying reflectance. In: Computer Vision and Pattern Recognition, pp. 1–8 (2008)
26. Wang, J., Zhao, S., Tong, X., Snyder, J., Guo, B.: Modeling anisotropic surface reflectance with example-based microfacet synthesis. In: ACM SIGGRAPH 2008 Papers, pp. 1–9. ACM, New York (2008)
27. Debevec, P., Tchou, C., Gardner, A., Hawkins, T., Poullis, C., Stumpfel, J., Jones, A., Yun, N., Einarsson, P., Lundgren, T., Fajardo, M., Martinez, P.: Estimating surface reflectance properties of a complex scene under captured natural illumination. Technical report ICT-TR-06, University of Southern California Institute for Creative Technologies Graphics Laboratory (2004)
28. Dong, Y., Wang, J., Tong, X., Snyder, J., Lan, Y., Ben-Ezra, M., Guo, B.: Manifold bootstrapping for svbrdf capture. ACM Trans. Graph. **29**(4) (2010)
29. Matusik, W., Pfister, H., Brand, M., McMillan, L.: Efficient isotropic BRDF measurement. In: The 14th Eurographics Workshop on Rendering, Aire-la-Ville, Switzerland, pp. 241–247. Eurographics Association, Geneva (2003)
30. Weyrich, T., Matusik, W., Pfister, H., Bickel, B., Donner, C., Tu, C., McAndless, J., Lee, J., Ngan, A., Jensen, H.W., Gross, M.: Analysis of human faces using a measurement-based skin reflectance model. ACM Trans. Graph. **25**(3), 1013–1024 (2006)
31. Oh, B.M., Chen, M., Dorsey, J., Durand, F.: Image-based modeling and photo editing. In: The 28th Annual Conference on Computer Graphics and Interactive Techniques, SIGGRAPH '01, pp. 433–442. ACM, New York (2001)
32. Dischler, J.-M., Maritaud, K., Ghazanfarpour, D.: Coherent bump map recovery from a single texture image. In: Graphics Interface, pp. 201–208 (2002)
33. Wang, X., Wang, L., Liu, L., Hu, S., Guo, B.: Interactive modeling of tree bark. In: 11th Pacific Conference on Computer Graphics and Applications, p. 83. IEEE Computer Society, Los Alamitos (2003)
34. Gilet, G., Dischler, J.-M.: An image-based approach for stochastic volumetric and procedural details. Comput. Graph. Forum **29**(4), 1411–1419 (2010)
35. Clark, R.: CrazyBump (2010). http://www.crazybump.com/
36. Fattal, R., Agrawala, M., Rusinkiewicz, S.: Multiscale shape and detail enhancement from multi-light image collections. In: ACM SIGGRAPH 2007 Papers, SIGGRAPH '07. ACM, New York (2007)
37. Fang, H., Hart, J.C.: Textureshop: texture synthesis as a photograph editing tool. In: ACM SIGGRAPH 2004 Papers, SIGGRAPH '04, pp. 354–359. ACM, New York (2004)
38. Zelinka, S., Fang, H., Garland, M., Hart, J.C.: Interactive material replacement in photographs. In: Graphics Interface 2005, GI '05, School of Computer Science, University of Waterloo, Waterloo, Ontario, Canada, pp. 227–232. Canadian Human-Computer Communications Society, Waterloo (2005)
39. Khan, E.A., Reinhard, E., Fleming, R.W., Bülthoff, H.H.: Image-based material editing. ACM Trans. Graph. **25**, 654–663 (2006)
40. Xue, S., Wang, J., Tong, X., Dai, Q., Guo, B.: Image-based material weathering. Comput. Graph. Forum **27**(2), 617–626 (2008)

Chapter 3
Efficient SVBRDF Acquisition with Manifold Bootstrapping

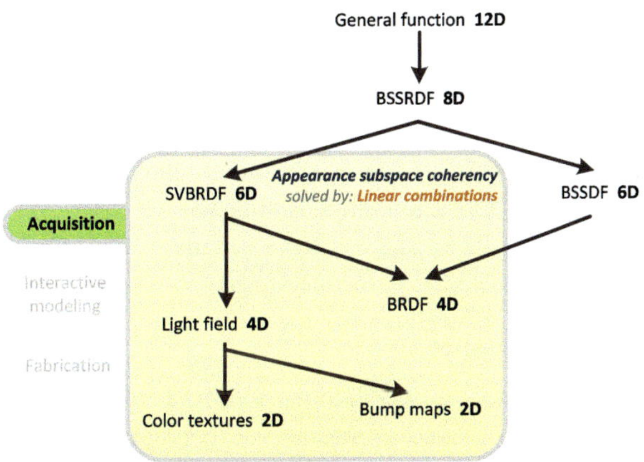

A major goal in this book is to simplify appearance measurement by avoiding collection of redundant data and by performing acquisition with inexpensive devices. At the same time, the acquired and reconstructed measurement data should faithfully represent the highly detailed appearance characteristics of the material sample. In this chapter, we focus on capturing spatially varying surface reflectance properties. Specifically, we will discuss efficient SVBRDF acquisition by fully utilizing the non-linear coherency of real-world surface appearance.

The key to efficient SVBRDF capture is to utilize the inherent coherence of material reflectance. Coherence in the form of spatial redundancy in reflectance has been exploited to expedite SVBRDF acquisition. Several methods have modeled reflectance at different surface points as linear combinations of representative BRDFs, and applied this idea to compress densely measured data [1–3]. Studies have shown that the BRDFs over a material surface are not globally coherent in a linear manner, since arbitrary linear combinations of BRDFs may result in implausible BRDFs [2, 4]. Rather, the spatially varying BRDFs of a material have non-linear

Y. Dong et al., *Material Appearance Modeling: A Data-Coherent Approach*,
DOI 10.1007/978-3-642-35777-0_3,

coherence and form a low-dimensional manifold in the high-dimensional BRDF space.

Though not globally linear, these low-dimensional manifolds have a locally linear structure. Via local linear embedding [5], BRDFs are well approximated by linear combinations of nearby manifold points. However, how to reconstruct the entire manifold of a material surface without full sampling is a major unsolved challenge in SVBRDF acquisition. Since the BRDF manifold is defined in a high-dimensional space, any direct measurement involves enormous data and lengthy capture times.

In this chapter, we propose an efficient bootstrapping scheme that separates data acquisition for a high-dimensional SVBRDF manifold into two lower-dimensional phases. The first phase captures the BRDF manifold structure of a given material sample according to *appearance subspace* coherency, while the second one determines the manifold point to which each surface position $\boldsymbol{x}$ corresponds using reconstruction by *linear combinations*. Specifically, the first phase captures a set of full-resolution BRDF representatives (hereafter referred to simply as representatives) at sparsely sampled points on the surface. The locations of these points need not be known. The second phase captures a set of reflectance measurements densely over the surface but sparsely in the angular domain, under only a few different lighting directions. This data we refer to as key measurements, which are arranged at each surface position $\boldsymbol{x}$ into a low-dimensional key vector. From a key vector, a high-resolution BRDF is inferred from representatives that have similar key vectors. The high-resolution BRDF is reconstructed by computing a linear combination of these representatives whose response to the key measurements matches the measured key at $\boldsymbol{x}$. The total amount of data acquired in the two phases is substantially less than full direct measurement of the SVBRDF, yet is sufficient for accurate SVBRDF reconstruction. Complex reflectance effects such as from anisotropic materials with spatially-varying normal and tangent vectors can be well modeled by this method.

To expedite data capture in the first phase, we present a technique to synthetically enlarge the representative set. For bumpy surfaces, a discrete series of normal tilts are applied to each original representative to obtain additional representatives. Similarly, for anisotropic surfaces we augment the representative set using discrete azimuthal rotations. Bootstrapping is then performed as before on the enlarged set.

The remainder of this chapter is organized as follows. We review related works in the first section. The second section introduces the basic components of manifold bootstrapping, such as representative and key measurements, and then presents the theoretical framework of manifold bootstrapping including the reconstruction method and an analysis of coherence in reflectance. In Sect. 3.3, a practical acquisition approach is described, including the design of a portable BRDF sampling device and an on-site setup for capturing of reflectance maps. A validation of this method and experimental results are provided in Sect. 3.4. The chapter closes in Sect. 3.5 with a summary of the major points in this work.

3.1 Related Work

In previous work, redundancies in reflectance data have been exploited to simplify data acquisition. One class of methods exploits angular redundancy. An example is the work of Gardner et al. [6], which scans the surface of a material with a linear light source and captures its reflectance from a fixed viewpoint. An isotropic Ward model [7] is then fit to the captured data at each point, to extrapolate the measured data to unmeasured lighting and viewing angles. A parametric reflectance representation such as the Ward model, however, provides limited accuracy in representing the angular reflectance variations of many real-world materials.

Another class of methods exploits coherence in both the angular and spatial domain. Several of these techniques employ a single data collection pass in their acquisition process. Lensch et al. [8] reconstruct the SVBRDF of a real object of known geometry. BRDFs from different surface points are grouped into small sets, with each set fit using a Lafortune model [9] basis. The reflectance at each point is then represented as a linear combination over the basis. Goldman et al. [10] use the same linear combination idea but with an isotropic Ward model as the BRDF basis, to reconstruct both an object's shape and its SVBRDF from sparse measurements. These methods capture spatial variation, but miss details in the BRDF's anisotropy, specularity, and other types of angular variation, because they merge angular information from different spatial samples. Zickler et al. [11] model the SVBRDF using six-dimensional radial basis functions. By assuming isotropic reflectance that varies smoothly over space, BRDF fitting at each point can be done with sparse reflectance data by using information from neighboring points. Our approach makes no assumptions about the material's spatial distribution, which in general may not be spatially smooth. Recently, Alldrin et al. [12] extended the linear combination idea using an isotropic bivariate function as the BRDF basis. It is not clear how to extend this method to model anisotropic SVBRDFs. The method of Wang et al. [13] models anisotropic surface reflectance from data captured from a single view and dense lighting directions, based on the general microfacet model. Reconstruction involves merging data from surface points having consistent reflectance properties with respect to microfacet normal distributions, and requires dense measurements over both space and lighting directions.

In general, methods based on a single data collection pass cannot avoid capturing huge datasets to obtain both spatial and angular details of complicated reflectance. Acquiring data in two separate and much smaller passes, the first for angular variations and the second for spatial variations, our method takes advantage of both angular and spatial coherence to significantly reduce the data and time needed for capture.

Some recent methods also perform a sort of two-step bootstrapping. To obtain surface reflectance of large outdoor scenes, Debevec et al. [14] measure a set of representative BRDFs from small regions of the scene using controlled lighting, as well as images of the entire scene under natural lighting. At each scene point, the Lambertian color is recovered and its BRDF is modeled as a linear combination of two representative BRDFs whose diffuse colors are most similar to that of the point. This approach works well for the targeted application, but fails in general when surface points have similar diffuse colors but different specular reflectance. We generalize the concept of key measurement, as well as the bootstrapping procedure, to enable capture of a wide range of materials.

Matusik et al. [15] represent an isotropic BRDF as a linear combination of 100 BRDFs chosen from an existing database. Based on this reconstruction, another BRDF can be optimally projected using about 800 measurements. Similarly, Weyrich et al. [16] represent the reflectance of human skin as a linear combination of a set of isotropic BRDFs manually selected from an existing database. Weights for each surface point are computed via non-negative matrix factorization (NMF), based on data that is densely acquired from 15 views and 300 light directions. These methods assume only isotropic reflectance and acquire much denser key measurements than we do (by 1–2 orders of magnitude). More fundamentally, they assume that the existing database or set of parameterized radial basis function (RBF) models fill in the missing angular data. By contrast, we obtain high-resolution BRDF representatives from the actual target. These are especially effective when the BRDF space becomes large, complex, and anisotropic. A second difference is that our technique respects the nonlinear nature of the BRDF space and applies only local reconstruction.

3.2 SVBRDF Manifold Bootstrapping

This section introduces the basic theory of manifold bootstrapping for SVBRDF capture. Implementation details, synthetic enlargement of the representative set, and a validation of the key measurement approach are also presented.

3.2.1 Representative and Key Measurement

Representative Measurement In the first phase, we capture a set of M high-resolution representative BRDFs, indexed by p and denoted by $B^* = \{b_p^*(\mathbf{o}, \mathbf{i}) \mid p = 1, 2, \dots M\}$. To represent BRDFs, each *representative vector*, $\boldsymbol{b}_p^*$, comprises $N_b = N_\mathbf{o} \times N_\mathbf{i}$ samples, over $N_\mathbf{o}$ viewing directions and $N_\mathbf{i}$ lighting directions. We assume that this set of representatives adequately samples the BRDF manifold across the surface.

To uniformly sample the BRDF manifold, we cull nearly identical representatives if their distance is less than ε, fixed at 10 % of the average distance over all pairs of nearest neighbors.

Key Measurement The second phase measures a low-dimensional set of keys, or reflectance responses, over the whole sample. Critical to bootstrapping is a set of key measurements that is still able to accurately discriminate BRDF features. Previous work [3, 13] has shown that many BRDFs are well-characterized by a single 2D BRDF slice; i.e., by measurements with respect to varying lighting but a fixed view. This is because specular reflectance for many real-world materials can be represented using the *microfacet model* [17], which expresses a complex 4D BRDF in terms of a simpler, 2D normal distribution function (NDF). The NDF can then be inferred by measuring data which covers the hemisphere of *half-angle vectors* midway between view and light directions,

$$\mathbf{h} = (\mathbf{o} + \mathbf{i}) / \|\mathbf{o} + \mathbf{i}\|. \tag{3.1}$$

This is clearly possible from measurements which vary the lighting but fix the view. The microfacet model will be used again and discussed in more detail in the next section. Note that though real materials are captured by the microfacet model, this does not imply that they can be captured by simple parametric models: real-world NDFs are complicated and require tabulation or more sophisticated modeling [13, 18].

The view direction, $\mathbf{o}^*$, is chosen to be 45° from directly overhead. This provides the best coverage of half-angle vectors as the light source direction is varied.

Our key measurement captures N images of the material sample, each indexed by j and acquired from a fixed view direction $\mathbf{o}^*$ and under a known but varying source radiance field L_j. The measured reflectance responses at each point $\boldsymbol{x}$ provide constraints on integrals of the BRDF $b_{\boldsymbol{x}}(\mathbf{i}, \mathbf{o})$, via

$$\boldsymbol{r}_j(\boldsymbol{x}) = \int_{\Omega_+(\mathbf{n})} b_{\boldsymbol{x}}\big(\mathbf{i}, \mathbf{o}^*\big)(\mathbf{n} \cdot \mathbf{i}) L_j(\mathbf{i}) \mathrm{d}\mathbf{i}, \tag{3.2}$$

where $\mathbf{n}$ is the surface normal.

Assembling all N reflectance responses at surface point $\boldsymbol{x}$ into an N-dimensional *key vector*, $\boldsymbol{r}_{\boldsymbol{x}} = (r_1(\boldsymbol{x}), r_2(\boldsymbol{x}), \ldots, r_N(\boldsymbol{x}))^T$, we can represent Eq. (3.2) in matrix form as

$$\boldsymbol{r}_{\boldsymbol{x}} = \boldsymbol{R} \boldsymbol{b}_{\boldsymbol{x}}, \tag{3.3}$$

where $\boldsymbol{b}_{\boldsymbol{x}}$ is the BRDF vector at $\boldsymbol{x}$. The $N \times N_b$ *key measurement matrix*, $\boldsymbol{R}$, converts sampled BRDFs to key measurements and is given by

$$\boldsymbol{R}_{jk} = \begin{cases} (\mathbf{n} \cdot \mathbf{i}_{k_\mathbf{i}}) L_j(\mathbf{i}_{k_\mathbf{i}}), & \mathbf{o}_{k_\mathbf{o}} = \mathbf{o}^*, \\ 0, & \text{otherwise}. \end{cases} \tag{3.4}$$

The indices $k_\mathbf{o}$ and $k_\mathbf{i}$ decompose the overall index k of the packed BRDF vector $\boldsymbol{b}_{\boldsymbol{x}}$ into its constituent view and lighting directions, via $k = k_\mathbf{o} N_\mathbf{i} + k_\mathbf{i}$. In fact, the dimensionality of $\boldsymbol{R}$ is really only $N \times N_\mathbf{i}$ (not $N \times N_b$), because it is based on a single view and so has no response to view vectors other than $\mathbf{o}^*$.

3.2.2 Manifold Bootstrapping Overview

Given the previous two-phase measurement of a material sample, our method combines the two to reconstruct a high-resolution SVBRDF as shown in Fig. 3.1.

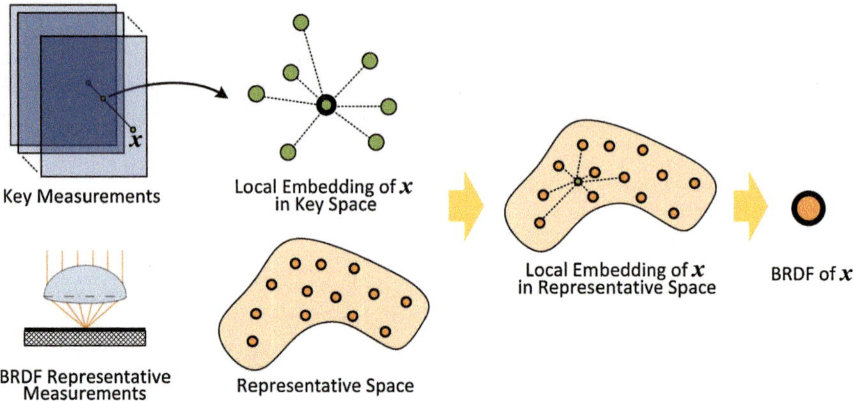

Fig. 3.1 SVBRDF bootstrapping. A key vector at each spatial position $\boldsymbol{x}$ is projected to the space of matching vectors to determine a local linear embedding. The linear weights and neighborhood indices are then applied to the full-resolution representatives to reconstruct the BRDF at $\boldsymbol{x}$

Local BRDF Reconstruction Interpolation of distant BRDFs leads to implausible reflectance, as demonstrated in [2] for isotropic BRDFs of different (spatially homogeneous) materials. For anisotropic BRDFs, the problem is even worse (see Fig. 3.9(f)). We solve this problem by bootstrapping using *local* reconstruction, which interpolates only over nearby representatives. We assume that the local dimensionality of the BRDF manifold is constant.

Mathematically, a particular BRDF $\boldsymbol{b}_{\boldsymbol{x}}$ at a spatial position $\boldsymbol{x}$ can be represented as a convex linear combination of a small number k of nearby representatives, called the *representative neighborhood*, $\boldsymbol{b}^*_p$, $p \in \delta(\boldsymbol{b}_{\boldsymbol{x}})$, $k = |\delta(\boldsymbol{b}_{\boldsymbol{x}})|$:

$$\boldsymbol{b}_{\boldsymbol{x}} \approx \sum_{p\in\delta(\boldsymbol{b}_{\boldsymbol{x}})} w_p \boldsymbol{b}^*_p, \qquad \sum_{p\in\delta(\boldsymbol{b}_{\boldsymbol{x}})} w_p = 1. \tag{3.5}$$

The neighborhood here is defined in terms of L2 distance in BRDF space, not spatial distance. This ensures that the linear combination produces a physically plausible result.

Representative Projection and Bootstrapping Substituting Eq. (3.5) into Eq. (3.3), we obtain a constrained linear equation on the weights w_p:

$$\boldsymbol{r}_{\boldsymbol{x}} = \sum_{p\in\delta(\boldsymbol{r}_{\boldsymbol{x}})} w_p \boldsymbol{r}^*_p, \qquad \sum_{p\in\delta(\boldsymbol{r}_{\boldsymbol{x}})} w_p = 1 \tag{3.6}$$

where

$$\boldsymbol{r}^*_p = \boldsymbol{R}\boldsymbol{b}^*_p. \tag{3.7}$$

The projection in Eq. (3.7) numerically applies the key lighting we captured in phase two to the representative BRDFs we captured in phase one, and also evaluates at the key viewing direction $\mathbf{o}^*$. It reduces an N_b-dimensional representative vector, $\boldsymbol{b}_p^*$, to an N-dimensional *matching vector*, $\boldsymbol{r}_p^*$. Equations (3.5) and (3.3) imply that the measured key vector $\boldsymbol{r}_x$ can be represented as a linear combination of neighboring matching vectors, $\boldsymbol{r}_p^*$, $p \in \delta(\boldsymbol{r}_x)$.

Because we do not know the entire BRDF vector $\boldsymbol{b}_x$ but instead only the key vector $\boldsymbol{r}_x$, we require that key vectors roughly preserve distance so that a neighborhood in key vector space corresponds to a similar neighborhood in the original BRDF space. This requires a sufficient number of key measurements.

3.2.3 Manifold Bootstrapping Details

Estimating Local BRDF Dimensionality We choose k based on an analysis of intrinsic local dimensionality of the representative set. The basic idea is to assemble a growing set of neighbors in terms of increasing distance around each representative, considered as a local center. We analyze dimensionality based on a singular value decomposition (SVD) of vector differences of all neighbors in the set to this center. Eliminating singular values less than a threshold (e.g., preserving 95 % of total energy), the number of significant singular values remaining forms an estimate of dimensionality. At first, dimensionality increases rapidly, since each new neighbor typically adds an entire new dimension. But after we have discovered a spanning set of neighbors, additional ones add no more significant dimensions to the space. We use a simple heuristic that fixes dimensionality when twice as many neighbors fails to increase the dimensionality estimate. We then average local dimensionality estimates over a random selection of representative centers.

Uniform Measurement Scaling Overlapping light sources and varying environmental lighting in key measurement produce a non-orthogonal key measurement matrix. This leads to ellipsoidal rather than spherical neighborhoods in key space, and so complicates the selection of neighbors and distorts the interpolation. We orthogonalize the projection by applying the SVD to $\boldsymbol{R}$, yielding

$$\boldsymbol{R} = \boldsymbol{U}_R \boldsymbol{\Lambda}_R \boldsymbol{V}_R \tag{3.8}$$

where $\boldsymbol{U}_R$ is an $N \times N$ orthogonal matrix of left-hand eigenvectors, $\boldsymbol{\Lambda}_R$ is an $N \times N$ diagonal matrix of eigenvalues, and $\boldsymbol{V}_R$ is an $N \times N_b$ (really $N \times N_\mathbf{i}$) orthogonal matrix of transposes of right-hand eigenvectors. $\boldsymbol{\Lambda}_R$ should contain no zero or very small elements; if it does, then we are measuring redundant (i.e., linearly dependent) lighting configurations, which add no new information to the key.

To remove non-uniform scaling in our key measurements, we apply the SVD in Eq. (3.8) to obtain the *uniform key vector*

$$\hat{\boldsymbol{r}}_x = \boldsymbol{\Lambda}_R^{-1} \boldsymbol{U}_R^T \boldsymbol{r}_x. \tag{3.9}$$

We also define the *uniform matching vector* $\hat{\boldsymbol{r}}_p^*$ as

$$\hat{\boldsymbol{r}}_p^* = \boldsymbol{V}_R \boldsymbol{b}_p^*. \tag{3.10}$$

Neighbors can now be found in the uniform key space using a simple distance threshold over these N-dimensional vectors, in order to match a linear combination of the $\hat{\boldsymbol{r}}_p^*$ to each $\hat{\boldsymbol{r}}_{\boldsymbol{x}}$.

Neighborhood Selection After uniform measurement scaling, the representative neighborhood δ is determined at each spatial position $\boldsymbol{x}$ by finding the k-nearest uniform matching vectors $\hat{\boldsymbol{r}}_p^*$ to the uniform key $\hat{\boldsymbol{r}}_{\boldsymbol{x}}$. We use approximated nearest neighbor (ANN) search [19] to accelerate finding the k-nearest neighbors. We also remove outliers having distance more than five times of the average distance over all neighborhoods.

Local Linear Combination We then determine the linear weights, w_p, based on the distance metric in each local neighborhood [5], via

$$w_p = \sum_{q \in \delta(\boldsymbol{r}_{\boldsymbol{x}})} \boldsymbol{C}_{pq}^{-1} \left(\hat{\boldsymbol{r}}_x \cdot \hat{\boldsymbol{r}}_q^* + \lambda \right), \tag{3.11}$$

$$\lambda = \frac{1 - \sum_{p,q \in \delta(\boldsymbol{r}_{\boldsymbol{x}})} \boldsymbol{C}_{pq}^{-1} (\hat{\boldsymbol{r}}_x \cdot \hat{\boldsymbol{r}}_q^*)}{\sum_{p,q \in \delta(\boldsymbol{r}_{\boldsymbol{x}})} \boldsymbol{C}_{pq}^{-1}}. \tag{3.12}$$

$\boldsymbol{C}_{pq} = \hat{\boldsymbol{r}}_p^* \cdot \hat{\boldsymbol{r}}_q^*$ denotes the covariance matrix of the neighborhood and $\boldsymbol{C}^{-1}$ is its inverse. We compute the inverse based on SVD, and clamp reciprocals of small singular values to 0. Though negative weight solutions are theoretically possible, we have not encountered negative weights in practice.

3.2.4 Synthetic Enlargement for Representatives

To handle bumpy surfaces, we enlarge the representative set by rotating each BRDF to align the vertical direction to a discrete set of tilted normals. The set is regularly sampled using 120 azimuthal angles and 30 polar angles in a 75° range, yielding an enlargement factor of 3600. The same bootstrapping algorithm is then applied to capture spatially-varying bumpy reflectance. After enlargement, nearly identical representatives are removed using distance culling as described in Sect. 3.2.1.

For anisotropic materials, we similarly rotate the derived BRDF around the normal direction by a discrete set of 360 azimuthal angles and add the corresponding BRDFs to the example set. We can then recover the anisotropic reflectance and local orientation angle at each spatial position.

Given a 3×3 rotation matrix $\mathscr{R}$, the rotated BRDF $b'(\mathbf{i}, \mathbf{o})$ is given by

$$b'(\mathbf{i}, \mathbf{o}) = b\left(\mathscr{R}^{\mathrm{T}} \mathbf{i}, \mathscr{R}^{\mathrm{T}} \mathbf{o}\right). \tag{3.13}$$

To handle tilts due to normal variation, representative BRDFs are defined on the full spherical domain, not just the upper hemisphere. The lower hemisphere of the original BRDF b is zeroed out before rotation. In our implementation, since our phase one capture relies on the microfacet model, we can simply rotate the NDF's half-angle vector **h**, and then convert the NDF to a full 4D BRDF, as later described in Sect. 3.3.1.

3.2.5 Key Measurement Validation

Key measurements must adequately discriminate BRDF features in two ways. First, they should ensure that representative neighborhoods in "key" space, $\delta(\boldsymbol{r_x})$, also correspond to neighborhoods in BRDF space, $\delta(\boldsymbol{b_x})$, so that distant BRDFs are not interpolated. Second, they should ensure that local distances in the BRDF manifold are preserved, to yield an accurate local reconstruction. This motivates an investigation of how well key measurements preserve distance in the original BRDF manifold, at both small and large length scales.

Overall distance preservation τ over a neighborhood of representatives of radius r, $\delta(p,r) = \{q \mid \|\boldsymbol{b}_p^* - \boldsymbol{b}_q^*\| < r\}$, can be measured by

$$\tau(p,r) = \frac{\sum_{i,j\in\delta(p,r)} \|\hat{\boldsymbol{r}}_i^* - \hat{\boldsymbol{r}}_j^*\|}{\sum_{i,j\in\delta(p,r)} \|\boldsymbol{b}_i^* - \boldsymbol{b}_j^*\|}. \tag{3.14}$$

In the uniformly-scaled space, we have $0 \le \|\hat{\boldsymbol{r}}_i^* - \hat{\boldsymbol{r}}_j^*\| \le \|\boldsymbol{b}_i^* - \boldsymbol{b}_j^*\|$. The closer τ is to 1, the better our key measurement is at discriminating between representatives in the neighborhood. Based on this, we examine average distance preservation at various length scales, r, via

$$\bar{\tau}(r) = 1/M \sum_{p=1}^{M} \tau\big(\delta(p,r)\big). \tag{3.15}$$

Finally, we define *global distance preservation*,

$$\tau_g = \bar{\tau}(\infty) \tag{3.16}$$

by calculating average distance over all pairs of representatives. We also define *local distance preservation*

$$\tau_l = \bar{\tau}(\bar{r}) \tag{3.17}$$

where $\bar{r}$ is the average local radius over all representative BRDFs. It is defined as the maximum distance over the k nearest neighbors to each representative, averaged over all representatives.

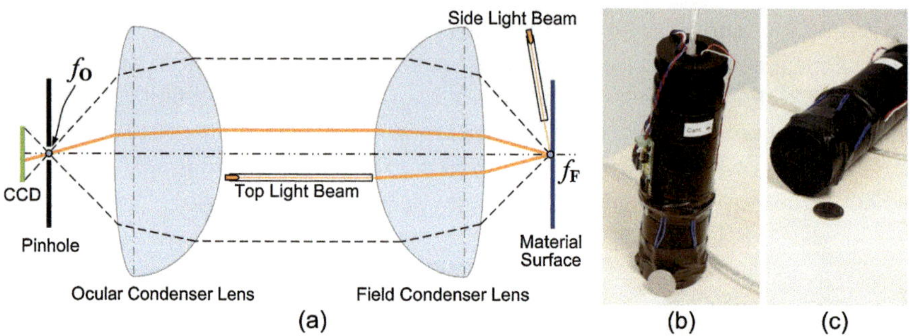

Fig. 3.2 Single point BRDF measurement device (phase 1). (**a**) Optical design. (**b/c**) Prototype from side/bottom view

3.3 SVBRDF Data Acquisition

Our approach captures two data sets from a flat sample of the target material. Typical sample dimensions are 10 cm × 10 cm. Our device setups are portable and handle natural background lighting and inexact lighting control, allowing materials to be captured on-site without the need to move them to a dedicated capture room.

3.3.1 Acquiring Representatives: BRDF Samples

We developed a portable device for capturing a hemispherical field of reflected rays emanating from a single point on the material sample using a single camera position. Data is acquired by illuminating the surface point using $n_l = 6$ lighting directions and capturing its resulting reflectance. A high-resolution general microfacet BRDF [20] is derived from this captured data. We scan the sample to acquire typically about hundreds of BRDFs scattered over its surface.

Device Setup Figure 3.2 shows the design of our single-point BRDF measurement device. Our setup includes a pair of Anchor Optics 47 mm condenser lenses with 21 mm focus length, a 200 μm pinhole and a Firefly$^{(R)}$ MV camera from Point Grey Research. These components are mounted along the same optical axis using a lens tube from Thorlabs. We use six high-brightness LEDs as light sources; each is attached to a carbon fiber tube to generate a light beam. One (top light beam) is mounted between the two condenser lenses and illuminates the capturing point at roughly a 10 degree bias from the vertical direction. The other five (side light beams) are mounted around the optical axis between the field condenser lens and the target surface, and illuminate the capturing point at 20 degrees above the horizontal plane.

A sample is placed at the focal plane of the field condenser lens, f_F. The pinhole is placed at the focal plane of the ocular condenser lens, f_O, and images the light field at a single point on the target surface onto a video camera. The acceptance angle of the condenser lens is 48° from the optical axis. The camera communicates with a laptop via an IEEE1394 cable, which also supplies power for the LEDs and their control unit. A housing ensures that the device is at the correct distance from the target sample.

Calibration The lens tube ensures optical alignment of the lenses, pinhole and camera. Distances between them are manually adjusted. The LED for the top light beam is held by an acrylic disc; its position is calibrated by measuring a mirror. Positions of the side LEDs are calibrated in manufacture. We calibrate the color and intensity of each LED by measuring a color checker pattern. Radial distortion of the dual condenser system is analytically calculated based on the specification from Anchor Optics, and determines the view direction at each pixel in the captured image.

Capturing The device is a cylinder 50 mm in diameter and 150 mm tall, and weighs about 500 g. We scan it over the sample to collect BRDFs at different locations. For each position, we acquire six images lit by each LED and two images per light for exposure bracketing. The camera captures images of resolution 320×240 at 135 Hz, yielding about 0.1 s per BRDF point capture. In a postprocess, each exposure pair is merged into a high dynamic range (HDR) image [21], and the resulting six images of 240×240 are used to derive a high-resolution BRDF. Figure 3.3(a) shows an example.

The top light LED component occludes a 3 mm diameter hole in the captured image. Since the top light beam does not coincide with the optical axis, this hole typically does not occlude the peak of the specular lobe. We obtain the occlusion mask when calibrating with the color checker. If the hole contains no high frequency features, we fill it with harmonic interpolation [22]. We detect this by querying the intensity range of pixels surrounding the hole and testing whether the max/min ratio exceeds 2. If it does, then we discard the sample.

Reflectance samples are then computed from the six HDR images by dividing by the cosine factor and light intensity:

$$\rho\big(\mathbf{o}(\boldsymbol{u}), \mathbf{i}_l\big) = \frac{G_l(\boldsymbol{u})}{(\mathbf{n} \cdot \mathbf{i}_l) L_l} \tag{3.18}$$

where $\boldsymbol{u}$ is the pixel position in the image corresponding to the view direction $\mathbf{o}(\boldsymbol{u})$, and $\mathbf{i}_l$ and L_l are the direction and intensity of the l-th LED. These quantities are all determined in calibration.

In sustained mode, we move the device continuously but slowly (e.g., around 1 mm/s) over materials with smooth spatial variations. For materials with piecewise reflectance discontinuities or small details, the device also runs in a triggering mode. Placing the device on the desired target location, the user triggers a single BRDF point capture using a UI on the computer connected to the device.

Reconstruction To reconstruct a high-resolution 4D BRDF from this captured data, we decompose the BRDF into diffuse and specular components. The diffuse

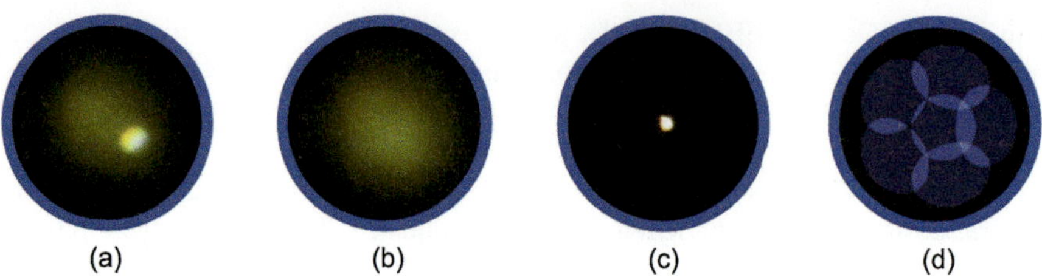

Fig. 3.3 NDF reconstruction. (**a**) 2D BRDF slice captured using top light beam. (**b**) Using side light beam. (**c**) Reconstructed NDF. (**d**) Covered region in the reconstructed NDF. BRDF slices from these six lighting directions cover most of the NDF domain

component ρ_d is determined by using a simple minimum filter on the samples ρ in Eq. (3.18), via

$$\rho_d = \frac{\sum_l \min_{\boldsymbol{u}}\{\rho(\mathbf{o}(\boldsymbol{u}), \mathbf{i}_l)\}}{n_l}. \tag{3.19}$$

The specular component is the residual after subtracting this diffuse term:

$$\rho_s\big(\mathbf{o}(\boldsymbol{u}), \mathbf{i}_l\big) = \rho\big(\mathbf{o}(\boldsymbol{u}), \mathbf{i}_l\big) - \rho_d. \tag{3.20}$$

We then represent the specular component with a general microfacet model [20] as

$$\rho_s(\mathbf{o}, \mathbf{i}) = c_s \frac{D(\mathbf{h})S(\mathbf{i})S(\mathbf{o})F(\mathbf{o}, \mathbf{i})}{\pi(\mathbf{i}\cdot\mathbf{n})(\mathbf{o}\cdot\mathbf{n})}. \tag{3.21}$$

This model is defined in terms of five factors: a microfacet normal distribution function D in terms of the half-angle vector from Eq. (3.1), its shadowing factor S, a Fresnel reflection factor F, and the scalar specular coefficient, c_s. We assume that the surface normal is aligned to the z axis: $\mathbf{n} = \mathbf{z} = (0, 0, 1)$. Since D dominates the other factors in determining the high-frequency characteristics of the BRDF, we follow [13, 20, 23] and tabulate it as a square image using the spherical parameterization in [24]. We fit this microfacet BRDF in Eq. (3.21) from the measured specular data ρ_s in Eq. (3.20) using the method described in [18]. In our case, the view direction, rather than the lighting direction, varies densely. Therefore we reconstruct the full NDF from partial NDFs inferred using a sparse set of n_l lighting directions. We represent the recovered NDF by a 400×400 square image using the spherical parameterization in [24]. Figure 3.3 summarizes the process and shows an example.

3.3.2 Acquiring Keys: Reflectance Maps

Keys are based on reflectance maps captured from a single view and lit by N different lighting configurations (Fig. 3.4). The lighting can include variable environmental/area sources and their inter-reflections off surrounding geometry, as shown

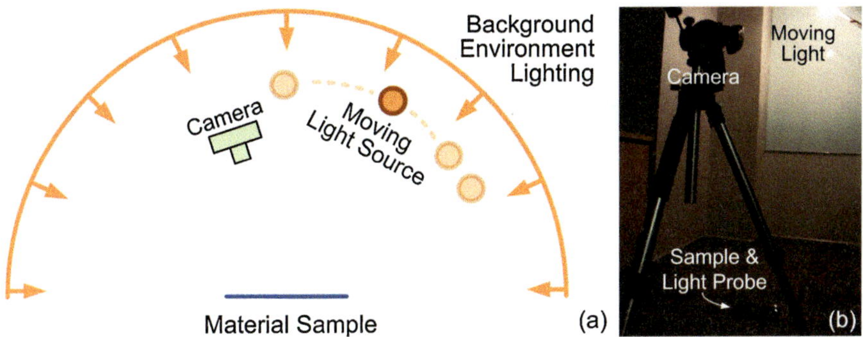

Fig. 3.4 Device setup for capturing reflectance maps (phase 2). (**a**) Diagram. (**b**) Photograph

Fig. 3.5 Lighting used for key measurement, L_j, visualized as hemicube maps

in Fig. 3.5. The light source is attached to a hand-held pole and moved in a 2D plane opposite the sample from the camera, about 1.5 m away from the sample center. We attempt to uniformly sample this plane, and ensure that the set of reflected directions are "covered" by a light direction (i.e., make a highlight appear on the sample). Precise lighting control is not necessary.

A mirror ball is used to probe the applied lighting. A Canon 30D camera with EF-100 2.8 lens is placed above and 2.0 m away from the center of the material sample. The image resolution is 3504×2336.

Before capturing, we calibrate the camera's position and orientation using the method in [25]. For each lighting change, we record an HDR image including the material and the mirror ball using exposure bracketing as in [21]. In our prototype system, we simply move the light source around the sample by hand.

The process is finished after capturing N images, resulting in the material's reflectance responses, $r_j(\boldsymbol{x})$, and reconstructed source radiance fields, $L_j(\mathbf{i})$, for $j \in 1, 2, \ldots, N$. The environmental lighting and moving area light source are far enough away to reasonably assume that the radiance field is constant over the entire material sample. We also compute the viewing direction $\mathbf{o}^\star$ at the sample center and assume it to be constant over all $\boldsymbol{x}$ as well.

Key Lighting Dimensionality To investigate the sufficiency of key lighting measurements, we captured 100 lighting conditions based on a small varying area light source, and randomly selected N as input to generate the matching vector space of 1200 BRDFs, sampled from the example in Fig. 3.10(b). Results are averaged over

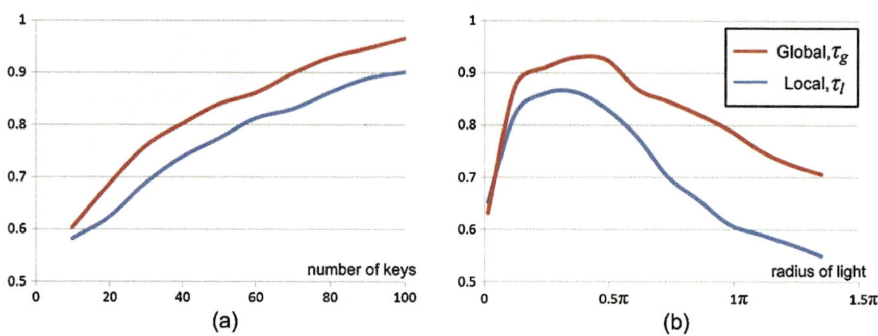

Fig. 3.6 Distance preservation from representative space to matching vector space. (**a**) With increasing number of key measurements. (**b**) With increasing size of light source. Light radius is a linear angle, measured in radians. The material used in this experiment is glossy paper, shown in Fig. 3.10(b). The distance preservations are computed from Eqs. (3.16) and (3.17)

ten trials of this random lighting selection. Figure 3.6(a) plots distance preservation as a function of N. Global and local distance preservation converge fairly quickly as N increases. In our experiments, convincing results are obtained with $\tau_g > 0.9$ and $\tau_l > 0.85$. Evaluating τ_l and τ_g at a few hundred representatives takes little time and indicates whether our lighting configuration and value for N are sufficient. So this validation can be applied between phase one and before phase two, to guide the key measurement.

Key Lighting Size In addition to the number of measurements, the size of the light source used also affects the sufficiency of our key measurement. To investigate this parameter, we performed an experiment on the material shown in Fig. 3.10(b), which mixes BRDFs of different specularity and color. We synthetically generated a series of matching vectors with a moving disk-shaped light source of varying radius. We then plot local and global distance preservation as a function of light source size. The result is shown in Fig. 3.6(b). Smaller light sources generate a higher-rank projection $\boldsymbol{V}_R$ from Eq. (3.10). However, their corresponding key space is also sparsely supported, so significant variation in the BRDF manifold can fall into its null space. Light sources of medium extent (e.g., 0.4π) provide an optimal balance between subspace dimensionality and wideness of support, and so they best preserve distance.

3.4 Experimental Results

We implemented our SVBRDF bootstrapping algorithm on an Intel Core(TM)2 Duo 2.13 GHz PC with 2 GB memory. Core capturing for BRDF representatives and reflectance map keys takes 10–20 minutes, excluding time for setting up the material target, camera, and light source. Subsequent data processing takes less than 10

Table 3.1 Statistics for our examples. The M column shows number of representatives before enlargement. Materials using synthetic enlargement are marked with † for normal and S for tangent enlargement

Material sample	Reflectance maps		Representative BRDFs		
	Resolution	# (N)	# (M)	τ_g/τ_l	k
glossy paper (Fig. 3.10(b))	1000×1000	50	30	0.90/0.87	10
wrinkled paper (Fig. 3.12(c))	1000×600	200	30 †	0.90/0.83	13
weathered copper (Fig. 3.12(d))	2000×2000	80	1200	0.93/0.85	21
aluminum pan (Fig. 3.12(a))	2000×2000	200	10 S	0.99/0.85	15
satin (Fig. 3.12(b))	2000×2000	90	30	0.99/0.85	15
wrinkled satin (Fig. 3.14)	1500×1500	200	30 †S	0.91/0.85	19

minutes. Table 3.1 lists the parameters used in capturing. We infer 2D NDFs of resolution 400×400, yielding 4D BRDFs with more than ten million angular samples in viewing and lighting direction. The spatial resolution ranges from one to four million samples.

3.4.1 Method Validation

Test on Fully-Sampled SVBRDF We tested our bootstrapping method on fully sampled anisotropic SVBRDF data (greeting card from [3]). The experiment selected 1000 BRDFs from random positions as the representatives. Reflectance map capture was simulated by applying the Grace Cathedral environment map [21] along with a disk light source with angular radius 0.4π at a controlled direction. We then measured the reconstruction error of our bootstrapping method as a function of the number N of different key measurements (light directions). For each N, we average over ten randomly generated sets of light directions. Figure 3.7(a) shows the average reconstruction error, which falls quickly as N increases. The rightmost two columns of the figure compare rendered results between the original data (b) and our reconstructed SVBRDF (c), at a view not used in the second phase capture. An accurate match is obtained.

Comparison with Microfacet Synthesis We compared our method with microfacet synthesis [13]. Results are shown in Fig. 3.8. We made $N = 20 \times 20$ lighting measurements for microfacet synthesis, as suggested in [13], requiring capture of 400 reflectance images. Our method was based on $N = 50$ key measurements. Both methods applied point source lighting. Even with such a large data set, microfacet synthesis generates results with grid artifacts on highly specular texels. The artifacts are caused by point light source sampling, which aliases specular peaks. By reconstructing based on full-resolution BRDFs acquired in a separate step, our method is able to avoid such artifacts with a greatly reduced measurement.

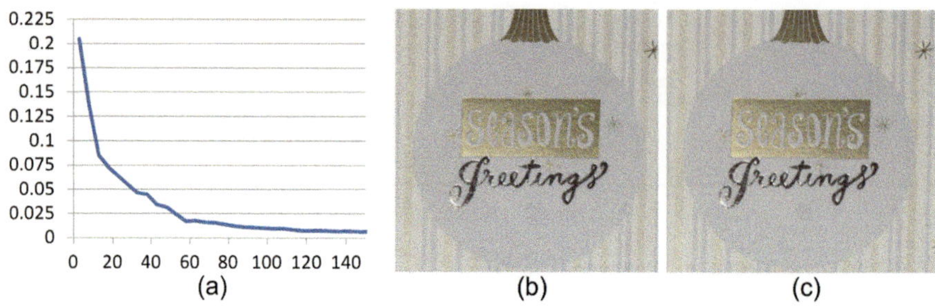

Fig. 3.7 Validation example. (**a**) Reconstruction error as a function of number of lighting measurements, N. (**b**) Rendering with original SVBRDF. (**c**) Rendering with reconstructed SVBRDF

Fig. 3.8 Comparison with result by microfacet synthesis [13]. (**a**) Ground truth. (**b**) Our result. (**c**) Result of microfacet synthesis

Effect of Neighborhood Size We also investigated how k affects reconstruction quality. Our experiment is based on the brushed aluminum sample with $N = 100$ key measurements. We used representative set enlargement based on tangent rotation as described in Sect. 3.2.4. Using a total of $M = 3600$ representatives, we compared reconstruction error from local linear combination as k varied from 1 to 3600. Results at a typical texel are shown in Fig. 3.9(a). The ground truth BRDF is acquired at that point by the device described in Sect. 3.3.1. As expected, increasing k always reduces the fitting error between the key vector and the linear combination of matching vectors. When $k = N$, the number of parameters matches the number of constraints and the error drops to 0. This does not imply a corresponding reduction in error for the final BRDF, because reconstruction is based on a sparse key measurement and so becomes extremely under-determined. As discussed, the BRDF manifold is not globally linear so such under-determined linear combinations generate results off the BRDF manifold and provide a poor fit. A very large k thus generates an implausible BRDF with ghosting artifacts and high error, as shown in Fig. 3.9(e, f). Over a broad range (4–60), the choice of k has little effect on reconstruction quality.

3.4.2 SVBRDF Capture Results

Figure 3.10 shows results for different material samples. We compare the rendered result of our reconstructed SVBRDFs to photographs of the captured sample with

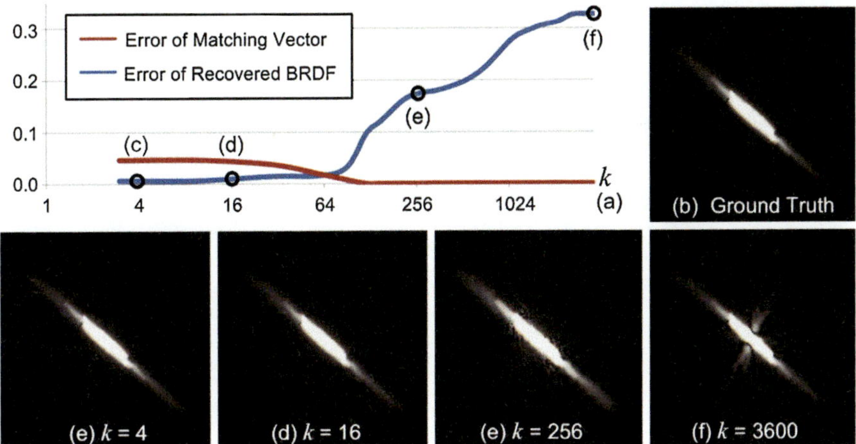

Fig. 3.9 Local linear reconstruction with different neighborhood sizes, k. Error is measured by sum of squared differences (squared L2), normalized to the signal's sum of squares. BRDFs are visualized as 2D NDFs inferred from the microfacet model. (**a**) Matching vector and final BRDF reconstruction error vs. k. (**b**) BRDF ground truth. (**c–f**) Reconstructed BRDF with different k, as marked in (**a**)

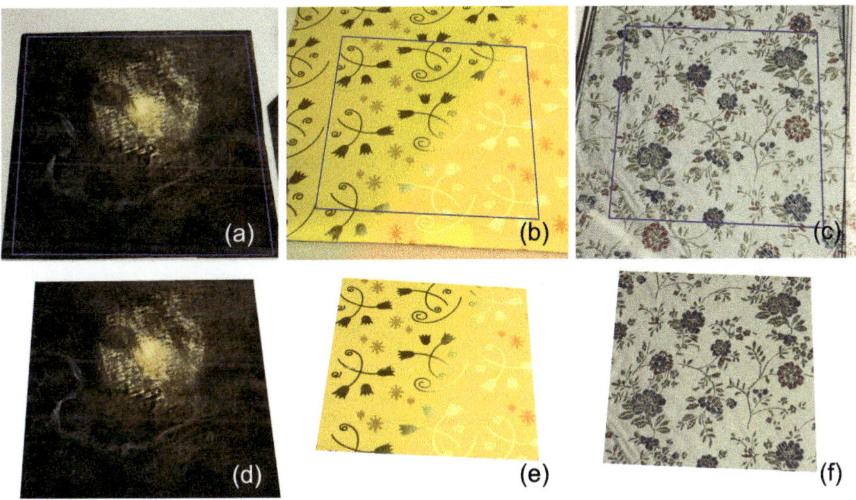

Fig. 3.10 SVBRDF examples. *Top row* shows an original image for each example; *bottom row* shows the reconstructed SVBRDF rendered with the same lighting condition. (**a**, **d**) Weathered copper plate. (**b**, **e**) Glossy paper. (**c**, **f**) Satin

the same lighting conditions. Materials with smooth (a/d) and sharp (b/e) spatial variation are both handled. The leftmost two columns show isotropic materials, while the rightmost column shows anisotropic satin. The comparison is made under

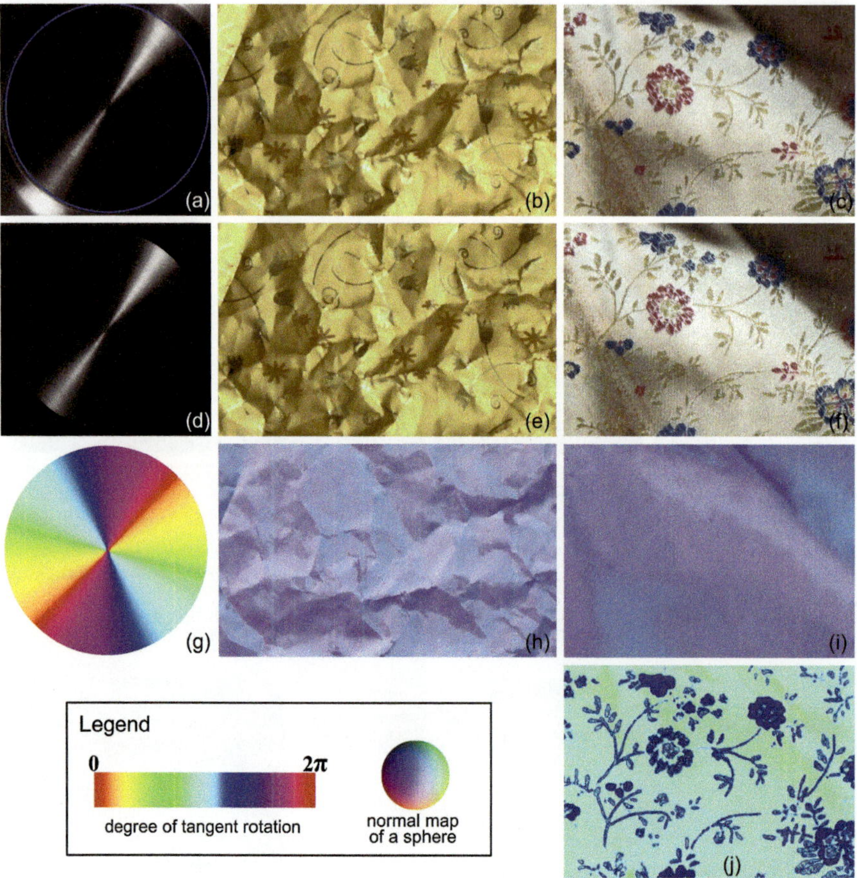

Fig. 3.11 Enlarged SVBRDF examples. *Top row* shows an original image of each example; *second row* shows reconstructed SVBRDFs rendered with the same lighting condition. *Third* and *fourth rows* show inferred normal and tangent maps. (**a**, **d**) Brushed aluminum pan. (**b**, **e**) Wrinkled glossy paper. (**c**, **f**) Wrinkled satin. Image (**g**) shows the tangent map of (**a**); (**h**) shows the normal map of (**b**); (**i**/**j**) shows the normal/tangent map of (**c**)

a novel view and light which does not correspond to any view or light conditions used in capture.

Figure 3.11 shows results for a bumpy isotropic material (b), an anisotropic material with spatially varying tangents (a), and a material with both spatially-varying normals and tangents (c). Rendering results with reconstructed SVBRDFs match well with the ground truth, as shown in the second row. The number of representatives before enlargement is listed in Table 3.1. The wrinkled satin example is enlarged based on both normal and tangent rotation; we reduced its enlargement factors to 72× for tangent and 400× for normal rotations, yielding 864k total representatives after enlargement. All other examples use 3600× for normal and 360×

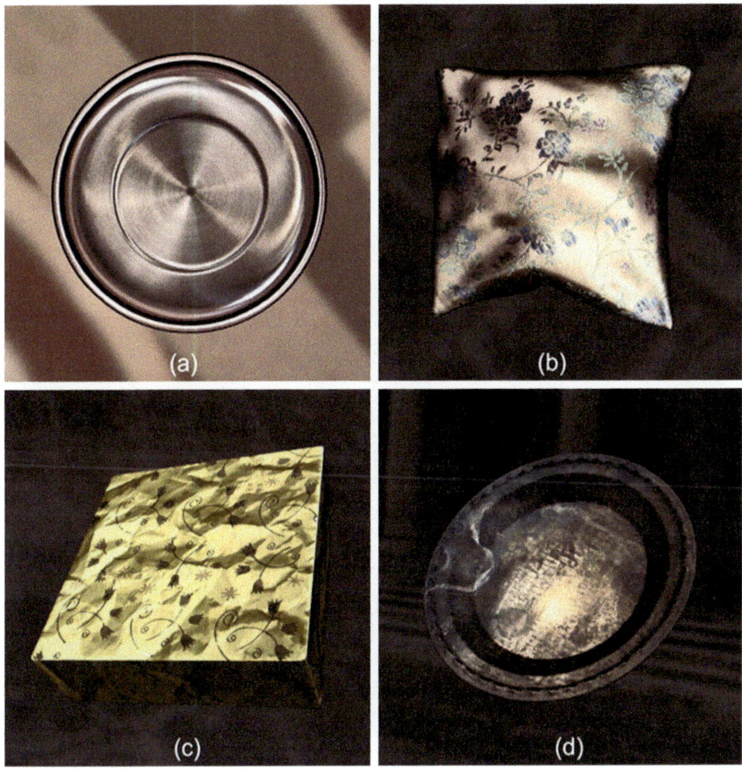

Fig. 3.12 Renderings of high-resolution SVBRDFs reconstructed by our method from two-phase, low-dimensional captured data. (**a**) Anisotropic brushed metal. (**b**) Satin with complex needlework. (**c**) Wrinkled glossy paper. (**d**) Weathered copper

for tangent enlargement, as mentioned in Sect. 3.2.4. The figure also shows normal/tangent maps inferred by applying the same linear combination used to reconstruct each SVBRDF texel to the representative normal/tangent vectors themselves. Such vectors provide a good, low-dimensional proxy to visualize our method's output.

Figures 3.12 and 3.13 show rendered results of the acquired SVBRDFs mapped on objects, from two different views. A brushed aluminum pan is shown in (a); the fan-shaped highlight and detailed brushing pattern create a realistic appearance. A satin pillow with complex needlework is rendered with environment lighting in (b), and exhibits complex appearance changes as the view and light varies. Wrinkled glossy paper with sharp reflectance changes is rendered in (c). Progressively changing reflectance captured from a weathered copper plate is shown in (d). Figure 3.14 shows rendered results from the wrinkled satin SVBRDF capture.

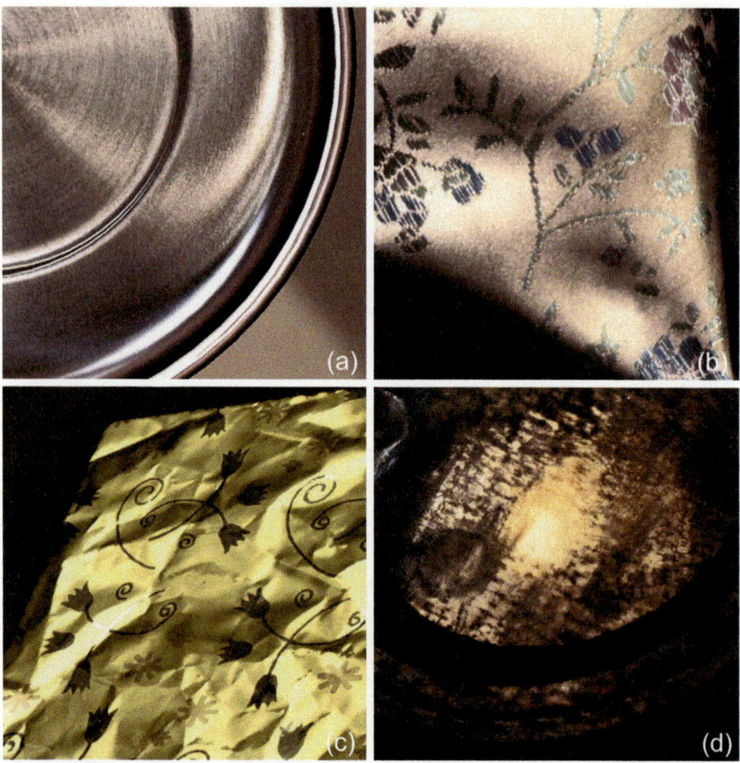

Fig. 3.13 Zoomed results. (**a**) Brushed aluminum. (**b**) Satin. (**c**) Wrinkled glossy paper. (**d**) Weathered copper

Fig. 3.14 Rendering results for wrinkled satin

3.5 Conclusion

Manifold bootstrapping simplifies and accelerates the capture of complex reflectance by decomposing data acquisition into two phases. One captures the overall BRDF manifold while the other maps this manifold over the surface. Both phases make only sparse measurements of the overall 6D SVBRDF. We propose a new compact device based on a pair of condenser lenses to scan BRDF point samples in the first phase. Using local linear embedding and representative set enlargement, we produce SVBRDFs of high resolution in both the spatial and angular domains from this sparse data. Captured materials exhibit convincing realism, isotropic and anisotropic specularity, and spatial detail.

Our method is general and may have application to other sorts of data capture, whenever representatives form a low-dimensional manifold in a high-dimensional space. It can also accommodate different methods for phase one and phase two measurement. Our hand-held BRDF scanner measures only a few light directions, and so requires amplification via the (single-bounce) microfacet model. Though this model has wide applicability [13, 20], it does prohibit anomalous materials such as retro-reflective ones. Our method for acquiring reflectance maps is limited to flat surfaces without significant self-shadowing and self-masking. We would like to address these drawbacks in future work.

References

1. Lensch, H.P.A., Goesele, M., Bekaert, P., Magnor, J.K.M.A., Lang, J., Seidel, H.-P.: Interactive rendering of translucent objects. Comput. Graph. Forum **22**, 195–205 (2003)
2. Matusik, W., Pfister, H., Brand, M., McMillan, L.: A data-driven reflectance model. ACM Trans. Graph. **22**(3), 759–769 (2003)
3. Lawrence, J., Ben-Artzi, A., DeCoro, C., Matusik, W., Pfister, H., Ramamoorthi, R., Rusinkiewicz, S.: Inverse shade trees for non-parametric material representation and editing. ACM Trans. Graph. **25**(3) (2006)
4. Wang, J., Tong, X., Lin, S., Pan, M., Wang, C., Bao, H., Guo, B., Shum, H.-Y.: Appearance manifolds for modeling time-variant appearance of materials. ACM Trans. Graph. **25**(3), 754–761 (2006)
5. Roweis, S.T., Saul, L.K.: Nonlinear dimensionality reduction by locally linear embedding. In: Science, pp. 2323–2326 (2000)
6. Gardner, A., Tchou, C., Hawkins, T., Debevec, P.: Linear light source reflectometry. ACM Trans. Graph. **22**(3), 749–758 (2003)
7. Ward, G.J.: Measuring and modeling anisotropic reflection. In: Proceedings of the 19th Annual Conference on Computer Graphics and Interactive Techniques, pp. 265–272. ACM, New York (1992)
8. Lensch, H.P.A., Kautz, J., Goesele, M., Heidrich, W., Seidel, H.-P.: Image-based reconstruction of spatial appearance and geometric detail. ACM Trans. Graph. **22**(2), 234–257 (2003)
9. Lafortune, E.P.F., Foo, S.-C., Torrance, K.E., Greenberg, D.P.: Non-linear approximation of reflectance functions. In: Proceedings of the 24th Annual Conference on Computer Graphics and Interactive Techniques, pp. 117–126. ACM/Addison-Wesley, New York (1997)
10. Goldman, D.B., Curless, B., Hertzmann, A., Seitz, S.M.: Shape and spatially-varying BRDFs from photometric stereo. In: International Conference on Computer Vision, pp. 341–348 (2005)
11. Zickler, T., Enrique, S., Ramamoorthi, R., Belhumeur, P.: Reflectance sharing: image-based rendering from a sparse set of images. In: Bala, K., Dutré, P. (eds.) Eurographics Symposium on Rendering, Konstanz, Germany pp. 253–264. Eurographics Association, Geneva (2005)
12. Alldrin, N., Zickler, T.E., Kriegman, D.: Photometric stereo with non-parametric and spatially-varying reflectance. In: Computer Vision and Pattern Recognition, pp. 1–8 (2008)

13. Wang, J., Zhao, S., Tong, X., Snyder, J., Guo, B.: Modeling anisotropic surface reflectance with example-based microfacet synthesis. In: ACM SIGGRAPH 2008 Papers, pp. 1–9. ACM, New York (2008)
14. Debevec, P., Tchou, C., Gardner, A., Hawkins, T., Poullis, C., Stumpfel, J., Jones, A., Yun, N., Einarsson, P., Lundgren, T., Fajardo, M., Martinez, P.: Estimating surface reflectance properties of a complex scene under captured natural illumination. Technical report ICT-TR-06, University of Southern California Institute for Creative Technologies Graphics Laboratory (2004)
15. Matusik, W., Pfister, H., Brand, M., McMillan, L.: Efficient isotropic BRDF measurement. In: Proceedings of the 14th Eurographics Workshop on Rendering, Aire-la-Ville, Switzerland, Switzerland, pp. 241–247. Eurographics Association, Geneva (2003)
16. Weyrich, T., Matusik, W., Pfister, H., Bickel, B., Donner, C., Tu, C., McAndless, J., Lee, J., Ngan, A., Jensen, H.W., Gross, M.: Analysis of human faces using a measurement-based skin reflectance model. ACM Trans. Graph. **25**(3), 1013–1024 (2006)
17. Cook, R.L., Torrance, K.E.: A reflectance model for computer graphics. ACM Trans. Graph. **1**(1), 7–24 (1982)
18. Ngan, A., Durand, F., Matusik, W.: Experimental analysis of BRDF models. In: Eurographics Symposium on Rendering (2005)
19. Mount, D., Arya, S.: Ann: A library for approximate nearest neighbor searching. In: 2nd CGC Workshop on Computational Geometry (1997)
20. Ashikhmin, M., Premoze, S., Shirley, P.: A microfacet-based BRDF generator. In: Siggraph 2000, Computer Graphics Proceedings, pp. 65–74. ACM/Addison-Wesley Longman, New York (2000)
21. Debevec, P.E., Malik, J.: Recovering high dynamic range radiance maps from photographs. In: ACM SIGGRAPH, pp. 369–378 (1997)
22. Schuster, W.: Harmonische Interpolation. In: Math. Semesterber., pp. 1–27. Springer, Berlin (2001)
23. Debevec, P., Hawkins, T., Tchou, C., Duiker, H.-P., Sarokin, W., Sagar, M.: Acquiring the reflectance field of a human face. In: Proc. SIGGRAPH 2000, pp. 145–156 (2000)
24. Shirley, P., Chiu, K.: A low distortion map between disk and square. J. Graph. Tools **2**(3), 45–52 (1997)
25. Zhang, Z.: A flexible new technique for camera calibration. IEEE Trans. Pattern Anal. Mach. Intell., **22**, 1330–1334 (2000)

Chapter 4
Interactive SVBRDF Modeling from a Single Image

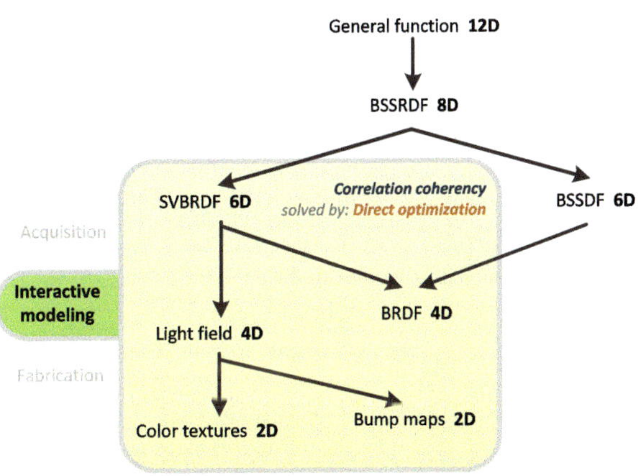

In the previous chapter, we presented an efficient method for capturing and representing an SVBRDF with the BRDF manifold model, which greatly simplifies the measurement process and accelerates acquisition speed. In many instances though, one wishes to model the appearance of a material for which a physical sample is not readily available. All that one may have is just an image of the desired material from an online photo gallery. For cases like this, manual modeling by artists is needed to generate an appearance model of the material for computer graphics. Software design tools like Photoshop, CrazyBump and Maya are often used for manual modeling from an image, but require considerable time and skill to generate materials with a reasonably convincing appearance.

This chapter presents an efficient and easy-to-use system called *AppGen* for interactive material modeling from a single image. We focus on modeling spatially-varying surface reflectance and normal variations from a texture image that is captured from a nearly planar surface lit by directional lighting. Such images are easily found in texture collections used by artists for material modeling. In this work, our

Y. Dong et al., *Material Appearance Modeling: A Data-Coherent Approach*,
DOI 10.1007/978-3-642-35777-0_4, © Springer-Verlag Berlin Heidelberg 2013

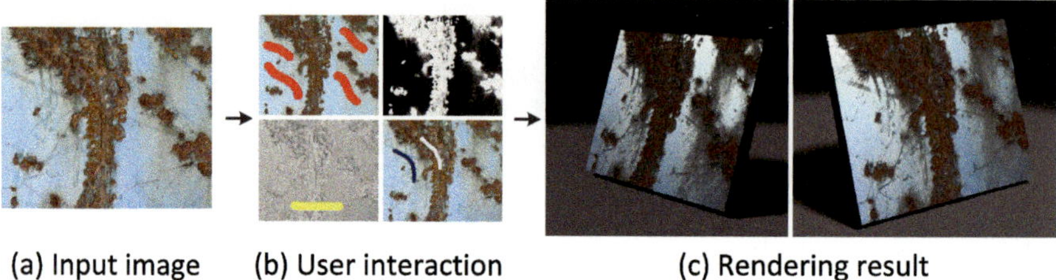

Fig. 4.1 Given a single image (**a**), our system models the spatially varying reflectance properties and normals with a few strokes specified by the user (**b**). The resulting material can be rendered under different lighting and viewing conditions (**c**)

goal is not to determine the exact reflectance and normals from such single images, which is well-known to be an ill-posed problem. Instead, we aim to obtain a material that is visually consistent with the photo while significantly speeding up the workflow of artists. To keep user interaction minimal, the key idea is to require the user to specify shading or reflectance information on only a few pixels with sparse strokes, while our algorithm employs *direct optimization* in efficiently inferring the reflectance and normal details for all pixels in the image based on this input. This inference uses two forms of *inter-attribute correlation* coherence: between diffuse and specular reflection, and between the chroma and albedo of surface points. The outcome of this process is exemplified in Fig. 4.1, which exhibits a material modeled using our system with just a few user strokes. With *AppGen*, an artist can quickly produce a highly detailed, realistic output material that is comparable in appearance to what he or she would generate with traditional software tools in substantially more time, as shown in Fig. 4.2.

What makes it possible for our system to reconstruct a material's spatially varying appearance from very little user input is the strong coherence in reflectance over a surface. By identifying the exact form of coherence that exists among the different surface points, our system is able to enforce corresponding constraints on the solution and also propagate the user-supplied reflectance data over the entire material accordingly.

Our system consists of four steps, illustrated in Fig. 4.3. (1) First, we remove highlight and shadow pixels in the input image and fill them by image inpainting. After that, we are left with an image of only the diffuse contribution. (2) We present an algorithm for interactively separating the texture image into the product of shading and diffuse albedo. We assume that in each local region pixels with the same chroma value belong to the same material and have the same albedo intensity, while groups of pixels with different chroma values share the same global geometry and thus have the same average shading. Based on these two assumptions, we formulate the separation as an optimization problem and solve it via an Expectation-Maximization (EM) like algorithm. We ask the user to interactively mark regions that violate our assumptions using a few rough strokes and augment our optimization procedure with these constraints to further refine the separation results. The result of this step is a diffuse color map and a shading map caused

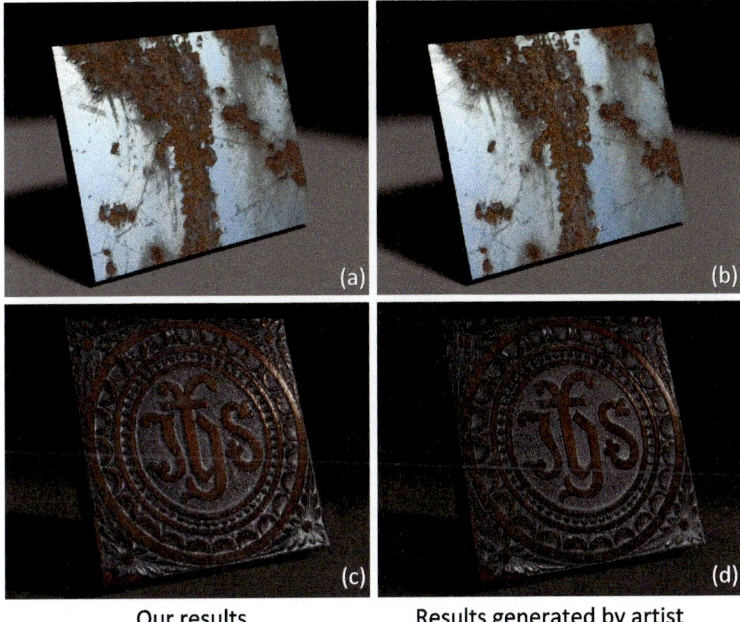

Fig. 4.2 Comparisons between the materials modeled by our method and materials manually modeled by an experienced artist. The results generated by the two methods are similar. Our system generated each result within five minutes, while the artist took about one hour to generate each result

by normal variations. (3) We recover the per-pixel normals from the shading map by representing the underlying geometry as a height field (to capture the overall shape) with perturbed normals over it (to fit the remaining fine-scale shading variations). In general, splitting the shading map into a height field and perturbed normals contribution is an ill-posed problem. In our case though, since we assume that the contributions of the perturbed normals are subtle high frequency effects, we remove them from the shading map by smoothing. Based on this observation, we introduce a two-scale normal reconstruction algorithm. We first compute a height field that best fits the smoothed shading image, and then solve for a detailed normal map over the height field that best fits the detailed shading map. The geometry features at different scales are well recovered in this way and generate consistent shading results under different lighting conditions. (4) Finally, we assign the proper specular properties to each pixel based on the diffuse albedo and the specular properties of a sparse set of pixels that are assigned by the user with rough strokes.

With this technique, materials with compelling appearance can be generated with only a few minutes of interaction. As we will later demonstrate, our system works well for a variety of material types, including natural surfaces (metals, woods, rocks, leathers) and man-made ones (textiles, papers, concrete).

4.1 Related Work

Several previous works have aimed to decompose an input image into a lighting and a reflectance component, commonly referred to as *intrinsic images*. Without prior knowledge about the scene and its objects, decomposition of a single input image into intrinsic images cannot be solved due to its inherent ill-posedness [1]. Methods that tackle this problem incorporate additional constraints to make the decomposition tractable. Horn [2] makes the assumption that the illumination varies smoothly over the surface, which is generally not true for bumpy surfaces. Tappen et al. [3] use color information and a pre-trained classifier to label gradients in the input image as either reflectance or albedo changes. Shen et al. [4] detect similar local neighborhoods (i.e., textons) over the image and assume these areas to have a similar reflectance. However the texton clustering used in their method can lead to banding artifacts in the resulting shading map. Recently, Bousseau et al. [5] decoupled intrinsic images from a single input image with user assistance. Their method assumes that the reflectance of pixels in a local window lies in a plane. Although this assumption is valid for natural images, it will fail in a texture image with rich reflectance details. All of these methods are designed for natural images and cannot work well for images of materials with rich variations in both albedo and shading. Our separation algorithm targets such texture images. With few assumptions and sparse user input, our method optimally decomposes the reflectance from shading while preserving both albedo and shading details in the result. In contrast to the diffuse shading separation method of Xue et al. [6] for images of weathered surfaces, our method does not assume surface reflectance to form a 1D manifold in color space. Our method provides a general solution to the separation problem, as well as an efficient refinement scheme.

In the field of computer vision, methods have been proposed for estimating surface shape from its shading in a single image. As in intrinsic image decomposition, this problem is also ill-posed and requires additional constraints. Horn and Brooks [7] recover the normals from a shading image by regularizing the problem with smoothness constraints. The resulting normals tend to be noisy and biased toward the lighting direction. Later methods [8, 9] assume the underlying surface to be integrable and solve a height field from the shading image. Although these methods work well for reconstructing the overall surface geometry, they fail to fit the shading details and thus cannot reproduce detailed normal variations over the surface. Our two-step normal reconstruction approach accurately recovers both surface geometry and detailed normal variations from a single shading image and generates consistent shading results under different lighting directions.

Recently, Glencross et al. [10] hallucinated a surface height field from an image captured under diffuse ambient lighting. Another image with flash illumination of the same scene is needed for separating the albedo from the input image. Our system uses a single input image under directional lighting for modeling both albedo variations and normal variations. Moreover, our normal reconstruction method accurately recovers detailed normal maps and preserves details in the shading map.

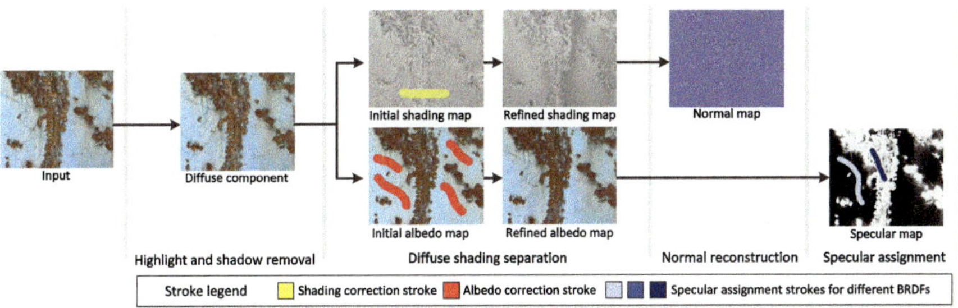

Fig. 4.3 Overview of our system. In the preprocessing step, we remove highlight and shadow pixels. After that, with user assistance, we decompose the diffuse component into the product of a diffuse albedo map and a diffuse shading map. We then assign specular reflectance guided by the albedo map and user strokes. Finally, we reconstruct geometry details from the diffuse shading map. A legend of color coded strokes used in this chapter is shown at the bottom

4.2 System Overview

Our system takes as input a texture image I of a nearly planar surface with spatially-varying reflectance and normal variations that is illuminated by a directional light. Since the underlying surface is nearly planar, we further ignore occlusion and inter-reflections between geometry details on the surface. Although this lighting model is not physically accurate, it nevertheless produces plausible results for many input images as later shown.

Without losing generality, we model the BRDF $\rho(x)$ at pixel x as the sum of a Lambertian component, with albedo $\rho_d(x)$, and a specular component, with specular coefficient $\rho_s(x)$ and lobe shape $f_r(x)$. Under directional lighting, the image value $\mathbf{I}(x)$ at x can be computed as the sum of the diffuse contribution $\mathbf{I}_d(x)$ and the specular highlights $\mathbf{I}_s(x)$ as

$$\mathbf{I}(x) = \mathbf{I}_d(x) + \mathbf{I}_s(x), \tag{4.1}$$

where

$$\mathbf{I}_d(x) = \rho_d(x)\mathbf{S}_d(x) = \rho_d(x)\big(\mathbf{N}(x) \cdot L\big)I_l, \tag{4.2}$$

$$\mathbf{I}_s(x) = \rho_s(x)\mathbf{S}_s(x) = \rho_s(x) f_r\big(\mathbf{N}(x), L, V\big)\big(\mathbf{N}(x) \cdot L\big)I_l. \tag{4.3}$$

The diffuse shading $\mathbf{S}_d(x)$ is determined by the local normal $\mathbf{N}(x)$, the light direction L and light intensity I_l, while the specular shading $\mathbf{S}_s(x)$ is additionally related to the viewing direction V.

Given input image $\mathbf{I}$, the goal of our system is to model spatially-varying diffuse albedos $\rho_d(x)$, specular coefficients $\rho_s(x)$, lobe shapes $f_r(x)$, and normals $\mathbf{N}(x)$ with the help of a few user strokes. Figure 4.3 shows an overview of our system that is composed of the following steps:

- *Highlight and Shadow Removal.* We first identify the highlight $\mathbf{I}_s(x)$ and shadow pixels $\mathbf{I}_o(x)$ by thresholding the pixel values ($I(x) > 235$ for highlights and

$I(x) < 25$ for shadows for 8-bit images) and fill these pixels by image inpainting [11]. After that, the image only contains the diffuse component $\mathbf{I}_d$. Any other shadow removal and specular separation method could be used instead in this step.

- *Diffuse Shading Separation* (Sect. 4.3). We decompose $\mathbf{I}_d$ obtained from the last step into the product of a diffuse albedo map ρ_d and a diffuse shading map $\mathbf{S}_d$. We formulate this separation as an optimization problem and compute the initial shading and diffuse albedo maps. After that, the user quickly refines the initial separation results by drawing sparse strokes in regions that violate our assumptions and thus exhibit artifacts.
- *Normal Reconstruction* (Sect. 4.4). We reconstruct a normal map $\mathbf{N}$ from the diffuse shading map $\mathbf{S}_d$ with a two-scale normal reconstruction approach. After the user specifies the lighting direction, we first compute a height field that fits a smoothed shading map. We then recover fine geometric variations by fitting detailed normals over the height field to match the detailed input shading map $\mathbf{S}_d$.
- *Specular Assignment* (Sect. 4.5). We assign the specular reflectance properties (ρ_s and f_r) of a fixed set of specular basis BRDFs to each pixel, guided by user strokes that assign the basis BRDFs to just a few pixels. A material classification algorithm determines the material type of all pixels, according to the diffuse color and stroke location, and uses this to assign a specular BRDF to each pixel.

4.3 User-Assisted Shading Separation

In this step, we decompose the diffuse components $\mathbf{I}_d$ into a shading map $\mathbf{S}_d$ and a diffuse albedo map ρ_d. These two components will serve as the input of the following steps for normal reconstruction and specular assignment.

For this purpose, we represent the image value $\mathbf{I}_d = (\mathbf{I}_d^r, \mathbf{I}_d^g, \mathbf{I}_d^b)$ by its intensity $\mathbf{I}_d^i = (\mathbf{I}_d^r + \mathbf{I}_d^g + \mathbf{I}_d^b)/3$ and chroma value $\mathbf{I}_d^c = (\mathbf{I}_d^r/\mathbf{I}_d^i, \mathbf{I}_d^g/\mathbf{I}_d^i, 3 - \mathbf{I}_d^r/\mathbf{I}_d^i - \mathbf{I}_d^g/\mathbf{I}_d^i)$. We assume the light is white $I_l = (1.0, 1.0, 1.0)$ so that the image chroma comes from the chroma of the diffuse albedo $\rho_d^c(x) = \mathbf{I}_d^c(x)$, while the image intensity is the product of shading and albedo brightness:

$$\mathbf{I}_d^c(x) = \rho_d^c(x), \qquad \mathbf{I}_d^i(x) = \rho_d^i(x)\mathbf{S}_d^i(x). \tag{4.4}$$

Our goal is to decompose the diffuse intensity $\mathbf{I}_d^i$ into an albedo intensity map ρ_d^i and a shading intensity map $\mathbf{S}_d^i$. To this end, we formulate the separation as an optimization problem and solve the initial albedo map and shading map by an EM (Expectation-Maximization) like algorithm. After that, we refine the results with the constraints specified by sparse strokes.

4.3.1 Separation as Optimization

We first assume that in each local region Ω, pixels with the same chroma value $\mathbf{I}_d^c(x) = \rho_d^c(x) = c$ belong to one material and thus have the same albedo intensity i_c. Based on this *local albedo assumption*, we have

$$\rho_d^i(x) = i_c, \quad x \in \Omega_c, \tag{4.5}$$

where Ω_c refers to the set of pixels that are in Ω and have the same chroma value c. For shading caused by the geometric details in Ω, our key observation is that although the spatial patterns and amplitudes of the geometric details of each material (i.e., pixels in each Ω_c) may be different from one another, the large scale geometry in Ω is almost flat. As a result, the average normals of the geometric details of all materials in Ω are almost the same and the shading estimation of each material is equivalent to the shading estimation of all pixels in Ω. Based on this *local shading assumption*, we have

$$E\big(\mathbf{S}_d^i(x)\big|x \in \Omega_c\big) = E\big(\mathbf{S}_d^i(x')\big|x' \in \Omega\big). \tag{4.6}$$

Given Eqs. (4.5) and (4.6), the intensity estimation of pixels in Ω_c can be computed as

$$\begin{aligned} E\big(\mathbf{I}_d^i(x)\big|x \in \Omega_c\big) &= \frac{\sum_{x\in\Omega_c}(\rho_d^i(x)\mathbf{S}_d^i(x))}{N_{\Omega_c}} = \frac{i_c \sum_{x\in\Omega_c} \mathbf{S}_d^i(x)}{N_{\Omega_c}} \\ &= i_c E\big(\mathbf{S}_d^i(x)\big|x \in \Omega_c\big) = i_c E\big(\mathbf{S}_d^i(x')\big|x' \in \Omega\big), \end{aligned} \tag{4.7}$$

where N_{Ω_c} is the number of pixels in Ω_c. So the albedo intensity $\rho_d^i(x)$ of a pixel x in region Ω_c should satisfy

$$\rho_d^i(x) = \frac{E(\mathbf{I}_d^i(x')|x' \in \Omega_c)}{E(\mathbf{S}_d^i(x'')|x'' \in \Omega)}, \quad x \in \Omega_c. \tag{4.8}$$

Since the shading intensity is $\mathbf{S}_d^i(x) = \mathbf{I}_d^i(x)/\rho_d^i(x)$, we can rewrite the right side of the equation as a function of image intensities and albedo intensities of pixels in Ω as

$$E_0\big(\Omega, c, \mathbf{I}_d^i, \rho_d^i\big) = \frac{E(\mathbf{I}_d^i(x')|x' \in \Omega_c)}{E(\mathbf{S}_d^i(x'')|x'' \in \Omega)} = \frac{\frac{1}{N_{\Omega_c}} \sum_{x'\in\Omega_c} \mathbf{I}_d^i(x')}{\frac{1}{N_\Omega} \sum_{x''\in\Omega} \frac{\mathbf{I}_d^i(x'')}{\rho_d^i(x'')}}. \tag{4.9}$$

Based on this local constraint, we formulate the separation as an optimization problem by minimizing the following energy function of $\rho_d^i(x)$:

$$F_0\big(\rho_d^i(x)\big) = \sum_{\Omega\in\Omega^\dagger} \big\|\rho_d^i(x) - E_0\big(\Omega, \rho_d^c(x), \mathbf{I}_d^i, \rho_d^i\big)\big\|^2, \tag{4.10}$$

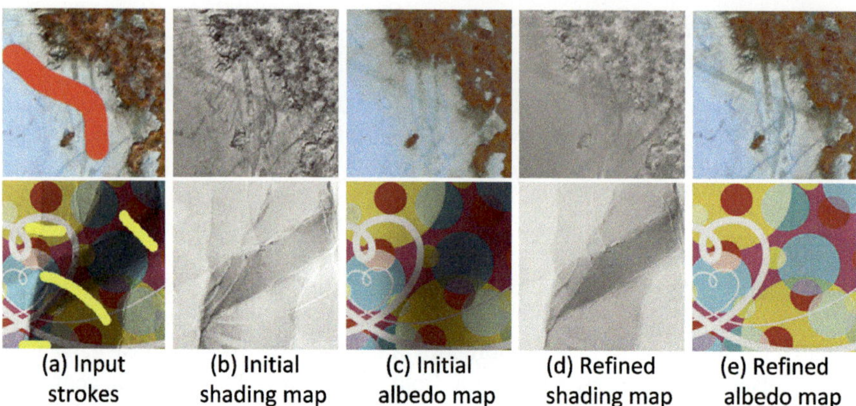

Fig. 4.4 Interactive refinement. Given the initial shading map (**b**) and albedo map (**c**) separated from the input image, the user draws sparse strokes in regions that violate our assumptions to refine the results. The top row shows the effect of an *Albedo correction stroke*, and the bottom row shows the effect of *Shading correction strokes*. Artifacts in the initial results (**b**) and (**c**) are fixed in (**d**) and (**e**) after refinement

where $\Omega^{\dagger}$ is the collection of all fixed sized local regions that contain x. In practice, we define Ω as a $W \times W$ window and solve this optimization using an iterative algorithm similar to Expectation-Maximization. In the E-step, given $E_0(\Omega, \rho_d^c(x), \mathbf{I}_d^i, \rho_d^i)$ computed from the current albedo intensity map, we update $\rho_d^i(x)$ by solving the linear equations that result from the differentiations of $F_0(\rho_d^i(x))$ with respect to $\rho_d^i(x)$. Then in the M-step, we update $E_0(\Omega, c, \mathbf{I}_d^i, \rho_d^i)$ for each window and each chroma value from the new albedo intensity map according to Eq. (4.9). We repeat these two steps iteratively until convergence. After obtaining the albedo intensity $\rho_d^i(x)$, we compute the shading intensity $\mathbf{S}_d^i(x) = \mathbf{I}_d^i(x)/\rho_d^i(x)$. Figure 4.4(b, c) illustrate the shading intensity map and albedo intensity map separated by our optimization algorithm.

In practice, we set the region size to $W = 20$ and initialize the optimization by setting the albedo intensity to the image intensity (i.e., the shading intensity is 1.0 everywhere). To determine whether two pixels have the same chroma value, we uniformly subdivide the first two channels of chroma vectors into 20 bins and quantize each pixel's chroma value to one of 400 quantized chroma values.

4.3.2 Interactive Refinement

Although our method generates reasonable results in most image regions, it will fail and generate artifacts in regions that violate our assumptions. Specifically, in regions that violate the *local albedo assumption*, pixels with the same chroma value have different albedo intensities. In this case, our method will leave image intensity variations of these pixels to the shading map and thus generate undesired shading details in flat regions (shown in the top row of Fig. 4.4(b, c)). In regions that violate the *local shading assumption*, the shading estimate of each material is different from each other and thus is also different from the shading estimate of the local region. In this case, our method will compute a biased albedo intensity for each pixel and thus introduce undesired variations in regions with constant albedo (shown in the bottom row of Fig. 4.4(b, c)). This case often happens in regions where the material distribution is correlated to large scale geometric structures.

User Strokes We design a user stroke for each type of artifact for users to quickly specify artifact pixels. Based on sparse strokes specified by the user, our algorithm automatically removes the artifacts and refines the separation results.

To fix the artifacts in regions that violate the *local albedo assumption*, we ask the user to draw *albedo correction strokes* over artifact pixels to indicate that locally the underlying geometry is flat and the shading details of a pixel should be moved to its albedo intensities. As a result, each albedo correction stroke defines the following constraint:

$$\rho_d^i(x) = E_S\big(\Omega, x, \mathbf{I}_d^i, \rho_d^i\big) = \frac{\mathbf{I}_d^i(x)}{E(\mathbf{S}_d^i(x')|x' \in \Omega)} = \frac{\mathbf{I}_d^i(x)}{\frac{1}{N_\Omega}\sum_{x'\in\Omega}\frac{\mathbf{I}_d^i(x')}{\rho_d^i(x')}} \tag{4.11}$$

and an energy term F_S for optimization:

$$F_S\big(\rho_d^i(x)\big) = \sum_{\Omega\in\Omega^\dagger} w(x)\big\|\rho_d^i(x) - E_S\big(\Omega, x, \mathbf{I}_d^i, \rho_d^i\big)\big\|^2, \tag{4.12}$$

where $w(x) = \lambda e^{-\|x-x_s\|^2/\sigma}$ is a weight function to control the importance of the stroke constraint at x, which is determined by the distance between x and its closest stroke pixel x'. In practice, we set $\lambda = 10.0$ and $\sigma = 3.0$.

To fix artifacts in regions that violate the *local shading assumption*, we ask the user to draw *shading correction strokes* over artifact pixels to indicate that locally the albedo intensity of a pixel with chroma c should be the same as the albedo intensity of stroke pixels that have the same chroma c. If no pixel in the stroke has chroma c, the pixel keeps its original albedo. So each shading correction stroke defines the following constraint:

$$\begin{aligned}\rho_d^i(x) &= E_A\big(\Omega_s, c, \rho_d^i\big) = E\big(\rho_d^i(x')\big|x' \in \Omega_{sc}\big)\\ &= \frac{1}{N_{\Omega_{sc}}}\sum_{x'\in\Omega_{sc}} \rho_d^i(x'), \quad \rho_d^c(x) = c,\end{aligned} \tag{4.13}$$

where Ω_s is the set of all pixels in the stroke, Ω_{sc} refers to all pixels in Ω_s that have chroma c, and $N_{\Omega_{sc}}$ is the number of pixels in Ω_{sc}. We thus define the following energy term F_A for optimization:

$$F_A\big(\rho_d^i(x)\big) = \sum_{\Omega\in\Omega^\dagger} w(x)\big\|\rho_d^i(x) - E_A\big(\Omega_s, \rho_d^c(x), \rho_d^i\big)\big\|^2. \tag{4.14}$$

Result Refinement To refine the separation result with user specified strokes, we minimize the following energy function that combines the energy terms defined by all strokes and F_0:

$$F_0\big(\rho_d^i(x)\big) + \lambda_S \sum_{j=0}^{N_S} F_{S,j}\big(\rho_d^i(x)\big) + \lambda_A \sum_{k=0}^{N_A} F_{A,k}\big(\rho_d^i(x)\big), \tag{4.15}$$

where $F_{S,j}$ denotes the j-th shading correction stroke, and $F_{A,k}$ is the k-th albedo correction stroke. N_S and N_A are the numbers of strokes of the two types. λ_S and λ_A weight the constraints specified by the two types of strokes respectively in optimization, both of which are set to 1.0 in practice.

We adapt our iterative solver for this new energy function. In the E-step, we update the albedo intensity $\rho_d^i(x)$ by solving the sparse linear system resulting from the differentiations of the new energy function with respect to $\rho_d^i(x)$. In the M-step, we update the functions E_0, E_S and E_A with the new albedo intensity values according to Eqs. (4.9), (4.11), and (4.13) respectively. We repeat these two steps iteratively until convergence. The spatial weights w for each stroke are computed before the optimization. Figure 4.4(d, e) illustrate refined separation results, where the artifacts are removed with the help of sparse user strokes.

4.3.3 Discussion

Different from previous intrinsic images methods [1] mainly designed for natural images, our method targets texture images with details in both reflectance and shading. On one hand, our local albedo assumption allows arbitrary chroma variations in the local region and thus can well handle complicated reflectance details. On the other hand, our local shading assumption only constrains the average shading of each material in the local region and thus well preserves the complicated shading details in the input. Moreover, we design two types of strokes for the user to quickly remove artifacts and refine results. We compare our method with two automatic intrinsic images methods [4, 12] in Fig. 4.5. The color retinex method [12] generates visible artifacts in the separated results. Although the non-local texture used in [4] improves the results, the separation artifacts still cannot be fully removed. By contrast, our method can automatically recover the shading/albedo in images with both shading and albedo variations. Figure 4.6 compares the results generated by our method with ones generated by the user-assisted intrinsic images method in [5]. Note that in [5] the local reflectance plane assumption cannot guarantee the shading/albedo to be constant in regions with constant shading/albedo. User inputs are always necessary for generating reasonable results and become cumbersome as the detail in the input image increases, while in our method the automatic solution already generates convincing results for most image inputs. User input is only needed to fix artifacts in the results.

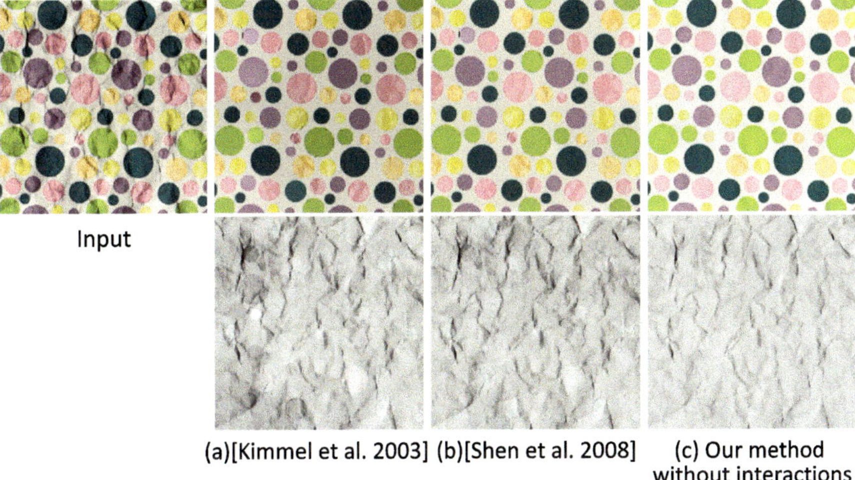

Fig. 4.5 Comparisons to automatic intrinsic image algorithms. (**a**) Color retinex [12] has artifacts in the separated results. (**b**) Even if combined with non-local texture cues [4] these artifacts cannot be fully removed. (**c**) Without user interaction, our method already produces reasonable results

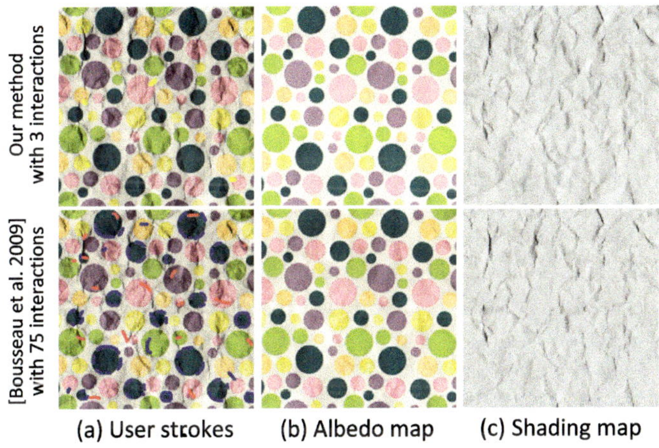

Fig. 4.6 Comparisons to user-assisted intrinsic images. Our method is shown in the top row, while the results of [5] are shown in the bottom row. With only three interactions, our method can generate high quality separation results, while [5] requires many more input strokes to get a reasonable separation

4.4 Two-Scale Normal Reconstruction

To model the geometry details of the input surface, we reconstruct a normal map $\mathbf{N}(x)$ from the diffuse shading map $\mathbf{S}_d(x)$ and a lighting direction L roughly specified by the user.

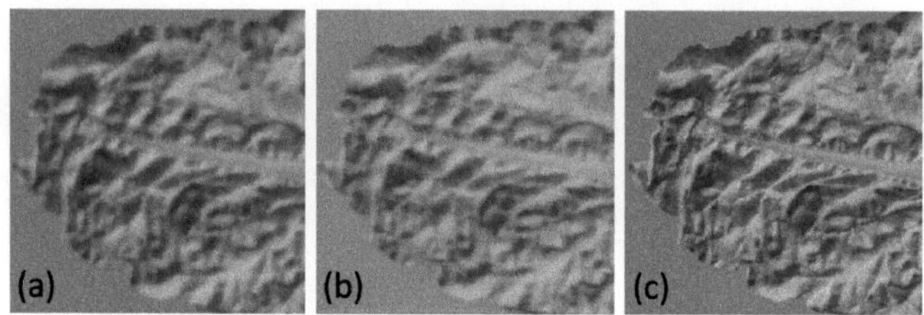

Fig. 4.7 Two-scale normal reconstruction. (**a**) Filtered shading map. (**b**) Result rendered from the reconstructed height field. (**c**) Result rendered from the final normal map

For this purpose, we represent the surface geometry as a height field with perturbed normals over it and develop a two-scale normal reconstruction algorithm. The key observation of this approach is that the shading details produced by the normal perturbations in $\mathbf{S}_d(x)$ are always subtle and high-frequency, and as such can be filtered out by smoothing. Based on this observation, we first filter the input shading map $\mathbf{S}_d$ with a 3×3 Gaussian filter ($\sigma = 0.4$ in our implementation) and recover a height field $\mathbf{H}$ from the filtered shading map $\mathbf{S}_d^{'}$ via shape from shading. We follow the method in [13] to compute a height field $\mathbf{H}$ in our current implementation, but other shape from shading methods can be used instead here. After that, we compute the perturbed normals defined over the height field by minimizing the energy function:

$$E_n = \sum_x \left\| \mathbf{N}(x) \cdot L - \mathbf{S}_d(x) \right\|^2 + \lambda \sum \left\| \mathbf{N}(x) - \mathbf{N}_h(x) \right\|^2. \tag{4.16}$$

The first term constrains the shading result of $\mathbf{N}$ with lighting direction L to fit the input shading map $\mathbf{S}_d$, while the second regularization term minimizes the difference between the resulting normal $\mathbf{N}$ and the normal $\mathbf{N}_h$ computed from the height field $\mathbf{H}$. The weight λ is a regularization term, which is set to 0.001 for all results shown in this chapter. This optimization can be done by solving a sparse linear system. In practice, we initialize the optimization by setting $\mathbf{N}(x) = \mathbf{N}_h(x)$ and compute the normal via a Gauss-Seidel solver with successive over-relaxation. The results of these two steps are illustrated in Fig. 4.7. Note that the normal map recovered by our method well preserves geometric details and generates convincing rendering results under different lighting conditions.

Discussion Our method is not sensitive to the accuracy of the light direction L specified by the user in that the error of light direction will lead only to a global rotation of all normals over the surface but has no effect on the relative normal variations. Since our method assumes that the underlying geometry is almost flat, we rotate the initial normals and lighting in the first step so that the average normal of the underlying geometry is always upward. Figure 4.8 illustrates results generated from one input shading map but with different lighting directions specified by the user. As the error of the specified lighting direction becomes larger, the error of the resulting normal map is small and almost unchanged.

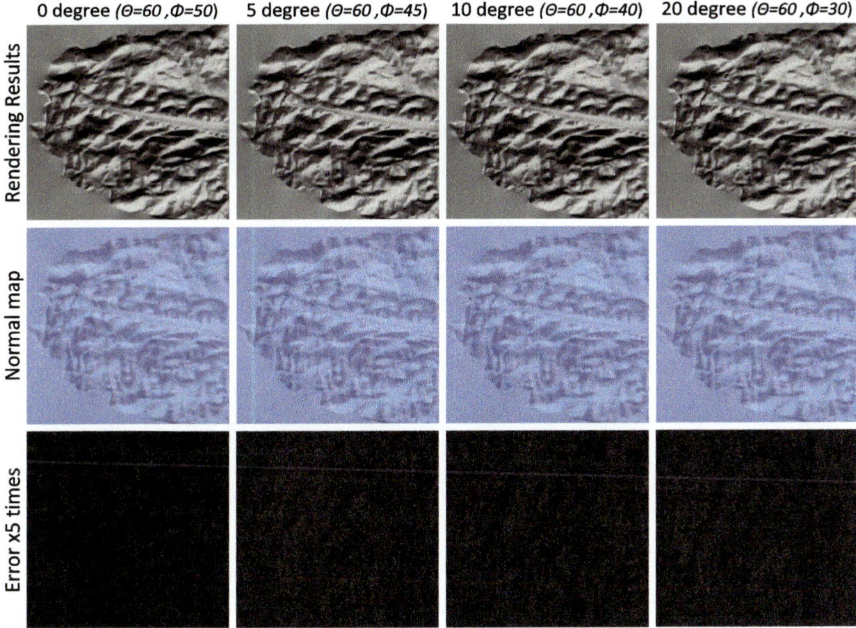

Fig. 4.8 Normal maps reconstructed from the same shading map, but with different lighting directions rotated respectively by 0, 5, 10, and 20 degrees. The rendering results are shown in the *top row*. The *middle row* displays a visualization of the reconstructed normal map. The *bottom row* shows the 5× magnified reconstruction error, measured as the length of the cross product between the resulting normal map and the normal map at 0 degrees. Note how our method is robust to the input light directions

In Fig. 4.9, we compare the result generated by our method (Fig. 4.9(g)) with the ones generated by other existing normal reconstruction methods. A straightforward solution would be to directly reconstruct the normal map from $\mathbf{S}_d$ with a regularization term as in [7]. Although the resulting normal map well fits the input shading image, it is biased toward the lighting direction L and generates artifacts under other lighting directions (Fig. 4.9(c)). Other shape from shading approaches assume the surface to be integrable and reconstruct a height field from the input shading map. Although these methods can reconstruct the overall surface geometry, the detailed normal perturbations over the surface are smoothed out. Figure 4.9(d) shows a rendering result of the height field reconstructed using [13]. Although the height field generates reasonable results under different lighting directions, the shading details caused by detailed normal variations are lost. Figure 4.9(e) illustrates the result generated by the shading-as-depth method used in [14]. Although the shading-as-depth method works well for many smooth surfaces, it fails to model the geometric features in this input. We also compare the results generated by our method with one (Fig. 4.9(f)) generated by the photometric method in [15]. While the photometric method can well recover the normal map, it needs many more images (12 images in

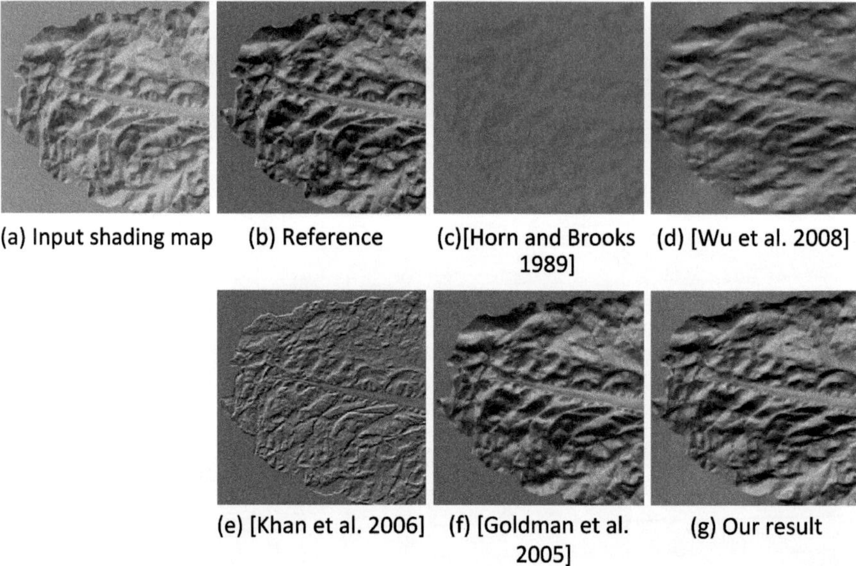

Fig. 4.9 Comparisons of different normal reconstruction methods. (**a**) is the input shading map rendered from a ground truth normal map. (**b**) is a reference image rendered from the ground truth under a novel lighting direction. (**c**) to (**g**) are images rendered from results generated by different normal reconstruction methods. The lighting directions used in rendering are the same as the one used in (**b**). Previous shape from shading methods either generate biased results (**c**), or smooth out the detailed normal variations (**d**). Simply taking the shading as depth [14] in (**e**) does not generate a reasonable result. The photometric stereo method [15] (**f**) can accurately reconstruct the normal map, but requires much more input data. Our normal reconstruction algorithm can well preserve normal details and generate a convincing result in (**g**) from a single input image

this example) as input, which are not always available in our application. Instead, our method generates convincing results from just a single input image.

4.5 User-Assisted Specular Assignment

In this step, we assign a specular coefficient ρ_s and lobe shapes f_r to each pixel. Based on the observation that the specular properties at each pixel mostly depend on the underlying material type (e.g., whether a pixel is metal or rust) rather than detailed diffuse color variations, we ask the user to assign the specular BRDF to a sparse set of pixels, using rough strokes, and then automatically determine the specular BRDF for other pixels. The user strokes not only determine the specular reflectance of the underlying pixels, but also assign the same material type to these pixels. With N_M BRDFs and N_M corresponding material types assigned by the strokes, we classify each pixel's material type by computing the probability that it belongs to each material type. After that, we assign the specular BRDF to each pixel based on the material classification results. This process is illustrated in Fig. 4.10.

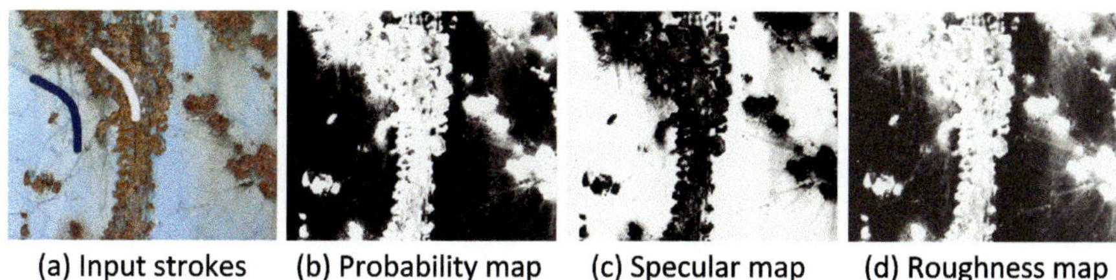

(a) Input strokes (b) Probability map (c) Specular map (d) Roughness map

Fig. 4.10 Specular assignment. We ask the user to assign single BRDFs to pixels that belong to the same material type by sparse strokes (**a**). Our algorithm then classifies the material type of pixels and determines the probability map (**b**). Finally, the specular (**c**) and roughness (**d**) coefficient of each pixel are calculated based on the probability map (**b**) and assigned BRDFs

Material Classification Given the set of pixels that belongs to each material type i (i.e., the pixels in the same-BRDF strokes), we construct the sets M_i of their diffuse colors. We remove the outliers in each set M_i by checking each diffuse albedo in the set and finding whether its $k = 10$ nearest diffuse albedos are in the same material set. If more than 50 % of them come from material sets other than M_i, we remove this diffuse color value from M_i. After that, we compute the probability $p_i(x)$ that each pixel x belongs to the i-th material type by using Shepard's method [16]:

$$p_i(x) = \frac{d_i(x)^{-p}}{\sum_{j=1}^{m} d_j(x)^{-p}}, \tag{4.17}$$

where m is the total number of material types and $d_i(x)$ is the distance from pixel x's diffuse color to the i-th material type's material set, which is computed by

$$d_i(x) = \frac{1}{10}\sum_{j=0}^{10}\left\|\rho_d(m_j) - \rho_d(x)\right\|, \tag{4.18}$$

where $\rho_d(m_j)$ is the ten diffuse albedos in M_i that are closest to $\rho_d(x)$. In practice, we pick $p = 1$ for all the results. Although it is possible to apply other edit propagation methods [17, 18] for determining the d_i for each pixel, we apply Shepard's method in our current implementation because of its simplicity.

Specular Coefficient Assignment After material classification, we assign the specular coefficient $\rho_s(x)$ and specular roughness $\alpha(x)$ to each pixel by

$$\rho_s(x) = \sum_{i=1}^{M} \rho_i p_i(x), \qquad \alpha(x) = \sum_{i=1}^{M} \alpha_i p_i(x), \tag{4.19}$$

where $p_i(x)$ is the probability that pixel x belongs to the i-th material, and ρ_i and α_i are the specular coefficient and roughness of the i-th material respectively.

In our implementation, the specular BRDFs are selected from 120 pre-defined specular BRDFs extracted from measured materials. We represent the specular lobe

Fig. 4.11 Images rendered from the results generated with different stroke inputs. The user stroke inputs are shown in the *bottom right*. Although the stroke inputs are different, the results generated by our method are similar

shapes f_r by using the Ward model controlled by the roughness parameter $\alpha(x)$ ranging from 0.005 to 0.5. When necessary, the user can fine-tune the parameters as well as the specular color of the selected BRDF. We use the Ward model as it can be easily adjusted by the user to fine-tune the lobe shape. Our method itself is not constrained to a parametric specular model.

4.6 Experimental Results

Performance We performed our tests on a PC with an Intel Xeon 2.83 GHz CPU and 4 GB RAM. For a typical input image of size 768×768, the albedo and shading separation runs within 1.8 seconds, the two-step normal map reconstruction converges within 1.5 seconds, depending on the input shading map, and the specular assignment step takes less than 0.2 seconds for material classification and reflectance coefficient blending. The fast computations in each step provide responsive feedback for user interaction.

User Input All results shown in this chapter are generated by an artist in one to five minutes. Depending on the complexity of the input image, up to nine strokes were used for diffuse shading separation, while one to four strokes were drawn for specular assignment. For all results shown in Figs. 4.13 to 4.17, we display all the strokes used for modeling in the input image. Different types of strokes are rendered in different colors. Similar to other stroke based methods, our method does not require accurate user strokes. Figure 4.11 illustrates the results generated from the same input but with different input strokes. Provided that the user intention was the same, these different user strokes generate similar results.

Comparison with Standard Toolsets Figure 4.12 compares a ground truth rendering with the result generated by our method, a combination of [5] and [13], and CrazyBump. We use an RGBN dataset from [19] to render the input image under directional lighting. We then compare the rendering of the ground truth data

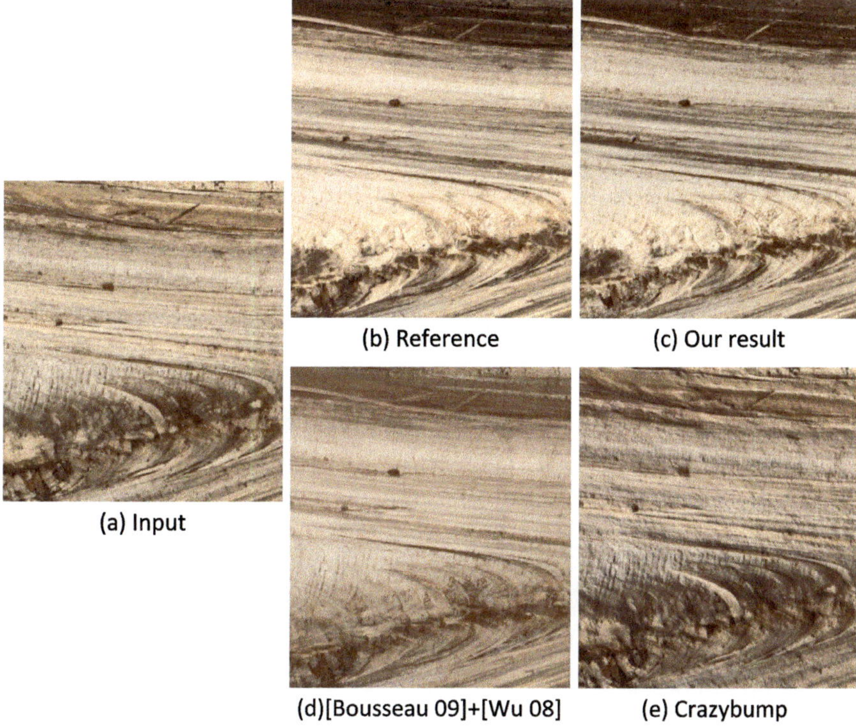

Fig. 4.12 Comparison with prior work. (**a**) Input image rendered from ground truth data [19]. (**b**) Reference image rendered from ground truth data lit from different lighting direction. (**c**) Rendering results of our method. (**d**) Results generated by a combination of [5] and [13]. (**e**) Results modeled by an artist using Crazybump. (**b**)–(**e**) are rendered under the same light direction, but different from (**a**). The result generated by our method is closer to the ground truth, while other methods fail to recover the shading and reflectance presented in the input image

and the data reconstructed by the different methods under a new lighting direction. In generating these images, we assume that the surface presented by the RGBN data is diffuse and take the RGB value as the albedo. To generate the result shown in Fig. 4.12(d), we applied the algorithm in [5] to separate the input image and then computed the normals from the resulting shading map with [13]. As shown in Fig. 4.12, both CrazyBump and the combination of [5] and [13] fail to recover the reflectance and normals from the input. By contrast, our method recovers the reflectance and normal details well.

Figure 4.2 illustrates two results generated by an experienced artist, in about one hour each, using standard image manipulation tools, including Photoshop and CrazyBump. With our method, the user generates similar results using a few user strokes within five minutes. Although a more systematic user study would be needed to derive formal results, we feel that this comparison is typical of our experience and shows the efficiency of our approach.

Fig. 4.13 Natural materials with complex geometric details generated by our system. (**a**, **b**) Rock. (**c**, **d**) Raw wood

Results We tested our system with a wide variety of input images, shown in Figs. 4.13–4.17 together with user strokes and the final materials, rendered under different viewing and lighting. We show user input as yellow strokes for *shading correction strokes*, red strokes for *albedo correction strokes*, and blue ones with different intensity to indicate the strokes that mark the placement of the different specular BRDFs.

We chose input images that correspond to a wide range of materials, ranging from man-made materials such as paper (Fig. 4.14) and wood carving (Fig. 4.17(a)), to natural materials like wood (Figs. 4.13(c), 4.15(a)), stone (Fig. 4.13(a)), asphalt (Fig. 4.16(c)), and rusted metals (Figs. 4.15(c), 4.16(a)). These input images and corresponding materials show a wide range of spatial distributions of geometry and reflectance, demonstrating the wide applicability of our approach.

Figure 4.13 shows results of two natural materials with complex geometric details. Note how the large scale geometry variations of the rock and the sharp cracks in the raw wood are modeled well by our method.

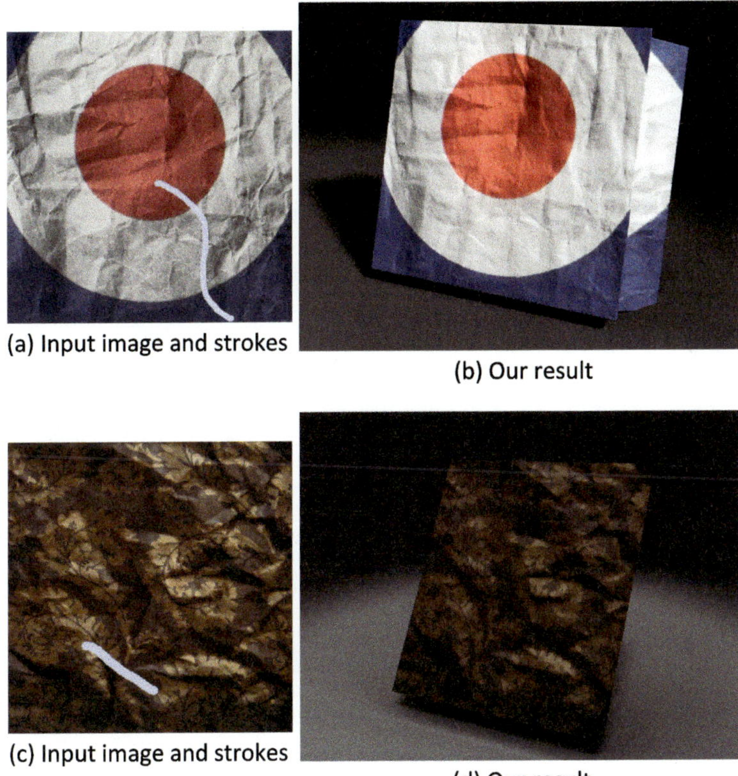

Fig. 4.14 Wrinkled paper results generated by our system

Figure 4.14 shows two results of wrinkled papers, which consist of sharp color variations and rich geometric details at multiple scales. Our method captures well these reflectance and normal variations and generates convincing rendering results.

In many natural materials, such as wood and rust, complex reflectance and normal variations are often combined. Figure 4.15 shows two typical images of these material types. Note that with minimal interaction, our method models well the spatially-varying highlights of the finished wood and the rich color and reflectance details in the rust.

Figures 4.16 and 4.17 demonstrate examples of surfaces composed of multiple material types, each of which exhibits its own spatially-varying appearance. The rusted metal in Fig. 4.16 has shiny specular highlights in the metallic regions, while the rusted parts are nearly diffuse with strong normal variations. Our result reproduces realistic appearance for both the metallic and rusted regions. Note the natural variations of the highlights in the final rendered images. For the asphalt in Fig. 4.16, our method successfully reveals the detailed bump variations of the surface while preserving the global structure of the yellow paint.

Fig. 4.15 Finished wood (**a**, **b**) and rusted metal (**c**, **d**) generated by our system

Figure 4.17 shows two materials that have man-made global structure and detailed natural textures. Our system reproduces the geometry variations for both man-made carvings and natural textures. In the wood carving, the specular reflectance of the polished red wood and matte reflectance of the dusted part are well preserved by our specular assignment. For the rock wall example, the rich albedo variations and sharp boundaries between rock and cement are well modeled in our result.

Limitations Although our system works well for a wide variety of texture images, we made several assumptions that might be violated by some input, as shown in Fig. 4.18. First, we assume that the input comes from a nearly planar surface lit by directional lighting. For images that violate this assumption, our algorithm may fail to produce convincing results (e.g., Fig. 4.18(a)). Second, our method mostly uses the diffuse component of the input image for material modeling. For images that contain large highlight and shadow regions (e.g., Fig. 4.18(b)), that are often clamped, the material variations in these regions cannot be reconstructed

Fig. 4.16 Rusted metal (**a**, **b**) and asphalt with yellow paint (**c**, **d**) generated by our system

well by our method. Finally, our interactive shading separation method relies on chroma variations during initialization. For materials with grayscale albedo, our separation method fails to generate the initial separation result, thus potentially requires too much user input for diffuse shading separation. Figure 4.18(c) illustrates a typical case: an image of a wrinkled paper with grayscale text on it, where our method generates artifacts in the resulting normal map and albedo map.

4.7 Conclusion

In this chapter, we presented *AppGen*, an interactive system for modeling materials from a single image. Given an input texture image of a nearly-planar surface lit by directional lighting, our system allows artists to efficiently model the spatially-varying reflectance and normals from only a few minutes of interaction to place a few rough strokes. A diffuse shading separation algorithm and a two-

Fig. 4.17 Carved wood plate (**a**, **b**) and concrete rock wall (**c**, **d**) generated by our system

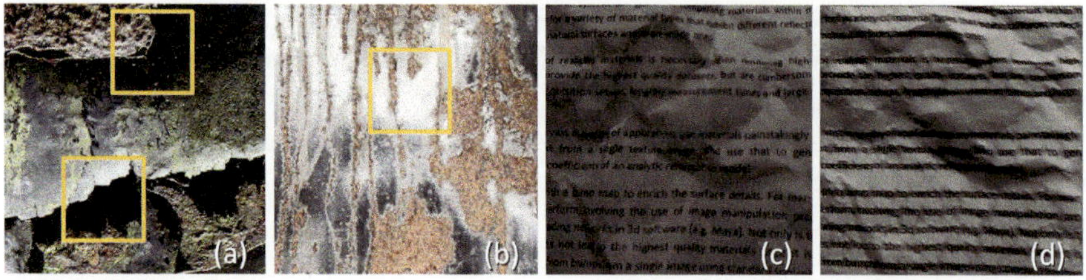

Fig. 4.18 Failure cases of our method. (**a**) Image with strong geometric structures. (**b**) Image containing large highlight regions. (**c**) Grayscale image, where the albedo only has grayscale variations. (**d**) Our method fails to separate the black text from shading variations and generates artifacts in the normal map

step normal reconstruction method are presented for deriving the normal and reflectance details from the texture input. We illustrate the capability of our method by modeling a wide variety of materials generated from images with different reflectance and normal variations. We believe that our system can greatly speed up the workflow of expert artists and might allow novices to start modeling materials.

Our method assumes that the input image is lit with directional lighting. One direction for future work is to extend our system to model materials from images taken under environment lighting. We are also interested in investigating the modeling of materials with complex meso-structure, that produce images with complex shadowing and inter-reflection. Finally, we are interested in developing methods that leverage measured material datasets when available in order to speed up the material modeling process.

References

1. Grosse, R., Johnson, M.K., Adelson, E.H., Freeman, W.T.: Ground truth dataset and baseline evaluations for intrinsic image algorithms. In: IEEE 12th International Conference on Computer Vision 2009, pp. 2335–2342 (2009)
2. Horn, B.K.P.: Robot Vision. MIT Electrical Engineering and Computer Science. MIT Press, Cambridge (1986)
3. Tappen, M.F., Adelson, E.H., Freeman, W.T.: Estimating intrinsic component images using non-linear regression. In: IEEE Computer Society Conference on Computer Vision and Pattern Recognition, 2006
4. Shen, L., Tan, P., Lin, S.: Intrinsic image decomposition with non-local texture cues. In: IEEE Conference on Computer Vision and Pattern Recognition, CVPR 2008, pp. 1–7 (2008)
5. Bousseau, A., Paris, S., Durand, F.: User-assisted intrinsic images. ACM Trans. Graph. **28**, 130 (2009)
6. Xue, S., Wang, J., Tong, X., Dai, Q., Guo, B.: Image-based material weathering. Comput. Graph. Forum **27**(2), 617–626 (2008)
7. Horn, B.K.P., Brooks, M.J.: Shape from Shading. MIT Press, Cambridge (1989)
8. Zhang, R., Tsai, P.-S., Cryer, J.E., Shah, M.: Shape from shading: a survey. IEEE Trans. Pattern Anal. Mach. Intell. **21**, 690–706 (1999)
9. Durou, J.D., Falcone, M., Sagona, M.: Numerical methods for shape-from-shading: a new survey with benchmarks. Comput. Vis. Image Underst. **109**(1), 22–43 (2008)
10. Glencross, M., Ward, G.J., Melendez, F., Jay, C., Liu, J., Hubbold, R.: A perceptually validated model for surface depth hallucination. ACM Trans. Graph. **27**, 59 (2008)
11. Bertalmio, M., Sapiro, G., Caselles, V., Ballester, C.: Image inpainting. In: The 27th Annual Conference on Computer Graphics and Interactive Techniques, SIGGRAPH '00, pp. 417–424. ACM Press/Addison-Wesley, New York (2000)
12. Kimmel, R., Elad, M., Shaked, D., Keshet, R., Sobel, I.: A variational framework for retinex. Int. J. Comput. Vis. **52**, 7–23 (2003)
13. Wu, T.-P., Sun, J., Tang, C.-K., Shum, H.-Y.: Interactive normal reconstruction from a single image. ACM Trans. Graph. **27**(5), 1–9 (2008)
14. Khan, E.A., Reinhard, E., Fleming, R.W., Bülthoff, H.H.: Image-based material editing. ACM Trans. Graph. **25**, 654–663 (2006)
15. Goldman, D.B., Curless, B., Hertzmann, A., Seitz, S.M.: Shape and spatially-varying brdfs from photometric stereo. IEEE Trans. Pattern Anal. Mach. Intell. **32**(6), 1060–1071 (2010)
16. Shepard, D.: A two-dimensional interpolation function for irregularly-spaced data. In: Proceedings of the 1968 23rd ACM National Conference, ACM '68, pp. 517–524. ACM, New York (1968)

17. An, X., Pellacini, F.: AppProp: all-pairs appearance-space edit propagation. ACM Trans. Graph. **27**(3), 40 (2008)
18. Xu, K., Li, Y., Ju, T., Hu, S.-M., Liu, T.-Q.: Efficient affinity-based edit propagation using k-d tree. ACM Trans. Graph. **28**(5), 118 (2009)
19. Fattal, R., Agrawala, M., Rusinkiewicz, S.: Multiscale shape and detail enhancement from multi-light image collections. In: ACM SIGGRAPH 2007 Papers, SIGGRAPH '07. ACM, New York (2007)

Part II
Modeling and Rendering of Subsurface Light Transport

For objects and materials that are not opaque, their appearance is influenced not only by surface reflections, but also by the transport of light beneath the surface. Many materials, ranging from marble to human skin, exhibit translucency due to the light penetration and scattering within the volume, and capturing this effect is critical for producing realistic appearance.

The light transport in translucent materials is much more complicated than surface reflectance. For heterogeneous translucent objects, subsurface scattering is determined by the object geometry, the optical properties of constituent volumetric elements, and the spatial distribution of these elements in the volume. Because of the complex effects of these various factors on subsurface scattering, modeling of these materials has been challenging topic in computer graphics.

As discussed in Chap. 1, spatially varying subsurface scattering can be represented by the eight-dimensional Bi-Directional Surface Scattering Reflectance Distribution Function (BSSRDF) [2], which represents the appearance of a surface point with respect to light that enters the volume from other points. Although it records the light scattering effects within the material volume, the BSSRDF is a surface model, since all the light transport by a BSSRDF is defined between two surface points.

Since subsurface scattering is determined by the optical properties of the material volume, a very different modeling approach is to directly compute the translucent appearance from volumetric material properties. In contrast to the surface model, volumetric material data is independent of object shape, and such a material model can be used with arbitrary target objects. In addition, such volumetric data is intuitive for artists to manipulate, which facilitates interactive editing to create novel material volumes with a desired translucent appearance.

Although volumetric data has many advantages for modeling translucent appearance, a full resolution 3D material volume often requires substantial storage space and computation. Since the spatial distribution of optical properties within material volumes generally has strong coherency in terms of patterns and statistics, we can use a texture model to efficiently represent the 3D spatial distribution of material properties.

In this part of the book, we present techniques for all three of these forms of subsurface light transport modeling. These methods offer efficient modeling based on the inherent coherency of materials in the BSSRDF domain, in the material volume, or in its material element distributions. After an overview of related work in Chap. 5, we directly analyze in Chap. 6 the non-linear coherence properties in subsurface light transport between surface points using the kernel Nyström method [4]. *Appearance subspace* coherency is exploited to reconstruct the BSSRDF of a material by *linear combinations* from a relatively small number of images. Chapter 7 presents a system based on a volume-based representation that allows for capturing, editing and rendering of translucent materials [3]. This solution is built on the diffusion equation, which describes the scattering of light in optically dense media. With this equation and a volumetric model, our method uses *material attribute repetition* coherency in solving for the material volume whose appearance is consistent with image observations. While accounting for material coherency, we obtain a solution by *direct optimization* from only a sparse set of images that allows accurate reproduction of the material for novel viewing and lighting conditions. To further exploit the spatial coherency for texture-like translucent material, we present in Chap. 8 an algorithm to generate high-resolution material volumes from a small 2D slice [5]. We capitalize on the *material attribute repetition* coherence of textures and *subspace search* reconstruction to model the volume from little data. The translucent volume can be efficiently rendered using the TransCut technique [1], which enables interactive modeling of high-resolution translucent material volumes.

References

1. Li, D., Sun, X., Ren, Z., Lin, S., Guo, B., Zhou, K.: TransCut: interactive rendering of translucent cutouts. Technical Report (2011)
2. Nicodemus, F.E., Richmond, J.C., Hsia, J.J., Ginsberg, I.W., Limperis, T.: Geometric Considerations and Nomenclature for Reflectance. Monograph, vol. 161, pp. 1–67. Natl. Bur. of Standards, Washington (1977)
3. Wang, J., Zhao, S., Tong, X., Lin, S., Lin, Z., Dong, Y., Guo, B., Shum, H.-Y.: Modeling and rendering of heterogeneous translucent materials using the diffusion equation. ACM Trans. Graph. **27**(1), 9 (2008)
4. Wang, J., Dong, Y., Tong, X., Lin, Z., Guo, B.: Kernel Nyström method for light transport. ACM Trans. Graph. **28**(3), 29 (2009)
5. Dong, Y., Lefebvre, S., Tong, X., Drettakis, G.: Lazy solid texture synthesis. Comput. Graph. Forum **27**(4), 1165–1174 (2008)

Chapter 5
Overview of Subsurface Light Transport

Subsurface light transport within a material has often been represented with physically based models of radiative light transfer. Radiative transfer models were first introduced to computer graphics by Blinn [1] to represent the scattering of light in participating media. This technique addressed single scattering within a homogeneous medium such as dusty air. To render multiple scattering in optically thick participating media such as clouds, Stam [2] later presented an approximation of multiple scattering as a diffusion process, where the many and frequent collision events within the medium causes light intensity to become isotropic or directionally independent. For a detailed survey on techniques for modeling and rendering of participating media, we refer the reader to [3]. In the following, we present a short overview of light transport beneath the surface of translucent materials.

5.1 Computing Subsurface Light Transport

Radiative light transfer for subsurface scattering has been modeled for translucent material volumes with known optical properties [4–6]. Jensen et al. [7] later presented a model for homogeneous translucent materials that combines an exact solution for single scattering with an analytic dipole diffusion approximation for multiple scattering based on the diffusion approximation of Stam [2]. This method was later extended in [8], where a shading model was formulated from multipole theory for light diffusion in multi-layered translucent materials. The diffusion equation was later used to more generally model heterogeneous translucent materials [9].

The diffusion equation has also been used to compute subsurface light transport. Wang et al. [9] first solve the diffusion equation on a GPU with a finite-difference method (FDM) on polycube structures, and later extended this approach to tetrahedral meshes [10]. Arbree et al. [11] solve the differential equation using the finite element method (FEM) which yields a stable solver. Li et al. [12] proposed a novel FDM solver over a tetrahedral mesh and substantially increased the speed of convergence while preserving the result quality.

Y. Dong et al., *Material Appearance Modeling: A Data-Coherent Approach*,
DOI 10.1007/978-3-642-35777-0_5, © Springer-Verlag Berlin Heidelberg 2013

Aside from radiative transfer models, subsurface scattering has been simulated and rendered using Monte Carlo methods [5, 6] and photon tracing [13]. Physically based simulation of the numerous scattering events within a material provides a high level of realism, but entails a considerable expense in computation. Real-time rendering can be achieved through precomputation of light transport [14, 15]. However, light transport quantities that have been precomputed with respect to a given volumetric model become invalid after material editing.

5.2 Capturing Subsurface Scattering Effects

The subsurface scattering of heterogeneous materials may be acquired directly from image appearance. Acquisition methods have been presented for human faces [16], object-based models [17], material-based models for volumes with an even distribution of heterogeneous elements [18], and material models for general heterogeneous volumes [19]. These image-based representations are specific to the measured object or material. Although the appearance of a material could potentially be modified in these models, physical material properties cannot be edited in a meaningful way.

Models of subsurface scattering may also be acquired through estimation of scattering parameters from a material sample. Parameter estimation, however, is often confounded by multiple scattering, whose appearance arises in a complex manner from a material's scattering properties. For homogeneous materials, multiple scattering can be approximated with analytic models [7, 20], which have greatly facilitated estimation of scattering parameters. In [21], the effects of multiple scattering are avoided by diluting participating media to low concentrations, such that multiple scattering becomes negligible and scattering parameters can be solved from only single scattering. For heterogeneous, optically dense materials, multiple scattering cannot be addressed with such simplifications.

For heterogeneous translucent materials, several methods compute spatially varying scattering properties by fitting the dipole model to BSSRDFs at each point [22, 23] or per region [24, 25]. However, these methods can only represent materials with slowly varying properties such as skin, whose BSSRDF can be well approximated by a homogeneous BSSRDF computed from scattering properties at each point. It cannot be used for modeling many other heterogeneous translucent materials with sharp variations, such as marble and jade.

Many methods have been developed for editing BSSRDFs [26–28] and rendering BSSRDFs under different lighting conditions [14, 15, 29, 30]. Although these methods provide good solutions for modeling and rendering surface appearance caused by subsurface scattering, they all ignore the actual material properties inside the object volume.

References

1. Blinn, J.F.: Light reflection functions for simulation of clouds and dusty surfaces. In: SIGGRAPH, pp. 21–29 (1982)

2. Stam, J.: Multiple scattering as a diffusion process. In: Euro. Rendering Workshop, pp. 41–50 (1995)
3. Cerezo, E., Perez, F., Pueyo, X., Peron, F.J., Sillion, F.X.: A survey of participating media rendering techniques. Vis. Comput. **21**(5), 303–328 (2005)
4. Hanrahan, P., Krueger, W.: Reflection from layered surfaces due to subsurface scattering. In: SIGGRAPH, pp. 165–174 (1993)
5. Dorsey, J., Edelman, A., Legakis, J., Jensen, H.W., Pedersen, H.K.: Modeling and rendering of weathered stone. In: SIGGRAPH, pp. 225–234 (1999)
6. Pharr, M., Hanrahan, P.M.: Monte Carlo evaluation of non-linear scattering equations for subsurface reflection. In: SIGGRAPH, pp. 275–286 (2000)
7. Jensen, H.W., Marschner, S.R., Levoy, M., Hanrahan, P.: A practical model for subsurface light transport. In: SIGGRAPH, pp. 511–518 (2001)
8. Donner, C., Jensen, H.W.: Light diffusion in multi-layered translucent materials. ACM Trans. Graph. **24**(3), 1032–1039 (2005)
9. Wang, J., Zhao, S., Tong, X., Lin, S., Lin, Z., Dong, Y., Guo, B., Shum, H.-Y.: Modeling and rendering of heterogeneous translucent materials using the diffusion equation. ACM Trans. Graph. **27**, 9–1918 (2008)
10. Wang, Y., Wang, J., Holzschuch, N., Subr, K., Yong, J.-H., Guo, B.: Real-time rendering of heterogeneous translucent objects with arbitrary shapes. Comput. Graph. Forum **29** (2010)
11. Arbree, A., Walter, B., Bala, K.: Heterogeneous subsurface scattering using the finite element method. IEEE Trans. Vis. Comput. Graph. **17**(7), 956–969 (2011)
12. Li, D., Sun, X., Ren, Z., Lin, S., Tong, Y., Guo, B., Zhou, K.: Transcut: interactive rendering of translucent cutouts. IEEE Trans. Vis. Comput. Graph. (2012). doi:10.1109/TVCG.2012.127
13. Jensen, H.W., Christensen, P.: Efficient simulation of light transport in scenes with participating media using photon maps. In: SIGGRAPH, pp. 311–320 (1998)
14. Hao, X., Varshney, A.: Real-time rendering of translucent meshes. ACM Trans. Graph. **23**, 120–142 (2004)
15. Wang, R., Tran, J., Luebke, D.: All-frequency interactive relighting of translucent objects with single and multiple scattering. ACM Trans. Graph. **24**(3), 1202–1207 (2005)
16. Debevec, P., Hawkins, T., Tchou, C., Duiker, H.-P., Sarokin, W., Sagar, M.: Acquiring the reflectance field of a human face. In: Proc. SIGGRAPH 2000, pp. 145–156 (2000)
17. Goesele, M., Lensch, H.P.A., Lang, J., Fuchs, C., Seidel, H.-P.: DISCO: acquisition of translucent objects. ACM Trans. Graph. **23**(3), 835–844 (2004)
18. Tong, X., Wang, J., Lin, S., Guo, B., Shum, H.-Y.: Modeling and rendering of quasi-homogeneous materials. ACM Trans. Graph. **24**(3), 1054–1061 (2005)
19. Peers, P., vom Berge, K., Matusik, W., Ramamoorthi, R., Lawrence, J., Rusinkiewicz, S., Dutré, P.: A compact factored representation of heterogeneous subsurface scattering. ACM Trans. Graph. **25**(3), 746–753 (2006)
20. Narasimhan, S.G., Nayar, S.K.: Shedding light on the weather. IN: CVPR, pp. 665–672 (2003)
21. Narasimhan, S.G., Gupta, M., Donner, C., Ramamoorthi, R., Nayar, S.K., Jensen, H.W.: Acquiring scattering properties of participating media by dilution. ACM Trans. Graph. **25**(3), 1003–1012 (2006)
22. Tariq, S., gardner, A., Llamas, I., Jones, A., Debevec, P., Turk, G.: Efficiently estimation of spatially varying subsurface scattering parameters. In: 11th International Fall Workshop on Vision, Modeling, and Visualization, pp. 165–174 (2006)
23. Donner, C., Weyrich, T., d'Eon, E., Ramamoorthi, R., Rusinkiewicz, S.: A layered, heterogeneous reflectance model for acquiring and rendering human skin. ACM Trans. Graph. **27**(5), 140 (2008)
24. Weyrich, T., Matusik, W., Pfister, H., Bickel, B., Donner, C., Tu, C., McAndless, J., Lee, J., Ngan, A., Jensen, H.W., Gross, M.: Analysis of human faces using a measurement-based skin reflectance model. ACM Trans. Graph. **25**(3), 1013–1024 (2006)
25. Ghosh, A., Hawkins, T., Peers, P., Frederiksen, S., Debevec, P.: Practical modeling and acquisition of layered facial reflectance. ACM Trans. Graph. **27**(5), 139 (2008)

26. Xu, K., Gao, Y., Li, Y., Ju, T., Hu, S.-M.: Real-time homogenous translucent material editing. Comput. Graph. Forum **26**(3), 545–552 (2007)
27. Wang, R., Cheslack-Postava, E., Luebke, D., Chen, Q., Hua, W., Peng, Q., Bao, H.: Real-time editing and relighting of homogeneous translucent materials. Vis. Comput. **24**, 565 (2008)
28. Song, Y., Tong, X., Pellacini, F., Peers, P.: SubEdit: a representation for editing measured heterogeneous subsurface scattering. ACM Trans. Graph. **28**(3), 31–1319 (2009)
29. Lensch, H.P.A., Goesele, M., Bekaert, P., Magnor, J.K.M.A., Lang, J., Seidel, H.-P.: Interactive rendering of translucent objects. Comput. Graph. Forum **22**(2), 195–205 (2007)
30. d'Eon, E., Luebke, D., Enderton, E.: Efficient rendering of human skin. In: Eurographics Symposium on Rendering, pp. 147–157 (2007)

Chapter 6
Modeling Subsurface Light Transport with the Kernel Nyström Method

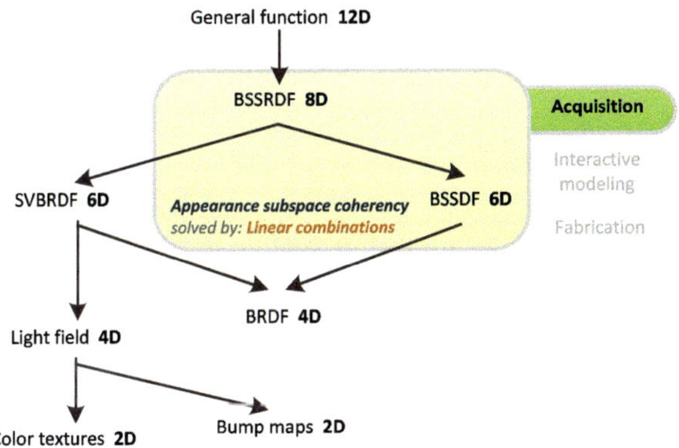

In this chapter, we present an image-based technique for modeling the subsurface light transport within a translucent object so that it can be regenerated with new illumination. Mathematically, the radiance from subsurface light transport can be formulated as the following equation [1, 2]:

$$\mathbf{b} = \mathbf{T} \cdot \mathbf{l}, \tag{6.1}$$

where $\mathbf{T}$ is the $n \times n$ light transport matrix that describes the diffuse BSSRDF between pairs of n surface points, $\mathbf{l}$ is the illumination condition represented by a vector of incident radiance at the n surface points, and $\mathbf{b}$ is the outgoing radiance observed in a camera image at the n points. We aim in this work to recover the matrix $\mathbf{T}$ for given real world object.

A special advantage of an image-based approach is that it provides accurate modeling without the need to directly recover the shape and optical properties of the object, which is often an arduous task. However, to generate high quality results, an extremely large number of images (e.g., on the order of tens of thousands [3, 4]) is

DOI 10.1007/978-3-642-35777-0_6, © Springer-Verlag Berlin Heidelberg 2013

often required for accurate reconstruction of the light transport matrix. Some techniques have aimed to reduce the number of required images, but they are either dedicated to specific light transport effects [5] or mainly effective only for simple object geometry [6, 7]. Applying these techniques to objects with complex subsurface scattering effects still requires a large number of input images and expensive reconstruction methods [2].

In this chapter we propose a *kernel Nyström* method for reconstructing the light transport matrix from a small number of images. We first acquire a small number of rows and columns of the light transport matrix of an actual object and then reconstruct the entire matrix from these sparse samples. This approach is inspired by the Nyström method proposed by Williams and Seeger [8] for reconstructing a low rank symmetric matrix using a linear combination of sparsely sampled rows and columns.

In the kernel Nyström method, the effectiveness of the Nyström method is enhanced by taking advantage of the non-linear coherence of the light transport matrix. This is done by employing a kernel function (the *light transport kernel*) to map the rows and columns in the light transport matrix to produce a matrix of reduced rank with *appearance subspace* coherence. This data specific kernel function can be estimated from sparse row and column samples in the light transport matrix. With this kernel mapping, a high quality matrix can then be reconstructed by *linear combinations* from sparse samples via the Nyström method. Finally, the light transport matrix is obtained from elements of the reconstructed matrix by inverse kernel mapping. By taking advantage of both the *linear* coherence and the *nonlinear* coherence of the light transport matrix in this way, the *kernel* Nyström method becomes much more powerful and the number of sampled rows and columns (and hence acquired images) needed for matrix reconstruction is greatly reduced.

A novel aspect of the kernel Nyström method is that it exploits the data coherence during the matrix reconstruction process, before the whole matrix is known. It has been recognized in the past that the data coherence in light transport can be used for data compression after the whole matrix is known [9, 10]. The kernel Nyström method takes a different approach and only uses the known rows and columns as representative samples for analyzing the data coherence and reconstructing the matrix. To this end, we develop an adaptive scheme for measuring the sparse row and column images of the light transport matrix and estimating the light transport kernel. Our experiments indicate that the kernel Nyström method can achieve good reconstruction of the light transport matrix with relatively few images and can lead to high quality renderings of subsurface light transport effects.

6.1 Related Work

We begin with a review of previous work on light transport matrix estimation both for subsurface scattering and for light transport in full scenes. The light transport matrix represents discrete samples of the reflectance field [3]. A complete 8D reflectance field, which describes the light transport from the incident light field to the outgoing light field [11], is difficult to capture and process due to the tremendous amount of data [12]. Therefore, most existing methods only consider simplified 4D [3, 6, 7, 13] and 6D reflectance fields [4, 14–16]. In this chapter, we focus on 4D reflectance fields with a fixed viewpoint and point light sources that lie in a 2D plane.

Existing methods for light transport acquisition may be categorized into three classes. We refer to the first as *brute force methods*, which directly measure the light transport matrix from the scene or object, where each column is an image of the scene lit by a single light source in the incident light domain. Debevec et al. [3] developed a light stage device for capturing 4D reflectance fields for a fixed viewpoint and distant lighting by moving a point light source around the object. They later improved the device for fast capturing [4]. Hawkins et al. [17] exploited Helmholtz reciprocity to capture the reflectance field of highly reflective objects. To obtain dense samples in the incident light domain, rows of the light transport matrix are captured by shooting rays from the viewpoint and capturing the high resolution image of the scene projected over the incident light domain. Reciprocity is also exploited in [16] for acquiring 6D reflectance fields. All these methods require tens of thousands of images for modeling a high quality light transport matrix. For subsurface scattering of similar quality, our approach requires only a few dozen images.

The second class, which we call *sparsity based methods*, model the light transport matrix with a set of basis functions defined over the incident light domain and assume that each row of the light transport matrix can be approximated by a linear combination of a sparse set of basis functions. Thus the light transport matrix can be reconstructed by deriving the sparse basis and their weights for each row from a set of images captured under special lighting conditions. Environment matting [5] models the reflectance of specular or refractive objects by representing the light transport of each pixel (i.e., a row of the transport matrix) with a single 2D box function. It was later extended to model glossy objects by replacing the box function with an oriented Gaussian kernel [18]. Matusik et al. [6] modeled the light transport matrix with hierarchical rectangular basis functions. An adaptive algorithm is developed for deriving the sparse basis and their weights for each pixel from images of the scene captured under various natural illumination conditions. Peers et al. [7] modeled the light transport matrix with wavelets and inferred the light transport matrix from images of the scene illuminated by carefully designed wavelet noise patterns. Both approaches apply a greedy strategy to find a suboptimal sparse basis for each pixel, which only works well for scenes with simple occlusions. Recently a compressive sensing approach [2] was proposed which computes the solution for each pixel from images captured from a scene illuminated by patterned lighting. However, the number of images needed for reconstruction depends on both the row length and the number of basis functions used for each row, which becomes quite large for scenes with complex occlusions. The reconstruction process is also time consuming.

Unlike the aforementioned sparsity based approaches, our method exploits the coherence in the matrix for reconstruction. It can well handle scenes with complex occlusions and caustics. The number of images needed for reconstruction is only proportional to the rank of the light transport matrix and independent of the size of the matrix. Moreover, our reconstruction algorithm consists of a set of matrix operations, which is simple and fast.

The third class, *coherence based methods*, acquire the light transport matrix by exploiting the coherence of reflectance field data. Masselus et al. [9] explored the interpolation and compression of reflectance fields. Fuchs et al. [19] proposed an adaptive sampling scheme for sampling the 4D reflectance field. The spatial coherence of the reflectance field in the incident domain is exploited for accelerating the acquisition process. Starting from a set of images taken with a sparse set of regularly distributed lighting directions, their algorithm analyzes the observed data and then captures more images in each iteration with the new lighting directions where the reflectance field is not smooth. We note that the smoothness of reflectance data among neighboring pixels is also exploited in [2, 6, 7] for improving the quality of the results.

While these methods only exploit the coherence in either rows or columns, our method exploits the data coherence in the entire light transport matrix for reconstruction. Since our approach makes no assumptions about the smoothness of the sampled reflectance field, it can effectively handle sharp variations of the light transport, such as shadows, caustics, and surface textures.

The Nyström method has been employed for various purposes besides reconstruction of low rank symmetric matrices. In the machine learning community, it has also been used for approximately computing the eigenvalues and eigenvectors of a symmetric matrix from sparse matrix samples [20]. In graphics research, An et al. [21] applied the Nyström method to accelerate appearance edit propagation by approximating the dense symmetric distance matrix with sparsely sampled rows and columns. For a given illumination, Hasan et al. [22] applied similar techniques to efficiently render synthetic scenes. In their approach, columns of the matrix are clustered in a small number of groups according to their values in the sparsely sampled rows. A representative column for each group is then sampled and weighted for approximating other columns in the same group. This approach only uses the coherence between columns in approximating the matrix. Coherence between rows is not exploited. Moreover, applying this approach to the light transport matrix may generate temporal artifacts under dynamic lighting, as noted in [23].

6.2 The Kernel Nyström Method

In this section, we introduce the kernel extension to the Nyström method, and present a method for estimating the light transport kernel. Let us first assume that a sparse set of columns of the light transport matrix is known. How to capture individual columns from a real world object is described in the next section.

The following notational convention is used throughout this chapter: a matrix is denoted by bold uppercase letters (e.g., $\mathbf{T}$), a vector is denoted by bold lowercase letters (e.g., $\mathbf{l}$), and a scalar or a scalar function is denoted by lowercase italic letters (e.g., f). Given a matrix $\mathbf{T}$, its element at row i and column j is denoted as $\mathbf{T}_{ij}$, while $f(\mathbf{T})$ denotes a matrix obtained by applying f to each element of the matrix $\mathbf{T}$.

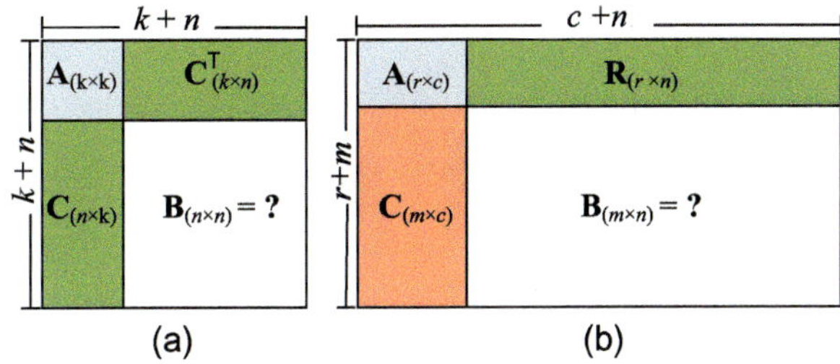

Fig. 6.1 Matrix reconstruction from sparsely sampled columns and rows. (**a**) Symmetric case. (**b**) Asymmetric case

6.2.1 Kernel Extension

The Nyström method in [8] reconstructs a low rank symmetric matrix from sparsely sampled columns. As shown in Fig. 6.1(a), an unknown $(n+k)\times(n+k)$ symmetric matrix $\mathbf{T}$ with k sampled columns $[\mathbf{A}\ \mathbf{C}^T]$ can be approximated as

$$\mathbf{T} = \begin{bmatrix} \mathbf{A} & \mathbf{C}^T \\ \mathbf{C} & \mathbf{B} \end{bmatrix} \approx \begin{bmatrix} \mathbf{A} & \mathbf{C}^T \\ \mathbf{C} & \mathbf{C}\mathbf{A}^{-1}\mathbf{C}^T \end{bmatrix}. \tag{6.2}$$

The reconstruction is accurate when the symmetric matrix $\mathbf{T}$ has a rank $d \le k$, except that the sampled columns $[\mathbf{A}\ \mathbf{C}^T]$ are of a rank smaller than d.

The Nyström method relies on the assumption that the ranks of $\mathbf{T}$ and $\mathbf{A}$ are identical, in order to achieve an exact reconstruction. In reality, this assumption may be violated, resulting in some reconstruction error. One possible way to make the Nyström method more effective is to apply a transformation to the entries in the matrix so that this low rank assumption is better satisfied, hence the reconstruction error can be expected to be minimized. As linear transforms do not change the rank of a matrix, nonlinear transforms are necessary.

In the machine learning literature, the "kernel trick" [24] is a standard approach for enhancing the performance of algorithms based on nonlinear transformations of the input data. The kernel trick is to map vectors in the data space to a (usually) higher dimensional feature space. Then the same procedures of the original algorithm done in the data space are transferred to the feature space. The key to the success of the kernel trick is that the mapping function need not be explicitly specified. Rather, a kernel function is sufficient for computing the inner products in the feature space.

Inspired by the success of the kernel trick, we consider using a nonlinear function f to change the values of the entries in light transport matrix $\mathbf{T}$ such that the rank assumption can be better fulfilled, i.e., the rank of $f(\mathbf{T})$ is as close to that of $f(\mathbf{A})$ as possible. We name this nonlinear function f the light transport kernel. After reconstructing $f(\mathbf{T})$ using the Nyström method, i.e.,

$$f(\mathbf{T}) \approx \mathbf{K} = \begin{bmatrix} f(\mathbf{A}) & f(\mathbf{R}) \\ f(\mathbf{C}) & f(\mathbf{C})(f(\mathbf{A}))^{-1}(f(\mathbf{RC}))^T \end{bmatrix}, \tag{6.3}$$

the original $\mathbf{T}$ can be recovered by an inverse mapping with f^{-1}: $\mathbf{T} \approx f^{-1}(\mathbf{K})$.

To see that the above nonlinear mapping process is a kernel method, one may regard $\mathbf{T}$ as an inner product matrix:

$$\mathbf{T}_{ij} = \phi_i \cdot \psi_j, \tag{6.4}$$

where $\{\phi_i\}$ and $\{\psi_j\}$ are two different point sets in a particular space.[1] This is slightly different from the traditional kernel method which requires $\{\phi_i\}$ and $\{\psi_j\}$ to be identical. We use different point sets because here $\mathbf{T}$ is asymmetric. The standard kernel method then uses an implicit mapping Γ to map the point sets to another space. Then the kernel matrix $\mathbf{K}$ in the mapped space, i.e. the inner product matrix of the mapped point sets, is

$$\mathbf{K}_{ij} = \Gamma(\phi_i) \cdot \Gamma(\psi_j). \tag{6.5}$$

To compute $\mathbf{K}$, one only has to prepare an explicit kernel function g such that $g(\phi_i, \psi_j) \equiv \Gamma(\phi_i) \cdot \Gamma(\psi_j)$, rather than explicitly specifying Γ, which is much more difficult. One of the most frequently used kernel functions is the polynomial kernel: $g(\phi_i, \psi_j) = (1 + \phi_i \cdot \psi_j)^p$. So one can choose the kernel g in such a form: $g(\phi_i, \psi_j) = f(\phi_i \cdot \psi_j)$. With this choice of the kernel function, we have that

$$\mathbf{K}_{ij} = f(\phi_i \cdot \psi_j) = f(\mathbf{T}_{ij}), \quad \text{i.e.,} \quad \mathbf{K} = f(\mathbf{T}). \tag{6.6}$$

6.2.2 *Estimating the Light Transport Kernel f*

To make the kernel Nyström method work, one has to specify the light transport kernel f. As the space of all monotonic smooth functions is of infinite dimension, one has to assume its form in order to narrow down the search space. In this work, we simply assume that f is a power function, $f(x) = x^\gamma$, as this family of functions has only one parameter and hence the optimal function is easy to find. Moreover, our experiments show that such a choice of the light transport kernel can indeed greatly enhance the reconstruction. We leave the problem of whether there are even better light transport kernel functions to future work.

As argued before, to reduce the reconstruction error, one has to make the rank of $f(\mathbf{T})$ as close to that of $f(\mathbf{A})$ as possible. However, we do not have the full information on $\mathbf{T}$. So the real rank of $f(\mathbf{T})$ is actually unknown. To overcome this difficulty, we choose to minimize the rank of $f(\mathbf{A})$ instead. The underlying philosophy is that if the rank of $f(\mathbf{A})$ is *much less* than $\min(r, c)$, then it is very likely that the rank of $f(\mathbf{T})$ does not exceed $\min(r, c)$. So the generalized kernel Nyström method can be effective. This leads to the rank minimization problem [25], which is usually formalized as minimizing the nuclear norm of a matrix. We seek a light

[1] As we will show, it is not necessary to specify what these two point sets are.

transport kernel f that minimizes the rank factor

$$e_r = \frac{\|f(\mathbf{A})\|_*}{\|f(\mathbf{A})\|_2}, \tag{6.7}$$

where the nuclear norm is defined as $\|\mathbf{X}\|_* = \sum_i \sigma_i$, the spectral norm is defined as $\|\mathbf{X}\|_2 = \max_i\{\sigma_i\}$ and σ_i are the singular values of the matrix $\mathbf{X}$. Note that here we normalize the nuclear norm with the largest singular value because we do not want to reduce the rank by mapping the entries to be close to zero (which corresponds to a small $\|f(\mathbf{A})\|_2$). Rather, we want to reduce the rank of $f(\mathbf{A})$ by enhancing the linear coherence of the rows/columns of $f(\mathbf{A})$.

It is easy to imagine that mapping all the entries to a constant can trivially reduce the rank of $f(\mathbf{A})$ to 1 or even 0. However, such a trivial mapping causes a problem in inverting from $\mathbf{K}$ to $\mathbf{T}$ by using the inverse function f^{-1}. To reduce the reconstruction error, we have to further make sure that this inversion is numerically robust. The robustness of inversion can be measured by the slope of f^{-1}: the steeper f^{-1} is, the less robust the inversion is. So we have to further minimize

$$e_s = \int_0^1 (f^{-1})'(x)p(x)\mathrm{d}x = \int_0^1 \frac{1}{f'(x)}p(x)\mathrm{d}x, \tag{6.8}$$

where the identity $(f^{-1})'(x) = \frac{1}{f'(x)}$ is used and $p(x)$ is the distribution density of the values in $\mathbf{A}$, which is estimated from the histogram of entry values of $\mathbf{A}$. $p(x)$ is assumed to be identical to that in $\mathbf{T}$, due to the random sampling of $\mathbf{A}$ from $\mathbf{T}$. We weight the slope of f^{-1} by $p(x)$ in order to achieve the best overall robustness for all entry values in $\mathbf{T}$.

Combining the above two criteria, our algorithm selects the light transport kernel function f whose parameter γ minimizes the objective function

$$g(\gamma) = e_r \cdot e_s = \frac{\|f(\mathbf{A})\|_*}{\|f(\mathbf{A})\|_2} \int_0^1 \frac{1}{f'(x)}p(x)\mathrm{d}x. \tag{6.9}$$

We use the golden section search [26] to search for the optimal γ within $[0.001, 1000]$ in logarithmic space. As $\mathbf{A}$ is of a relatively small size ($r \times c$), this optimization takes only a few seconds.

In summary, our kernel Nyström method works as follows. Given the matrices of sampled columns ($\mathbf{A}$ and $\mathbf{C}$), we estimate the light transport kernel f from $\mathbf{A}$ and map matrices of sparse samples to their kernel version $f(\mathbf{A})$ and $f(\mathbf{C})$ respectively. We then apply the Nyström method to reconstruct the kernel light transport matrix $\mathbf{K} = f(\mathbf{T})$. Finally, we obtain the light transport matrix $\mathbf{T}$ via the inverse kernel mapping $\mathbf{T} = f^{-1}(\mathbf{K})$.

6.3 Adaptive Light Transport Measurement

The kernel Nyström method requires a sparse set of columns of the light transport matrix as input for reconstruction. However, without any knowledge about the light

Fig. 6.2 Pseudo code of the adaptive capturing scheme

```
AdaptiveCapture( r', c', ε )
    finished = false
    capturing r' rows and c' columns
    r = r'; c = c'
    While(finished == false)
        estimating f from A
        estimating rank factor e_r of f(A)
        If( e_r / min(r, c) < ε )
            finished = true
        Else
            capturing r' rows and c' columns
            adding samples in sample set
            updating A
            r = r + r'; c = c + c'
```

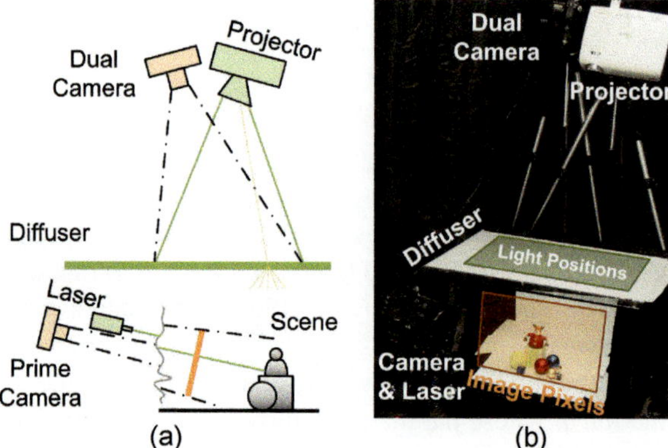

Fig. 6.3 Device setup for capturing sparse columns of the light transport matrix. (**a**) Illustration. (**b**) Photograph

transport within an object, it is difficult to determine the sample number in advance. To address this issue, we design an adaptive scheme for capturing sparse columns from the object, where the sample number is determined from the captured data. As shown in Fig. 6.2, after a batch of columns is sampled from the scene, we estimate the light transport kernel f from the matrix $\mathbf{A}$ of the current sample set and compute the rank factor e_c of $f(\mathbf{A})$ using Eq. (6.7). For a sample set that has c columns, if e_c/c is smaller than a pre-defined threshold ε, the rank of $f(\mathbf{A})$ is much less than c. Based on the same philosophy used in the kernel estimation, it is very likely the rank of $f(\mathbf{T})$ does not exceed c. Thus the sampled data are sufficient for reconstructing $f(\mathbf{T})$ and the capturing is finished. Otherwise, we capture a new batch of columns and repeat the above steps with the extended sample set.

A device setup is designed for acquiring a batch of column samples from the scene. As shown in Fig. 6.3, we focus on the light transport from point light sources on a 2D plane to image pixels captured from a fixed viewpoint. In our setup, a column of the light transport matrix is directly obtained from the image of the object under a virtual point light source.

Device Setup and Calibration In our implementation, we use a device setup similar to the one used in [27] for capturing. As shown in Fig. 6.3(b), our setup consists of an Optoma HD73 DLP projector, three laser emitters that can generate red, blue and green laser beams, and a Canon 20D camera. The three laser emitters are close to each other and shoot three color beams to points over the object surface. We control the laser beams to make sure that they focus on the same surface point. HDR images of the object surface are captured from a fixed viewpoint. We repeat this process by shooting the laser beams to a random set of surface points. With the calibrated camera position and known geometry of the object, we map the image pixels onto the object surface.

Before capturing, we calibrate the color and intensity of each point light source. In our implementation, we first calibrate the point light sources sampled on 40×40 regular grids by capturing the images of the diffuser plane lit with each of the 1600 point light sources from the object side. We then calibrate the other point light sources within the regular grid by interpolating the calibration results of the neighbor point light sources on the grid.

Column Sampling After calibration, we capture the columns of the light transport matrix with the projector and the camera. Without any knowledge on the light transport in the object, we acquire a set of columns from the camera with r illuminated points that are uniformly distributed over the surface. For each sampled point light source $\boldsymbol{l}_j$, eight images of different exposures are taken from the camera and then down-sampled and fused into HDR images as in [28]. The result is a set of column vectors $\mathbf{T}_{\cdot,j}$ of the matrix $\mathbf{T}$.

6.4 Results and Discussions

We implemented our kernel Nyström method on a PC with an Intel Core™2 Duo 3.2 GHz CPU and 4 GB of memory. In our implementation, we capture a batch of ten columns in each adaptive capture step and experimentally set the threshold as $\varepsilon = 0.05$. A typical acquisition session (including image acquisition, HDR reconstruction, and kernel estimation) takes about 45 minutes for capturing 50 columns from the object. The image resolution is 1752×1168, while the light sampling resolution is 1024×768. To reconstruct the light transport matrix for relighting, we store the sampled matrices (**C** and **A**) in memory and reconstruct all rows of the matrix during rendering. With 50 columns, our kernel Nyström method takes less than 5 minutes to estimate the kernel and reconstruct all rows of the light transport matrix of the scene. For samples that do not fit in memory, we store one matrix (**C** in our implementation) on disk and the other matrices in memory. An out-of-core implementation, which is dominated by the disk I/O, then takes about 30 minutes for reconstruction.

6.4.1 Method Validation

We validate the kernel Nyström method with the light transport matrices acquired from a star fruit and a piece of marble, in which the light sources are sampled on regular 35×35 grids. We simulate the adaptive sampling scheme for each object. In each iteration, we randomly pick ten columns that are not in the sample set from the acquired full matrix and add them in the sparse sample set. After that, we estimate the light transport kernel f and compute the rank of the kernel mapped matrix $f(\mathbf{A})$ of the sparse samples. The rank of a matrix is determined by the number of eigenvalues of the matrix that can preserve 95.0 % of the energy of the original matrix. We also reconstruct the light transport matrix from the sparse sample set via the kernel Nyström method. We repeat this process until the number of sparse samples reaches 300, which is more than the number of sparse samples n_s determined by the adaptive sampling scheme with the pre-defined ε.

Figure 6.4 shows plots of the ranks of kernel mapped matrices $f(\mathbf{A})$ of sparse sample sets with a different number of samples, where the number of sparse samples n_s determined by the adaptive sampling scheme is marked by an orange line. The blue line indicates the rank of the kernel mapped matrix $f(\mathbf{T})$, in which the kernel function is estimated from the sparse sample set with n_s samples. For both objects, the ranks of $f(\mathbf{A})$ of sparse samples grow as the number of samples increases and are close to that of $f(\mathbf{T})$ as the number of samples approaches n_s, which leads to a good reconstruction.

Figure 6.5 shows plots of the relative errors of the light transport matrices reconstructed from a different number of samples, where the relative reconstruction error is computed as

$$\varepsilon = \sqrt{\frac{\sum_{i,j} |B_{i,j} - \tilde{B}_{i,j}|^2}{\sum_{i,j} |B_{i,j}|^2}}. \tag{6.10}$$

Here $B_{i,j}$ is the ground truth submatrix element that is not in the sparse sample set and $\tilde{B}_{i,j}$ is the same submatrix element reconstructed using the kernel Nyström method. To further explore the impact of different sample sets on reconstruction quality, we execute the above experiment 16 times, each time with different rows and columns randomly selected from the matrix. As shown in Fig. 6.5, the relative error decreases quickly as the number of sparse samples increases. With the same number of sparse samples as we used in our capturing, the relative error of the reconstructed light transport matrix is below 5 %. Also note that the variance of the error under the same number of samples reduces quickly with the increasing number of samples, which guarantees the quality of the light transport matrix reconstructed from the random sampled rows and columns.

Figure 6.6(a) compares the performance of the Nyström method and the kernel Nyström method for a star fruit. For each sparse sample set, we reconstruct the light transport matrices using both the Nyström method and the kernel Nyström method. Their relative errors are shown in Fig. 6.6(a). Without the kernel

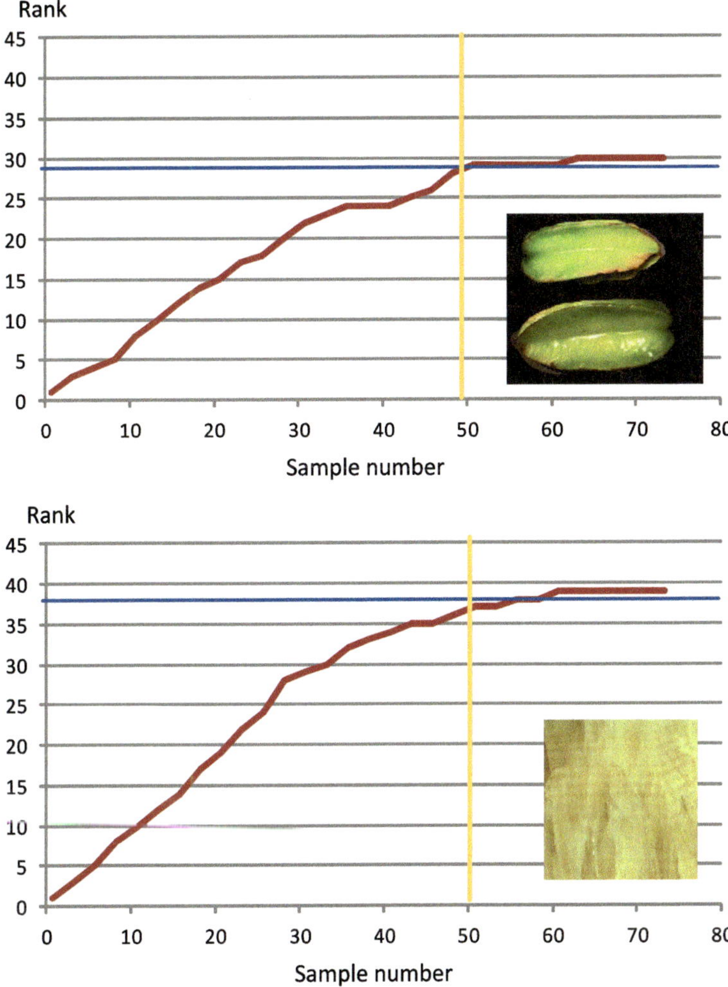

Fig. 6.4 Ranks of the kernel mapped matrices $f(\mathbf{A})$ of the sparse sample sets with different numbers of samples. The *orange line* indicates the sample number determined by the adaptive capturing scheme, while the *blue line* indicates the rank of the kernel mapped matrix $f(\mathbf{T})$

extension, the Nyström method requires roughly five to six times the number of samples to achieve the same reconstruction quality as the kernel Nyström method does.

Figure 6.6(b, c) compares the performance of the kernel Nyström method with different light transport kernels (i.e., different γ values) for the star fruit example. For each γ value, we reconstruct the light transport matrix from the same set of sparse samples (250 samples) with the kernel Nyström method. Figure 6.6(b, c) shows plots of the objective function $g(\gamma)$ and the relative error of the reconstructed

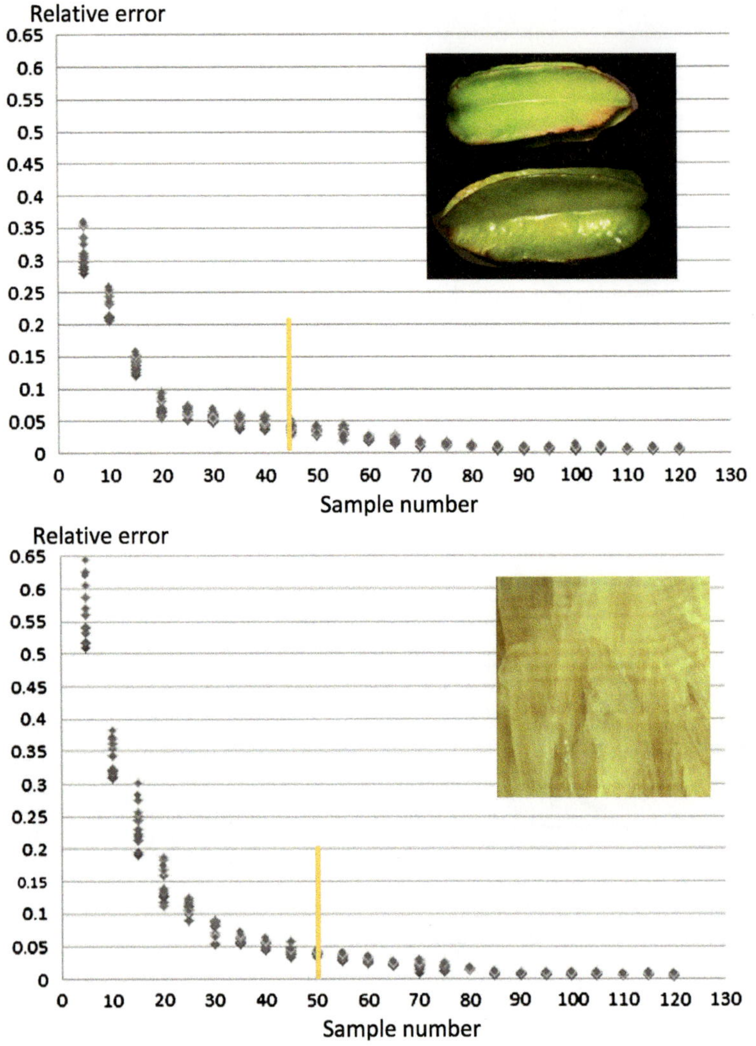

Fig. 6.5 Relative reconstruction errors of the light transport matrix reconstructed from sparse sample sets with different number of samples. The *orange line* indicates the sample number determined by the adaptive capturing scheme

light transport matrices as a function of γ. Note that the relative reconstruction error is minimal when the optimal γ value derived by our approach is used for reconstruction. Also, the light transport matrix is well reconstructed by the kernel Nyström method using the optimal γ value. However, the light transport matrices reconstructed with the kernel Nyström method using other γ values exhibit larger relative errors and visible artifacts.

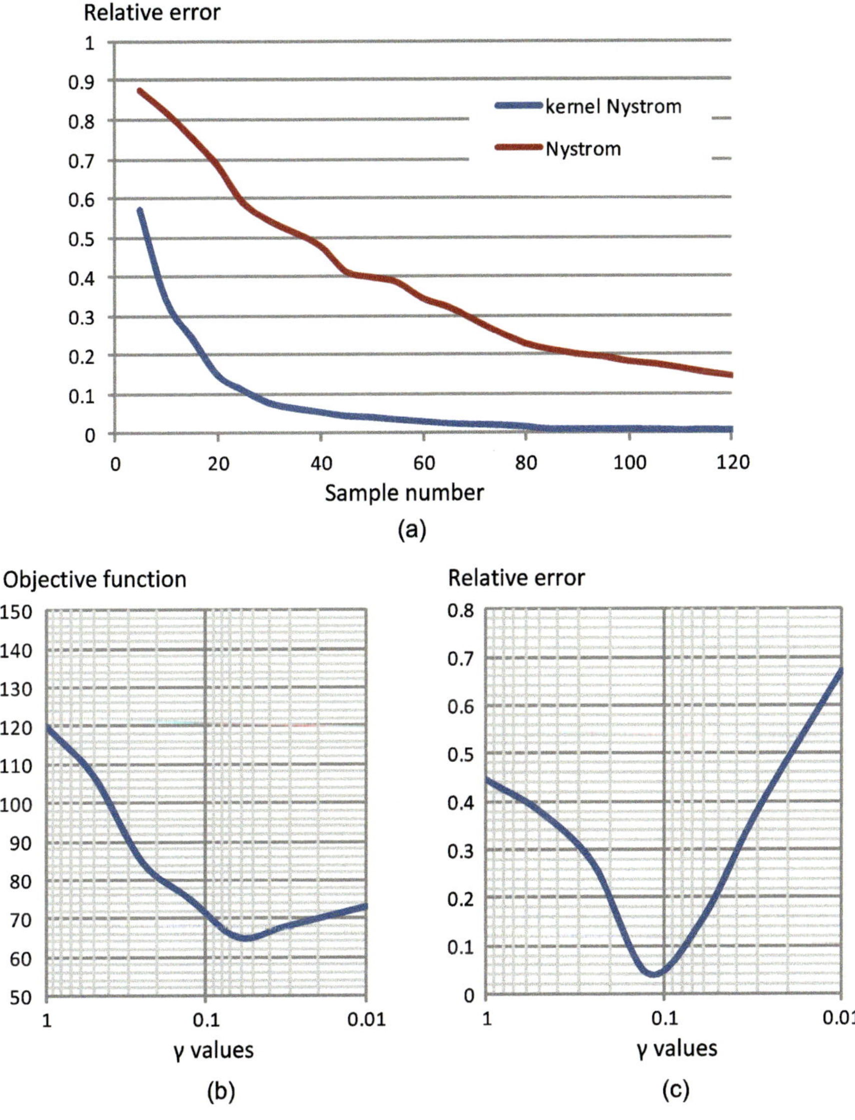

Fig. 6.6 Reconstruction results with the kernel Nyström method and with the Nyström method. The relative reconstruction errors with respect to the different numbers of samples are compared in (**a**). The reconstruction results of the kernel Nyström method with different light transport kernels are shown in (**b**, **c**). The objective function values with respect to different γ values are given in (**b**), while the relative reconstruction errors are shown in (**c**)

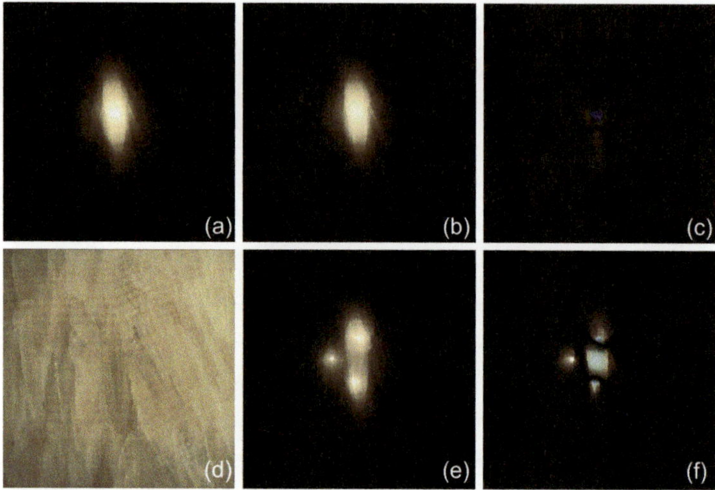

Fig. 6.7 Modeling subsurface light transport with the kernel Nyström method. (**a**) The image of marble lit by a laser beam at one point. (**b**) Image rendered with reconstructed light transport matrix with light on the same point. (**c**) The difference between (**a**) and (**b**), intensity of which is scaled by 10. (**d**) Photograph of the flat marble sample. (**e**) Image rendered by interpolating the nearby sample images. (**f**) The difference between (**a**) and (**e**), intensity of which is scaled by 10

6.4.2 Subsurface Scattering Results

We applied the kernel Nyström method for modeling the light transport due to subsurface scattering. The elements of the light transport matrix describe the diffuse BSSRDF R_d between the two surface points x_i and x_j as $\mathbf{T}_{ij} = R_d(\boldsymbol{x}_i, \boldsymbol{x}_j)$ [27].

With 50 sampled images, we reconstruct the light transport matrix of subsurface scattering using the kernel Nyström method. The coefficient of the light transport kernel used in reconstruction is $\gamma = 0.0625$. The resolution of surface points in the light transport matrix is the same as the image resolution. Figure 6.7 compares the rendering result of the reconstructed light transport matrix, the ground truth image captured from the object under the same lighting condition, and the result rendered by directly interpolating the nearby sample images. Note that the detailed spatial patterns and anisotropic subsurface scattering in the real material are well preserved with the reconstructed light transport matrix, while the results generated by interpolation clearly exhibit artifacts. Also note that to capture the light transport effects with a similar resolution, brute force methods [27, 29] need dense light sampling, which is prohibitively expensive and time consuming.

6.4.3 Discussion

The light transport matrix of an object exhibits both data coherence and sparsity. While sparsity based approaches exploit data sparsity for capturing the light transport matrix, the kernel Nyström method exploits the coherence in both rows and columns of the light transport matrix for the same task. For the low frequency light transport effects of subsurface scattering, light transport matrices always exhibit strong coherence in both rows and columns, which can be efficiently reconstructed using the kernel Nyström method with dozens of images, which is far fewer than that used in sparsity based methods.

6.5 Conclusion

We presented the kernel Nyström method for reconstructing the light transport matrix of subsurface scattering from a relatively small number of acquired images. While existing techniques typically require tens of thousands of images for accurate reconstruction of a light transport matrix, the kernel Nyström method can achieve a good reconstruction with a few dozen images and produces high quality relighting results. The kernel Nyström method is able to capture complex lighting effects which are particularly challenging for many existing techniques, especially various sparsity-based methods. The effectiveness of the kernel Nyström method comes from its ability to exploit both the linear and nonlinear coherence in the light transport matrix from a relatively small number of columns in the matrix.

In future work, we are interested in investigating better kernel estimation methods and designing new kernel functions for light transport matrix reconstruction. We also plan to apply the kernel Nyström method to model surface reflectance. Finally, we want to explore ways to extend the kernel Nyström method to handle high-dimensional tensor data.

References

1. Ng, R., Ramamoorthi, R., Hanrahan, P.: All-frequency shadows using non-linear wavelet lighting approximation. ACM Trans. Graph. **22**(3), 376–381 (2003)
2. Peers, P., Mahajan, D.K., Lamond, B., Ghosh, A., Matusik, W., Ramamoorthi, R., Debevec, P.: Compressive light transport sensing. ACM Trans. Graph. **28**(1), 3–1318 (2009)
3. Debevec, P., Hawkins, T., Tchou, C., Duiker, H.-P., Sarokin, W., Sagar, M.: Acquiring the reflectance field of a human face. In: Proc. SIGGRAPH 2000, pp. 145–156 (2000)
4. Wenger, A., Gardner, A., Tchou, C., Unger, J., Hawkins, T., Debevec, P.: Performance relighting and reflectance transformation with time-multiplexed illumination. ACM Trans. Graph. **24**(3), 756–764 (2005)
5. Zongker, D.E., Werner, D.M., Curless, B., Salesin, D.H.: Environment matting and compositing. In: Proceedings of SIGGRAPH 99. Computer Graphics Proceedings, Annual Conference Series, pp. 205–214 (1999)
6. Matusik, W., Loper, M., Pfister, H.: Progressively-refined reflectance functions from natural illumination. In: Rendering Techniques 2004: 15th Eurographics Workshop on Rendering, pp. 299–308 (2004)
7. Peers, P., Dutré, P.: Inferring reflectance functions from wavelet noise. In: Rendering Techniques 2005: 16th Eurographics Workshop on Rendering, pp. 173–182 (2005)

8. Williams, C., Seeger, M.: Using the Nyström method to speed up kernel machines. Adv. Neural Inf. Process. Syst. **13**, 682–688 (2000)
9. Masselus, V., Peers, P., Dutré, P., Willems, Y.D.: Smooth reconstruction and compact representation of reflectance functions for image-based relighting. In: Rendering Techniques 2004: 15th Eurographics Workshop on Rendering, pp. 287–298 (2004)
10. Mahajan, D., Shlizerman, I.K., Ramamoorthi, R., Belhumeur, P.: A theory of locally low dimensional light transport. ACM Trans. Graph. **26**(3), 62–16210 (2007)
11. Levoy, M., Hanrahan, P.M.: Light field rendering. In: Proceedings of SIGGRAPH 96. Computer Graphics Proceedings, Annual Conference Series, pp. 31–42 (1996)
12. Garg, G., Talvala, E.-V., Levoy, M., Lensch, H.P.A.: Symmetric photography: exploiting data-sparseness in reflectance fields. In: Eurographics Workshop/Symposium on Rendering, Nicosia, Cyprus, pp. 251–262. Eurographics Association Geneva (2006)
13. Lin, Z., Wong, T.-T., Shum, H.-Y.: Relighting with the reflected irradiance field: Representation, sampling and reconstruction. Int. J. Comput. Vis. **49**(2)
14. Matusik, W., Pfister, H., Ngan, A., Beardsley, P., Ziegler, R., McMillan, L.: Image-based 3D photography using opacity hulls. ACM Trans. Graph. **21**(3), 427–437 (2002)
15. Masselus, V., Peers, P., Dutré, P., Willems, Y.D.: Relighting with 4d incident light fields. ACM Trans. Graph. **22**(3), 613–620 (2003)
16. Sen, P., Chen, B., Garg, G., Marschner, S.R., Horowitz, M., Levoy, M., Lensch, H.P.A.: Dual photography. ACM Trans. Graph. **24**(3), 745–755 (2005)
17. Hawkins, T., Einarsson, P., Debevec, P.: A dual light stage. In: Rendering Techniques 2005: 16th Eurographics Workshop on Rendering, pp. 91–98 (2005)
18. Chuang, Y.-Y., Zongker, D.E., Hindorff, J., Curless, B., Salesin, D.H., Szeliski, R.: Environment matting extensions: Towards higher accuracy and real-time capture. In: Proceedings of ACM SIGGRAPH 2000, July 2000. Computer Graphics Proceedings, Annual Conference Series, pp. 121–130 (2000)
19. Fuchs, M., Blanz, V., Lensch, H.P.A., Seidel, H.-P.: Adaptive sampling of reflectance fields. ACM Trans. Graph. **26**(2), 10 (2007)
20. Platt, J.C.: Fastmap, metricmap, and landmark mds are all MNyström algorithms. In: 10th International Workshop on Artificial Intelligence and Statistics, pp. 261–268 (2005)
21. An, X., Pellacini, F.: AppProp: all-pairs appearance-space edit propagation. ACM Trans. Graph. **27**(3), 40 (2008)
22. Hašan, M., Pellacini, F., Bala, K.: Matrix row-column sampling for the many-light problem. ACM Trans. Graph. **26**(3), 26 (2007)
23. Hašan, M., Velazquez-Armendariz, E., Pellacini, F., Bala, K.: Tensor clustering for rendering many-light animations. Comput. Graph. Forum **27**(4), 1105–1114 (2008)
24. Cristianini, N., Shawe-Taylor, J.: An Introduction to Support Vector Machines and Other Kernel-Based Learning Methods. Cambridge University Press Cambridge (2000)
25. Fazel, M.: Matrix rank minimization with applications. PhD thesis, Stanford University (2002)
26. Press, W.H., et al.: Numerical Recipes in C, 2nd edn. (1992)
27. Goesele, M., Lensch, H.P.A., Lang, J., Fuchs, C., Seidel, H.-P.: DISCO: acquisition of translucent objects. ACM Trans. Graph. **23**(3), 835–844 (2004)
28. Debevec, P.E., Malik, J.: Recovering high dynamic range radiance maps from photographs. In: ACM SIGGRAPH, pp. 369–378 (1997)
29. Peers, P., vom Berge, K., Matusik, W., Ramamoorthi, R., Lawrence, J., Rusinkiewicz, S., Dutré, P.: A compact factored representation of heterogeneous subsurface scattering. ACM Trans. Graph. **25**(3), 746–753 (2006)

Chapter 7
Modeling and Rendering Subsurface Scattering Using Diffusion Equations

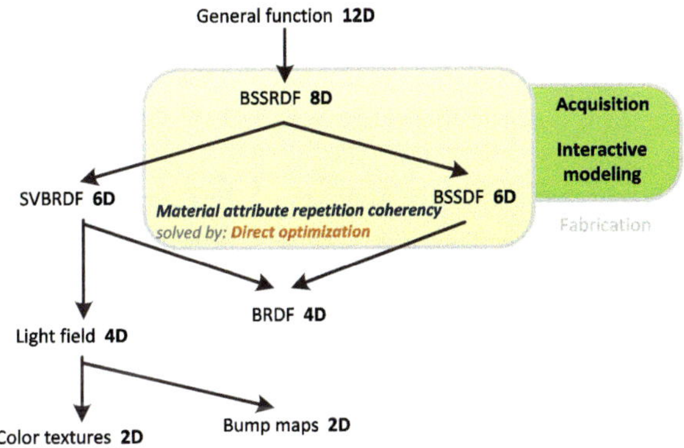

Surface based modeling of BSSRDFs, such as in the preceding chapter and in techniques that directly measure the BSSRDF under sampled lighting and viewing directions [1–3], has important drawbacks that can limit the use of these BSSRDFs. One is that a surface based BSSRDF is coupled with the object geometry, making it unsuitable to use with different surface shapes. Another is that rendering of such surface models involves an integration of BSSRDF contributions from all points on the surface, which is inefficient in practice without complex precomputations. Also, this form of reflectance data is difficult to manipulate if one wants to edit the material appearance.

In this chapter, we propose *volume based* techniques for modeling and rendering of heterogeneous translucent materials that enable acquisition from measured samples, interactive editing of material attributes, and real-time rendering. The material is represented as a discretized volume in which spatially-variant absorption and diffusion coefficients are associated with each volume element. In contrast to the previous chapter which extracts the non-linear coherency in the surface based BSSRDF, here we more directly model the coherency among optical properties of

Y. Dong et al., *Material Appearance Modeling: A Data-Coherent Approach*,
DOI 10.1007/978-3-642-35777-0_7, © Springer-Verlag Berlin Heidelberg 2013

the material volume, which through subsurface scattering among the different volumetric elements leads to the observed non-linearities.

We focus on multiple scattering and assume the material to be optically dense such that subsurface scattering becomes nearly isotropic and can be well approximated by a diffusion process [4]. This is called the diffusion approximation. In medical imaging, the diffusion approximation has been widely used to model the multiple scattering in heterogeneous human tissues [5, 6]. For rendering participating media, Stam [7] used the diffusion approximation to model the multiple scattering in heterogeneous clouds, where the absorption and diffusion coefficients can vary in the volume. For subsurface scattering, an analytic dipole model derived from the diffusion approximation was used by Jensen et al. [8] for multiple scattering in homogeneous materials. In this chapter, we also address subsurface scattering, but deal with the general case of multiple scattering in heterogeneous materials with the diffusion approximation.

For modeling heterogeneous materials, we present an algorithm for recovering a material model from appearance measurements by solving an inverse diffusion problem. For a given distribution of spatially-variant absorption and diffusion coefficients, the corresponding diffusion process that generates the material appearance can be expressed as a partial differential equation, defined over the volumetric elements, with the boundary condition given by the lighting environment. Acquiring a volumetric model from a material sample involves an inverse diffusion problem in which we search for a distribution of spatially-variant absorption and diffusion coefficients such that the corresponding diffusion process generates the material appearance that is most consistent with the measured surface appearance in captured images. Since the images record an actual material sample, a solution to the inverse diffusion problem certainly exists. This inverse problem, however, is well-known to be ill-posed, since a range of different volumetric models may have indistinguishable surface appearances [9]. Consequently, the diffusion equations and image measurements define a group of solutions. Since all solutions correspond to the same visual appearance, any solution from this group might provide a valid volumetric appearance model of the given material. To address this problem, we take advantage of the *material attribute repetition* coherency in material volumes, which generally consist of a limited number of distinct elements. Our method incorporates a smoothness constraint on the optical properties of neighboring voxels in order to favor solutions with substantial repetition, and in this way we obtain solutions by *direct optimization* that are more natural and provide more realistic results for novel viewing and lighting conditions. A material volume with greater coherence furthermore simplifies appearance editing.

Generally, finding a solution to the inverse diffusion problem is challenging due to the nature of the inverse problem and the large number of variables involved. The inverse diffusion problem is usually solved with an iterative optimization procedure, in which each iteration requires an expensive gradient evaluation. For a volume with elements on an n^3 grid, this gradient evaluation involves $n^3 \times M$ light diffusion computations, where M is the number of image measurements. The inverse diffusion problem is also ill-conditioned numerically, which presents convergence problems for the iterative solver. To ensure stable convergence, we incorporate the smoothness regularizer on the diffusion coefficients and use an effective initialization that assigns uniform diffusion coefficients among the voxels. We additionally employ an adjoint method [10], widely used in optimal control for gradient computation, to dramatically reduce the cost of the gradient evaluation down to $2M$ light diffusion computations. With these schemes and a GPU implementation of the diffusion computation, we show that finding a solution of the inverse diffusion problem becomes feasible for volumes of moderate size.

We also present an algorithm for rendering a volumetric model with known material properties by solving a diffusion equation whose boundary condition is defined by the given illumination conditions. That multiple scattering may be modeled as a diffusion process was first observed by Stam [7] in the context of participating media rendering. He solved the diffusion equation on a cubic volume using a regular grid and a finite difference method (FDM). Our rendering algorithm solves the diffusion equation on 3D volumes of arbitrary shape using a polygrid and an FDM. Our algorithm is centered around the polygrid representation, which facilitates the solution of the light diffusion equation in arbitrary volumes. A polygrid is a grid with regular connectivity and an irregular shape for a close geometric fit without fine sampling. The regular connectivity allows us to develop a hierarchical GPU implementation of our rendering algorithm for real-time performance. We describe how to construct a polygrid on an arbitrary 3D object, and present a technique for evaluating diffusion equations defined among the irregular intervals of polygrid nodes.

7.1 Related Work

Before presenting our system in detail, we briefly describe several works most relevant to ours.

In medical imaging, estimation of scattering properties within body tissue with multiple scattering effects has been examined as a general inverse diffusion problem [6]. For better conditioning of this inverse problem, special devices for measuring time domain and frequency domain information have been utilized in recent techniques [11]. In contrast to medical imaging applications, we do not aim to recover the actual scattering coefficients in a material volume, but instead seek a material model whose appearance is consistent with image measurements.

For rendering of BSSRDF models of subsurface scattering, several hierarchical schemes [12, 13] have been proposed to facilitate integration of BSSRDF contributions from all points on the surface. Since these hierarchical data structures need to be precomputed before rendering, they cannot be used in material editing. Mertens et al. [14] proposed a hierarchical scheme that supports real-time updates, but since this method is based on the dipole diffusion model, it can be used only for rendering homogeneous materials. In [15], local subsurface scattering is computed by a local image filter, while the global scattering is determined from vertex-vertex transport. Although this method can provide interactive rendering speed, precomputation of the local filter and global transport makes this approach unsuitable for material editing.

For radiance transfer modeled as a diffusion process, the set of partial differential equations may be numerically solved to determine material appearance. Multi-grid schemes and simplified volume representations have been employed to facilitate rendering of participating media in [7]. Haber et al. [16] used embedded boundary discretization to solve for light diffusion in object volumes of arbitrary shape, though not in real time. A finite element method (FEM) could also be used in computing light diffusion in an arbitrary object. However, FEMs require decomposition of the object into tetrahedra, whose irregular connectivity makes GPU implementation difficult. In our proposed approach, real-time evaluation of diffusion is achieved with a polygrid representation of the object volume and an adaptive hierarchical scheme for diffusion computation that has an efficient implementation on the GPU.

7.2 Overview

Figure 7.1 presents an overview of our approach. Let the object interior be volume V and the object surface be A. The outgoing radiance $L(x_o, \omega_o)$ at a surface point x_o in direction ω_o may be computed by integrating the incoming radiance $L(x_i, \omega_i)$ from all incident directions ω_i and points x_i on surface A:

$$L_o(x_o, \omega_o) = \int_A \int_\Omega S(x_i, \omega_i, x_o, \omega_o) L_i(x_i, \omega_i)(n \cdot \omega_i) \mathrm{d}\omega_i \mathrm{d}A(x_i),$$

where n is the surface normal at x_i and $S(x_i, \omega_i, x_o, \omega_o)$ is the BSSRDF. The outgoing radiance can be divided into single- and multiple-scattering components:

$$L_o(x_o, \omega_o) = L_s(x_o, \omega_o) + L_m(x_o, \omega_o).$$

The single-scattering component $L_s(x_o, \omega_o)$ accounts for light that interacts exactly once with the medium before exiting the volume, and may be evaluated by integrating the incident radiance along the refracted outgoing ray, as described in Eq. (6) of [8]. In our method, we focus on multiple scattering and use a highly simplified single scattering term that assumes scattering to be isotropic and occurring only at surface points x_o:

$$L_s(x_o, \omega_o) = \frac{\sigma_s(x_o) F}{4\pi} \int_{2\pi} L_i(x_o, \omega_i) \mathrm{d}\omega_i, \tag{7.1}$$

where σ_s is the scattering coefficient, and $F = F_t(\eta(x_o), \omega_o) F_t(\eta(x_o), \omega_i)$ is the product of incoming and outgoing Fresnel transmission terms with η being the refractive index.

The multiple-scattering component $L_m(x_o, \omega_o)$ consists of light that interacts multiple times within the object volume. For highly scattering, non-emissive materials, multiple scattering may be approximated by a diffusion process described by the following equation [4]:

$$\nabla \cdot \big(\kappa(x) \nabla \phi(x)\big) - \mu(x) \phi(x) = 0, \quad x \in V, \tag{7.2}$$

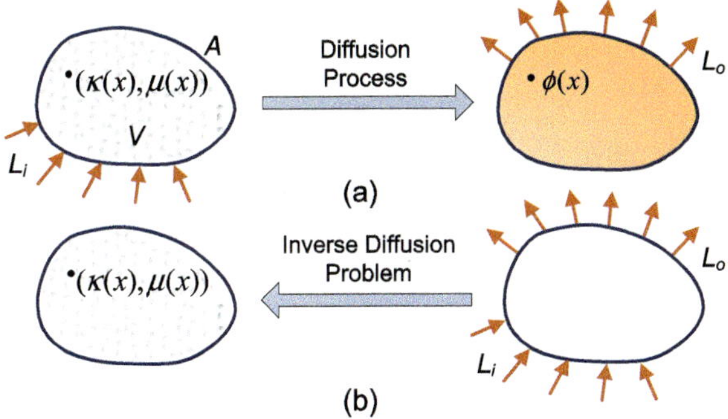

Fig. 7.1 Overview. (**a**) Rendering with forward diffusion, from the volumetric material properties ($\kappa(x)$ and $\mu(x)$) and illumination setting (L_i) to the outgoing radiance (L_o). (**b**) Model acquisition with inverse diffusion, from a set of illumination conditions (L_i) and measured outgoing radiances (L_o) to the volumetric material properties ($\kappa(x)$ and $\mu(x)$)

with boundary condition defined on the object surface A:

$$\phi(x) + 2C\kappa(x)\frac{\partial \phi(x)}{\partial n} = \frac{4}{1 - F_{dr}} q(x), \quad x \in A, \tag{7.3}$$

where $\phi(x) = \int_{4\pi} L_o(x, \omega) d\omega$ is the radiant fluence (also known as the scalar irradiance), $\kappa(x) = 1/[3(\mu(x) + \sigma_s'(x))]$ is the diffusion coefficient, $\mu(x)$ is the absorption coefficient, and $\sigma_s'(x) = \sigma_s(1 - g)$ is the reduced scattering coefficient with g being the mean cosine of the scattering angle. We define $C = (1 + F_{dr})/(1 - F_{dr})$, where F_{dr} is the diffuse Fresnel reflectance. The diffuse incoming light at a surface point x is given by $q(x) = \int_\Omega L_i(x, \omega_i)(n \cdot \omega_i) F_t(\eta(x), \omega_i) d\omega_i$. With the diffusion approximation, the multiple scattering component of the outgoing radiance is calculated as

$$L_m(x_o, \omega_o) = \frac{F_t(\eta(x_o), \omega_o)}{4\pi} \left[\left(1 + \frac{1}{C}\phi(x_o)\right) - \frac{4}{1 + F_{dr}} L_i(x_o) \right], \tag{7.4}$$

where $\phi(x_o)$ is computed from Eqs. (7.2) and (7.3).

Our work centers on modeling and rendering multiple scattering in a heterogeneous material using the diffusion approximation. For rendering an object with known $\mu(x)$ and $\kappa(x)$ throughout the object volume V, we solve the diffusion problem with a given illumination condition $q(x)$ on the object surface A. Once the solution $\phi(x)$ is found, the multiple scattering component of the outgoing radiance can be easily evaluated using Eq. (7.4). We note that the diffusion equation assumes scattering to be frequent enough to be considered isotropic and independent of the phase function.

In acquiring the material properties from measured appearance, we need to compute the absorption coefficients $\mu(x)$ and diffusion coefficients $\kappa(x)$ based on measured outgoing radiances $\{L_{o,m}(x, \omega_o) \mid x \in A, m = 0, 1, \ldots, M\}$ from the object surface due to multiple scattering under M different illumination conditions

$\{L_{i,m}(x,\omega_i) \mid x \in A, m = 0, 1, \ldots, M\}$ on the object surface. For this purpose, we solve the inverse diffusion problem to find $\kappa(x)$ and $\mu(x)$ such that the corresponding diffusion problem, which is expressed by Eqs. (7.2), (7.3), and (7.4), produces the outgoing radiance $L^R_{o,m}(x,\omega_o)$ that is most consistent to the measured outgoing radiance $L_{o,m}(x,\omega_o)$ under the same illumination conditions $L_{i,m}(x,\omega_i)$. The inverse diffusion problem is thus formulated as finding the values of $\kappa(x)$ and $\mu(x)$ throughout the volume that minimize the objective function

$$\sum_{m=1}^{M} \int_A \int_\Omega \left(L_{o,m}(x,\omega_o) - L^R_{o,m}(x,\omega_o)\right)^2 \mathrm{d}A(x)\mathrm{d}\omega_o. \tag{7.5}$$

To obtain multiple scattering components from image measurements, a cross-polarization approach as described in [17] may be employed. We instead utilize an image acquisition scheme described in the following section that minimizes the presence of single scattering and surface reflections in the image data.

7.3 Acquisition of Material Model

To acquire the volumetric material model of a real object, we obtain images of the object under different illumination conditions and then solve the inverse problem of light diffusion on the multiple scattering components. In solving the inverse diffusion problem, we search for the volumetric model $(\mu(x), \kappa(x))$ whose forward diffusion solution is most consistent with the acquired images. This procedure is described in the following subsections.

7.3.1 Data Capture

We use a Canon 30D digital camera with a 17–45 mm lens to record images of a material sample that is illuminated by an Optoma DLP projector with a 4500:1 contrast ratio. In our experiments, the material samples are all block-shaped and represented as a regular grid with $n \times m \times l$ sample points ($n \geq m \geq l$) on the grid nodes. As shown in Fig. 7.2, we utilize two setups depending on the thickness of the sample. In both setups, we position the sample so that one of the $n \times m$ faces is perpendicular to the optical axis of the projector. For thin material samples ($n, m \gg l$), the camera is placed facing the sample from the opposite side, such that the sample is imaged with back-lighting. For thick material samples with little transmission of light through the volume, we position the camera beside the projector as done in [3]. We will refer to the side of the sample facing the camera as the front face.

The camera and projector are calibrated prior to image acquisition. For radiometric calibration of the camera, we apply the method of [18]. Geometric calibration of both the camera and projector is done with the technique in [19], where for the projector we project a chessboard pattern onto different planes. The white balance of

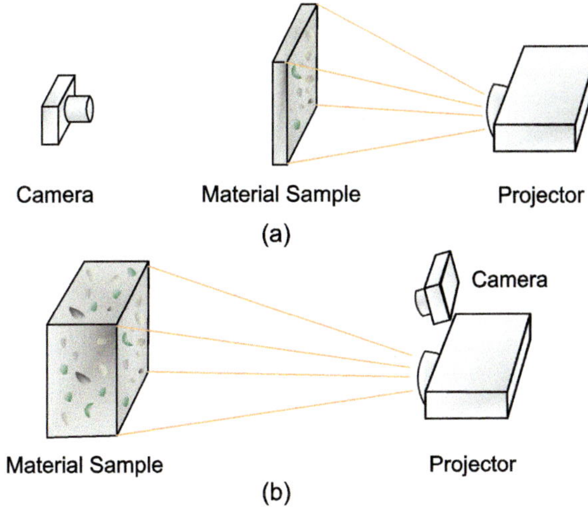

Fig. 7.2 Two experimental setups used for data acquisition. (**a**) Back-lighting setup for thin material samples. (**b**) Front-lighting for thick material samples

the camera is calibrated with respect to the projector, based on the projection of a white image onto a Macbeth Color Checker™ chart with known albedos. The color chart is also used in measuring the black level of the projector. To avoid interference effects from the projector's color wheel, we utilize exposure times of at least $1/30$ second.

In illuminating the sample, we subdivide the face that receives direct lighting into 4×4 regions, and separately project light onto each region while capturing an image sequence of the complete sample with a fixed aperture and variable exposure times ranging from $1/30$ to 8 seconds. Using the method in [18], we construct an HDR image from the image sequence for each illumination condition. Vignetting effects from the projector are minimized by illuminating the sample using only the center of the projector images. This capture process typically takes about half an hour.

With this capture process, we obtain images of multiple scattering data. In the thin-sample setup, the back-lighting is assumed to scatter multiple times before exiting from the front face, such that captured images contain only multiple scattering. In the setup for thick samples, we utilize image data only from surface points that are not directly illuminated by the projector. The appearance of these points is considered to result only from multiple scattering. Since the projector and camera are aligned perpendicularly to the material sample in both configurations, we can disregard the Fresnel transmittance effects on the measured multiple scattering, and drop the dependence on ω_o in Eq. (7.5). For all examples in this chapter, we set $C = 2.1489$ with $\eta = 1.3$.

To capture the approximate single scattering term in Eq. (7.1), we use the front-lighting setup and follow the method in [2], which records one image of the sample under uniform lighting. The single scattering term is obtained by subtracting the multiple scattering contribution from it.

Table 7.1 Conjugate gradient based algorithm for minimizing f_M

Set initial material properties: $\vec{\kappa}_0, \vec{\mu}_0$
Set initial search direction: $\vec{d}_0 = -\vec{z}(\kappa_0, \mu_0)$ and $\vec{p}_0 = \vec{d}_0$
Repeat following steps until $f_M < \varepsilon$
Compute gradient $\vec{z}(\kappa_t, \mu_t) = \left(\frac{\mathrm{d}f_M(\vec{\kappa},\vec{\mu})}{\mathrm{d}\kappa(x)}, \frac{\mathrm{d}f_M(\vec{\kappa},\vec{\mu})}{\mathrm{d}\mu(x)}\right)$
Set $p_t = -\vec{z}(\kappa_t, \mu_t)$
Update search direction $\vec{d}_t = \vec{p}_t + \beta \cdot \vec{d}_{t-1}$,
$\beta = \max\left(\frac{\vec{p}_t^T(\vec{p}_t - \vec{p}_{t-1})}{\vec{p}_{t-1}^T \vec{p}_{t-1}}, 0\right)$
Golden section search λ' by $\min_{\lambda'}[f_M((\vec{\kappa}_t, \vec{\mu}_t) + \lambda' \vec{d}_t)]$
Update solution $(\vec{\kappa}_{t+1}, \vec{\mu}_{t+1}) = (\vec{\kappa}_t, \vec{\mu}_t) + \lambda' \vec{d}_t$

7.3.2 Volumetric Model Acquisition

For each captured image and corresponding lighting condition, we map onto each grid node on the front and back faces its incoming light intensity and measured outgoing radiance. The material model is then acquired by solving for the scattering parameters (κ and μ) of each node in the volume that would result in image appearances most consistent with the measured data. With the M measured images of the material sample, we thus aim to minimize the following objective function:

$$f_M(\vec{\kappa}, \vec{\mu}) = \sum_{m=1}^{M} f_m(\vec{\kappa}, \vec{\mu}) + \lambda \sum_{x \in V} \left\| \nabla \kappa(x) \right\|^2,$$

where $f_m(\vec{\kappa}, \vec{\mu}) = \sum_{x \in A} (L_{o,m}(x) - L_{o,m}^R(x))^2$ measures the consistency between the measured outgoing radiance $L_{o,m}(x)$ from all frontal surface points x and the outgoing radiance $L_{o,m}^R(x)$ that is computed from the estimated scattering parameters with the illumination condition of image m. Note that in f_m we drop the dependence on ω_o that is present in Eq. (7.5) because of our imaging configuration. The vectors $\vec{\kappa}$ and $\vec{\mu}$ represent the set of diffusion and absorption coefficients defined over all the grid nodes. Since model acquisition is ill-conditioned with respect to κ, we add a regularization term $\sum_{x \in V} \|\nabla \kappa(x)\|^2$ based on material coherency to the objective function, where λ is set to 1e-5 in our implementation.

To minimize f_M, we employ the conjugate gradient algorithm outlined in Table 7.1. From an initialization of $\vec{\kappa}$ and $\vec{\mu}$, we first compute the gradient of f_M with respect to $(\vec{\kappa}, \vec{\mu})$ over the set of measured images. The search direction is then updated with the Polak-Ribiere method [20]. Subsequently, we perform a golden section search to find the optimal step size λ' along the search direction. Finally, we update $\vec{\kappa}$ and $\vec{\mu}$ using the computed gradient $\vec{z}(\kappa, \mu)$ and λ'. These steps are iterated to update $\vec{\kappa}$ and $\vec{\mu}$ until the objective function falls below a threshold set to $\varepsilon = 10^{-4} \times \sum_{x \in A} [L_{o,m}(x)]^2$ in our implementation. This optimization is performed separately on the RGB channels.

To initialize the scattering parameters in this optimization, we solve for the volumetric material model under the assumption that it is homogeneous, i.e., all the grid nodes have the same μ, κ. Since there exist only two unknowns in this case, they can be quickly computed using the conjugate gradient procedure with user-specified initial values.

A key step in conjugate gradient optimization is the computation of the f_M gradient relative to the unknown κ and μ values at each grid node. Since the diffusion equation has no analytic solution, we compute the gradients numerically. A straightforward approach for gradient computation is to perturb each of the variables and obtain the resultant change in objective function value. One forward diffusion simulation would then be necessary to compute each gradient. Although this method is feasible for a system with few parameters (e.g., a homogeneous volume), it is impractical for arbitrary heterogeneous volumes which have a large number of unknowns. Specifically, model acquisition for an $n \times m \times l$ grid with M measurements would require $2 \times n \times m \times l \times M$ forward diffusion simulations for each iteration, clearly a prohibitive expense.

7.3.3 Adjoint Method for Gradient Computation

To significantly expedite gradient computation, we take advantage of the adjoint method [21], a technique that has been widely used in optimal control [10]. We describe here how to directly use the adjoint method in our application.

To use the adjoint method in our solution, we first define the adjoint equation of the original diffusion equation as

$$\nabla \cdot \big(\kappa(x)\nabla\varphi(x)\big) - \mu(x)\varphi(x) = 0, \quad x \in V, \tag{7.6}$$

with boundary condition defined on the surface A:

$$\varphi(x) + 2C\kappa(x)\frac{\partial\varphi(x)}{\partial n} = \frac{8C}{\pi(1 - F_{dr})}\big(L_{o,m}(x) - L^R_{o,m}(x)\big), \quad x \in A, \tag{7.7}$$

where $(L_{o,m}(x) - L^R_{o,m}(x))$ is the difference between the measured outgoing radiance $L_{o,m}(x)$ from all frontal sample points x and the outgoing radiance $L^R_{o,m}(x)$ that is computed from the diffusion equation with the illumination condition q_m of image m. Given φ, the gradient of f_M with respect to κ and μ at each grid point is computed by

$$\begin{aligned} \mathrm{d}f_M(\vec{\kappa}, \vec{\mu})/\mathrm{d}\kappa(x) &= \sum_{m=1}^{M} \nabla\varphi_m(x) \cdot \nabla\phi_m(x) - 2\lambda\Delta\kappa(x), \\ \mathrm{d}f_M(\vec{\kappa}, \vec{\mu})/\mathrm{d}\mu(x) &= \sum_{m=1}^{M} \varphi_m(x)\phi_m(x), \end{aligned} \tag{7.8}$$

where $\phi_m(x)$ is determined from the diffusion equation with the illumination condition q_m of image m.

In contrast to the original diffusion equation, the adjoint method utilizes "virtual" illumination to define the boundary condition. This virtual illumination $(2C/\pi)(L_{o,m}(x) - L^R_{o,m}(x))$, which may be negative, and ϕ are computed from the diffusion equation using the actual illumination condition. With the virtual illumination, we solve the adjoint equation for φ, and then determine the gradient of f_M relative to κ and μ using Eq. (7.8). Using the adjoint method, only $2M$ forward diffusion simulations are needed for gradient computation. Because of its computational efficiency, the adjoint method has also been used in [22] for gradient computation in fluid control.

7.3.4 GPU-Based Diffusion Computation

In model acquisition, forward diffusion simulations are used not only in gradient computation, but also for evaluating the objective function in the golden section search. To solve the diffusion equation on a 3D regular grid, we discretize the diffusion equation over the grid nodes, and numerically solve this system using the multi-grid FDM scheme in [7].

This FDM technique involves considerable computation and is the bottleneck in model acquisition. For efficient processing, we present a GPU-based multiresolution scheme that simulates forward diffusion in the pixel shader on grid values of κ, μ, and q packed into separate 2D textures. This GPU-based method can be regarded as a regular-grid version of the rendering algorithm in Sect. 7.4, where we provide further details.

In solving the diffusion equation on the GPU, we upload all the relevant data from main memory to texture memory, and then output the radiant fluence results from the frame buffer back to main memory. The remaining optimization computations are all executed on the CPU. Despite some overhead for data transfer, an appreciable overall reduction in computation costs is obtained through GPU acceleration.

7.3.5 Discussion

In theory, the diffuse BSSRDF should be densely sampled to ensure that the acquired material volume generates accurate surface appearances for arbitrary illumination conditions. However, because of the redundancy in BSSRDF data, we have found that models acquired from sparsely sampled images provide good results in practice. Note that each image here corresponds to a 2D slice of the 4D BSSRDF.

To examine the relationship between the number of measurements and model quality, we applied our model acquisition algorithm on the synthetic volume shown in Fig. 7.3, which was modeled using a $72 \times 72 \times 10$ grid. We subdivide the front surface into $n \times n$ regions that are each separately illuminated. For different n, we generated images using the diffusion equation, and then used these images as input to our algorithm. Normalized errors were then computed as $E =$

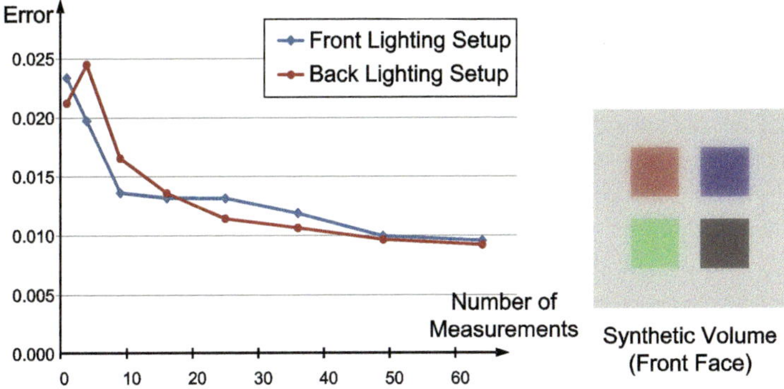

Fig. 7.3 Model quality vs. number of measurements. *Left*: errors of BSSRDFs computed from material volumes acquired using different numbers of measurements. *Right*: front face of the synthetic volume used in this analysis

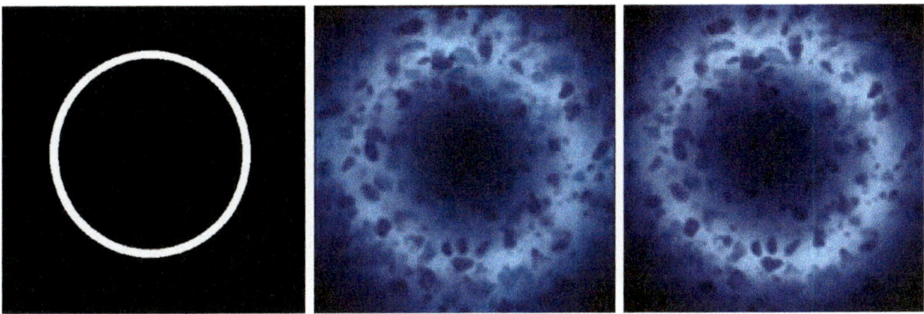

Fig. 7.4 Comparison of acquired model to ground truth. From left to right: illumination setting (behind the material sample); rendering of volume acquired from 16 images; real image of material

$\sum_{x_i,x_j \in A}[R'_d(x_i,x_j) - R_d(x_i,x_j)]^2 / \sum_{x_i,x_j \in A}[R_d(x_i,x_j)]^2$, where R_d is the diffuse BSSRDF computed from the original volume, and R'_d is that computed from the acquired material volume. The experiments are done with both the front-lighting and back-lighting setups. Figure 7.3 displays the error for $n = 1, 2, \ldots, 8$, which indicates that for 16 or more images, the error is comparable to that reported for the factorized BSSRDF representation in [3]. In our current implementation, we use 16 images under different illumination settings for model acquisition, which provides a level of rendering quality exemplified in Fig. 7.4.

7.4 Rendering and Editing

After acquiring a material model from a real sample, a volume of arbitrary shape can be formed with this material using the mapping techniques described in [23, 24]. These approaches map the material properties into a shell layer at the object surface, and construct the inner core volume by synthesizing a user-specified material texture or interpolating from the inner boundary of the shell layer using mean value coordinates [25].

With a given lighting condition and the material properties defined throughout the object volume, the subsurface scattering effects from the object can be rendered in a three-pass process. In the first pass, we compute the incoming radiance on the object surface, based on shadow map visibility for directional or point lighting, or from precomputed radiance transfer techniques [26, 27] for environment lighting. In the second pass, we render the multiple scattering effects by simulating light diffusion inside the object volume with the incident radiance on the surface as the boundary condition. Finally, we compute the single scattering term and surface reflectance from the incoming illumination, and obtain the final rendering result by adding these components together.

To efficiently solve for light diffusion on the GPU, we extend the FDM scheme on regular volumetric grids to handle a polygrid defined in the object volume. A polygrid is a grid with regular 6-connections among evenly distributed nodes inside the volume, and that has boundary nodes that are aligned with the object surface and are each connected to one interior node along the inward normal direction. With the polygrid representation of the object volume, we discretize the light diffusion equation and its boundary condition into a system of linear equations:

$$\begin{aligned} &\sum_{j=1}^{6} w_{ji}\kappa(v_j)\phi(v_j) - \left(\sum_{j=1}^{6} w_{ji}\right)\kappa(v_i)\phi(v_i) - u(v_i)\phi(v_i) = 0, \\ &\phi(v_i') + 2C\kappa(v_i')\frac{\phi(v_i') - \phi(v_j')}{d_{ji}} = \frac{4}{1-F_{dr}}q(v_i'), \end{aligned} \tag{7.9}$$

where v_j denotes one of six nodes directly connected to interior node v_i with a weight w_{ji} for the Laplacian operator. d_{ji} represents the distance between a boundary node v_i' and the closest interior node v_j' along the inward normal direction, and $q(v_i')$ denotes the incoming radiance at surface node v_i'.

In the remainder of this section, we describe how to construct the polygrid of an object volume and how to solve the diffusion equation on the GPU. We also present a hierarchical scheme for accelerating GPU evaluation of light diffusion on a polygrid.

7.4.1 Polygrid Construction

The steps in constructing a polygrid model of the object volume are shown in Fig. 7.5. We first manually assemble a polycube [28] of similar topology that approximates the volume. Within the cubes, we form regular grids of equal resolution, and connect the grids between adjacent cubes. The interior nodes directly linked to boundary nodes on the edges or corners of the cube have connectivity to multiple boundary nodes, which may lead to artifacts in the light diffusion computation.

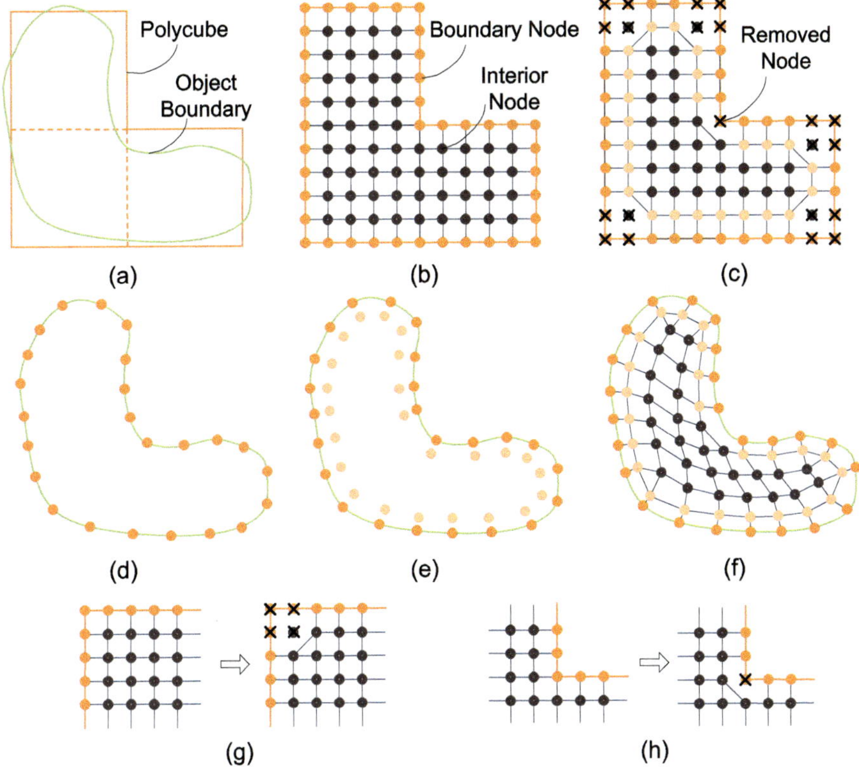

Fig. 7.5 A 2D illustration of polygrid construction. (**a**) Creating a polycube that approximates the object. (**b**) Generating a grid in the polycube. (**c**) Modifying the corner nodes. (**d**) Projecting boundary nodes to the object surface. (**e**) Mapping nodes connected to boundary nodes to the object volume. (**f**) Computing the final polygrid in the object volume. (**g**) and (**h**) are two schemes used to modify irregular corner nodes on 2D slices of the grid

We address this problem by removing certain nodes and adjusting the links to obtain single connections to boundary nodes. As shown in Fig. 7.5(g, h), we examine axis-aligned 2D slices of the grid and utilize different grid adjustment schemes depending on the grid convexity in each slice. This procedure yields a polygrid defined in the polycube.

We then map this polygrid to the object volume. To find a mapping, we first determine a projection of the polycube surface onto the object surface, using a PolyCube-Map [28] or other mesh cross-parameterization method (e.g., [29, 30]). The boundary nodes of the polygrid are then mapped to the object surface and adjusted to obtain an even distribution [31]. After that, the interior nodes directly connected to the boundary nodes are placed within the object volume at a distance d along the inward normal directions, where d is one-tenth the average distance between connected boundary nodes on the object surface. The close placement of these nodes to the boundary nodes is intended for accurate handling of the bound-

Fig. 7.6 The polygrid constructed in a 3D model

ary condition. The remaining interior nodes are then positioned within the volume in a manner that minimizes the variance of distances between connected nodes: $\min \sum_{i \in interior} \mathrm{Var}(\{\|v_i - v_j\| : j \bowtie i\})$, where $\mathrm{Var}(\cdot)$ denotes the variance of a set of scalars, v_i is the 3D position of node i, and $j \bowtie i$ indicates that node j is connected to node i. Figure 7.5 illustrates this construction procedure in 2D. In principle, a conformal mapping [32] should be used to preserve the orthogonality of the original grid connections and minimize distortion. However, this remains a challenging problem for 3D volumes, so in practice we utilize the presented variance minimization scheme which we have found to yield acceptable solutions.

This construction scheme maintains the regular connectivity of nodes and produces locally uniform distributions of interior grid nodes in the object volume. As exemplified in Fig. 7.6, all the interior grid nodes of the polygrid are 6-connected, and each boundary node is connected to exactly one interior node. The connectivity between the boundary grid nodes is not used in rendering and can be ignored in the diffusion computation.

7.4.2 GPU-Based Polygrid Diffusion Computation

With the constructed polygrid, we build a system of linear equations for light diffusion. The material properties for each grid node are sampled from the object volume, and the incoming illumination is computed for boundary nodes. Although a general purpose GPU-based linear system solver could be used for computation [33, 34], we have designed a more efficient GPU implementation that is specific to diffusion computation on a polygrid.

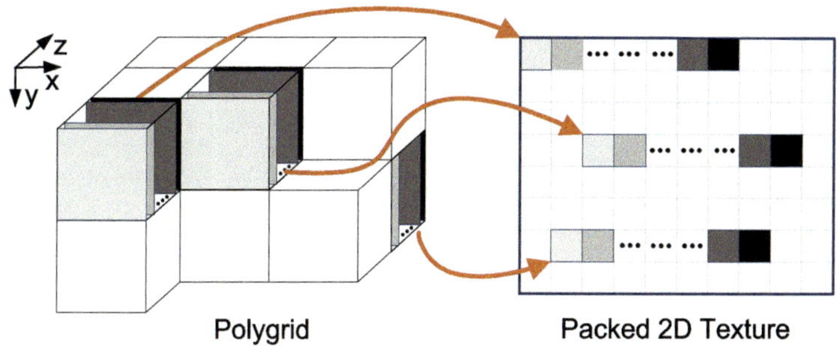

Fig. 7.7 Flattening a polygrid into a packed 2D texture

In this method, the polygrid material parameters are packed into a set of 2D textures for computation on the GPU. For efficient rendering, the textures must be packed such that the connected neighbors of each node are easily accessible. Towards this end, we organize each texture according to the positions of the polygrid nodes within the original polycube. We traverse the cubes in the polycube in scan-line order, and flatten the grid of each cube as shown in Fig. 7.7. The grid in each cube is divided into 2D x–y slices, which are each treated as a texture block and ordered in the texture by increasing z value. In packing the texture, we retain the empty positions of grid nodes that were previously removed, so that the cubes have slices of equal size. Two 2D textures T_κ and T_μ are created for the corresponding scattering parameters, and for the iterative computation we maintain two swap radiance buffers I_A and I_B that are organized in the same manner as T_κ and T_μ. In addition, we precompute the weights for the Laplacian operator, then similarly pack this data into two textures T_{w1} and T_{w2}. The incoming radiance is also packed into a 2D texture T_l according to access order as described later.

After texture packing, we solve the diffusion equations on the polygrid using the relaxation scheme in [7]. Starting from the initial radiant fluence values ϕ_0, we iteratively update the radiant fluence values in the two radiance buffers until convergence. With the radiant fluence at each node corresponding to one pixel in the radiance buffer, this computation can be executed in the pixel shader with parameters accessed from the textures. To reduce texture fetches in the pixel shader, we store $\phi' = \kappa\phi$ in the radiance buffer. In each step, the radiant fluence values are updated as follows:

$$\phi'_{n+1}(v_i) = \frac{\sum_{1\le j\le 6} w_{ji}(v_i)\phi'_n(v_j)}{\mu(v_i)/\kappa(v_i) + \sum_{1\le j\le 6} w_{ji}(v_i)},$$

$$\phi'_{n+1}(v'_i) = \frac{q(v'_i)\kappa(v'_i)\kappa(v'_j)d + 2C\kappa^2(v'_i)\phi'_n(v'_j)}{\kappa(v'_j)d + 2C\kappa(v'_i)\kappa(v'_j)},$$

where right-hand-side operators of the form $f(\cdot)$ involve a texture access, and the radiance buffer for ϕ'_n is used as the texture while the other radiance buffer is used as the rendering target for ϕ'_{n+1}.

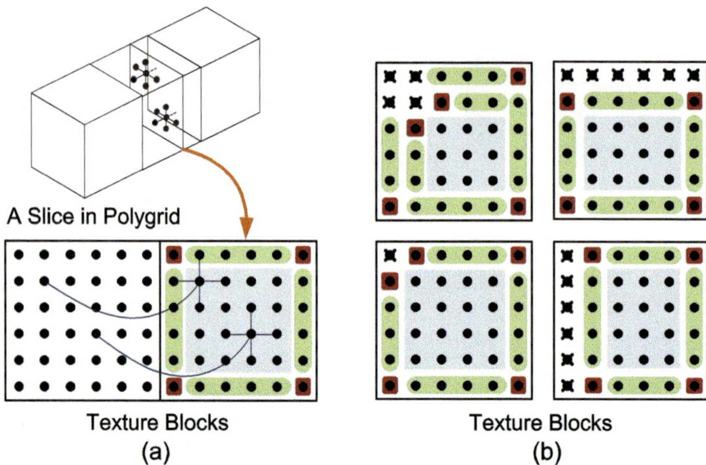

Fig. 7.8 Geometric primitives for nodes with different texture access patterns. (**a**) Three types of nodes, rendered using different geometric primitives. Each region is rendered by one primitive. (**b**) Geometric primitives for some texture blocks with removed nodes

As shown in Fig. 7.8, there exist three types of nodes/pixels in the radiance buffer, each with different texture access patterns for reaching connected nodes. We render each type of node using a different geometric primitive, represented by colored regions in the figure. For a (blue) node that lies in the interior of a texture block, four of its connected neighbors in the polygrid are also adjacent neighbors in the 2D texture, while the other two neighbors can be found with the same offset value in other texture blocks. We update the values of these nodes by rendering a quadrilateral with the texture offsets of the two non-adjacent neighbors as vertex attributes. After rasterization, this offset information can be interpolated from the vertices to each pixel in the quad. In a similar manner, the (green) nodes on each texture block edge are rendered with a line, where three neighbors are adjacent in the texture, and the texture offsets of the other three are stored as line vertex attributes. The (red) nodes of each texture block corner are rendered with points, with the texture offsets of all six neighbors stored as vertex attributes. Slices that contain removed nodes can also be rendered using these three primitives. All of these geometric primitives and their vertex attributes can be precomputed and loaded into graphics memory before rendering. Since the surface boundary nodes and the interior nodes are processed differently, we render their corresponding geometric primitives in two separate passes with different pixel shaders. After completing this computation, we calculate the output radiance on the surface by updating the boundary nodes in the radiance buffer as $L(v_i') = F_t(x_o, \omega_o)[\phi'(v_i) - q(v_i)\kappa(v_i)]/[2\pi\kappa(v_i)]$. These boundary node values are then used as a texture for surface vertices in the final pass.

With this packing and rendering scheme, the radiant fluence values are updated with ten texture fetches for interior nodes and five texture fetches for surface nodes. Our scheme avoids extra texture storage for node connectivity information and dependent texture accesses in rendering. We acknowledge that alternative schemes for

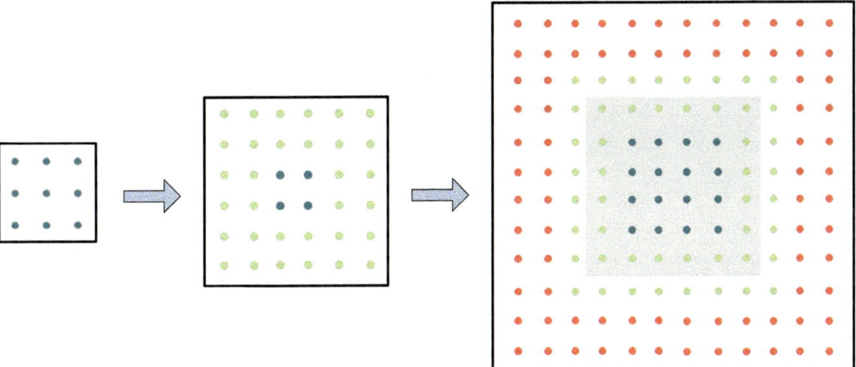

Fig. 7.9 A 2D illustration of the adaptive hierarchical technique used in diffusion computation. In this scheme, we fix the values of the *blue nodes* in the middle level after initialization from the coarsest level. The *blue* and *green nodes* at the finest resolution are also fixed after initialization. *Nodes in the gray region* are not used in the diffusion computation and are removed from textures

packing and rendering are possible and may be better. Nevertheless, we have obtained good performance with this method.

7.4.3 Hierarchical Acceleration

For greater efficiency in computing light diffusion, we employ a hierarchical scheme to accelerate rendering with the polygrid. In this scheme, we first construct a multiresolution polygrid in the object volume. Starting from the original polygrid, the positions and material properties of nodes at successively coarser levels are determined by averaging the positions and material properties of its eight children at the next finer level. For nodes whose children contain removed nodes, we normalize the result by the number of existing children. Before rendering, we pack the material properties at each resolution and generate texture pyramids for T_κ, T_μ, T_{w1} and T_{w2}. Pyramids need not be generated for the radiance buffers I_A and I_B, which can simply be reused for computation at each level. During rendering, we first solve the diffusion equations at the coarsest grid level, and then use the computed radiant fluence at each node as initializations for its children nodes at the next finer level. This process iterates until a solution at the original polygrid resolution is obtained.

The hierarchical algorithm can be accelerated by employing an adaptive scheme in which light diffusion is computed to different resolutions at different depths in the volume. Since material variations deeper inside the object volume have more subtle effects on surface appearance, it is sufficient to approximate light diffusion at deeper nodes with coarser-resolution solutions. As shown in Fig. 7.9, after we obtain the solution at a coarse resolution and copy it to a finer resolution, the radiant fluence values at nodes below a certain depth are fixed, while the nodes closer to boundary are updated. In our implementation of this adaptive scheme, the computed

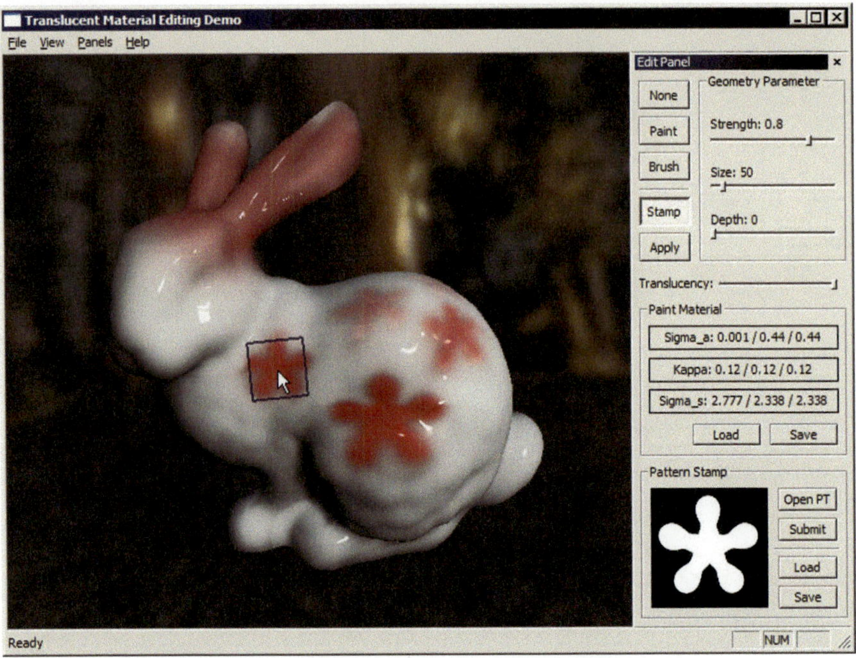

Fig. 7.10 User interface for material editing

resolution at different depth levels is given by the user. Texture blocks whose nodes are not used in computation at a given level are removed to save on texture storage.

In our current implementation, we do not use the V-cycle multi-grid algorithm to speed up light diffusion computation, since the multigrid algorithm cannot easily be incorporated into our adaptive scheme. Also, V-cycle multi-grid algorithms require extra texture storage for residual and temporary radiant fluence values in each level. If all grid nodes are used in light diffusion, our hierarchical solution algorithm can be regarded as a simplified N-cycle multi-grid scheme without the V-cycles for each resolution [20].

A favorable property of the light diffusion algorithm is that the coherence between frames can be exploited to facilitate rendering. For applications in which the lighting or material changes gradually, the rendering result of the last frame provides an excellent initialization for the current frame. With good initial values, the number of iteration steps can be significantly reduced.

7.4.4 Editing

With this real-time rendering system, the acquired volumetric material model can be interactively edited with real-time feedback on the modified appearance. To illustrate this capability, we developed a simple editing system shown in Fig. 7.10.

In addition to painting new values for $\mu(x)$ and $\kappa(x)$, various ways to modify existing $\mu(x)$ and $\kappa(x)$ are supported. The user can directly adjust $\mu(x)$ and $\kappa(x)$ by multiplying them with or adding them to user-supplied constants. Alternatively, the user can modulate the μ and κ values within a pattern mask using a texture. With our volumetric representation, users can also modify a material at specific depth levels. For a demonstration of a material editing session, please view the supplemental video.

In our system, all editing operations are executed as pixel operations on the GPU. We maintain extra buffers T'_κ and T'_μ of the κ and μ textures as rendering targets for editing. In each frame, T'_κ and T'_μ are modified by user-specified operations, and then swapped to T_κ and T_μ for rendering. To support editing operations on local regions, we store the positions of grid nodes in a texture T_p. Then when the user selects a region on the screen for editing, we compute the screen projection of each grid node based on its position in the editing shader, and execute the editing operations only for the nodes within the user-specified local region. In material editing, we do not use the adaptive scheme, but instead take advantage of the coherence between frames to reduce rendering computation, which allows for more complex material editing operations to be executed on the GPU.

7.5 Experimental Results

We implemented our material acquisition and rendering system on a PC configured with an Intel Core2Duo 2.13 GHZ CPU, 4 GB memory, and a Geforce 8800GTX graphics card with 768 MB graphics memory. The GPU-based light diffusion and rendering algorithm was implemented in the OpenGL shading language. For the GPU-based light diffusion computation used in model acquisition, we represent all parameters and computation results as 32-bit floating-point values for high precision. For light diffusion computations on the polygrid, each channel of κ and μ is quantized into 8-bits and stored together in 24-bit textures. We use 16-bit floating-point values in rendering computations, which provides sufficient precision in appearance.

Figure 7.11 displays the material samples used in our experiments and the acquired κ and μ values along the surface of the material volume. For these samples, the grid resolutions, lighting configurations, and computation times are listed in Table 7.2. With GPU acceleration, the reconstruction algorithm gains a fifty-fold increase in speed over a CPU-based implementation on the same platform.

The effect of coherence-based regularization is illustrated in Fig. 7.12. Different solutions for the volumetric scattering parameters can give similar results for the measured lighting condition, as shown in the top row. However, our solution with greater material coherency as enforced by the regularization term provides a more natural looking result under a new lighting condition, in this case, ring lighting from behind. As commonly found in other aspects of nature, what is observed is often best represented with simplicity.

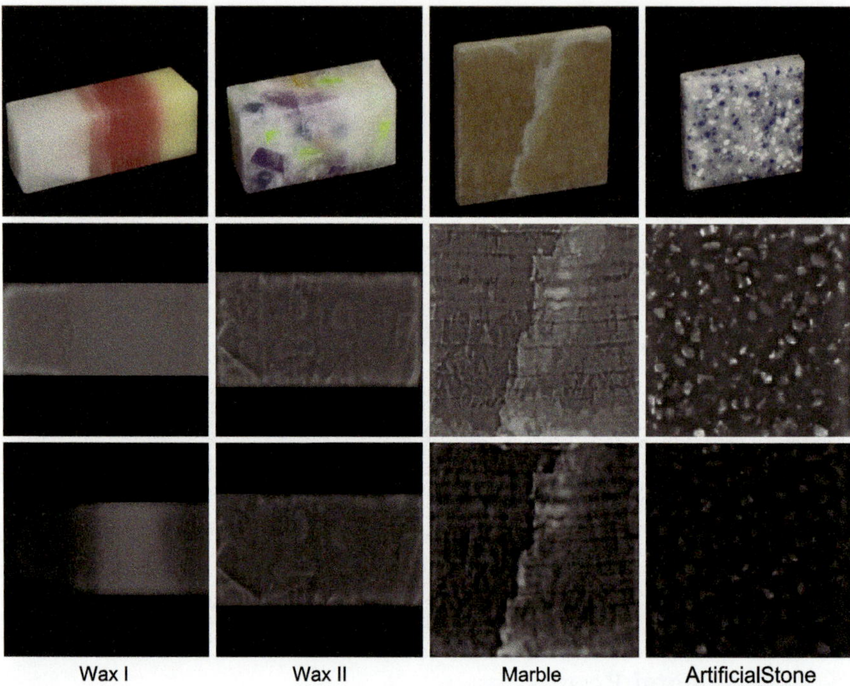

Fig. 7.11 Acquired material samples. *Top row*: real image of sample. *Middle row*: reconstructed κ along the surface. *Bottom row*: reconstructed μ along the surface. The values of κ and μ are scaled for better viewing

Table 7.2 Acquisition settings for the different materials

Material	Grid resolution	Illumination	Computation time (h)
Wax I	130 × 53 × 37	back	2.0
Wax II	140 × 75 × 48	front	4.0
Marble	256 × 256 × 20	back	11.0
Artificial Stone	128 × 128 × 41	back	3.0

Table 7.3 lists the polygrid resolution at the finest level, the texture size, and rendering performance for all the examples shown in this chapter. The polygrid resolution is the product of the number of cubes in the polycube and the grid resolution in each cube. The texture size includes all textures used for light diffusion computation. In this table, the rendering times are broken down into the three passes, for incident light computation (t_1), light diffusion (t_2), and final rendering (t_3). For the overall rendering speed, the first number reports the frame rate without frame coherence (i.e., radiances initialized to zero), while the second number in parentheses gives the speed with frame coherence. In rendering, we use the ambient occlusion to determine visibility for environment lighting, and the shadow buffer for visibil-

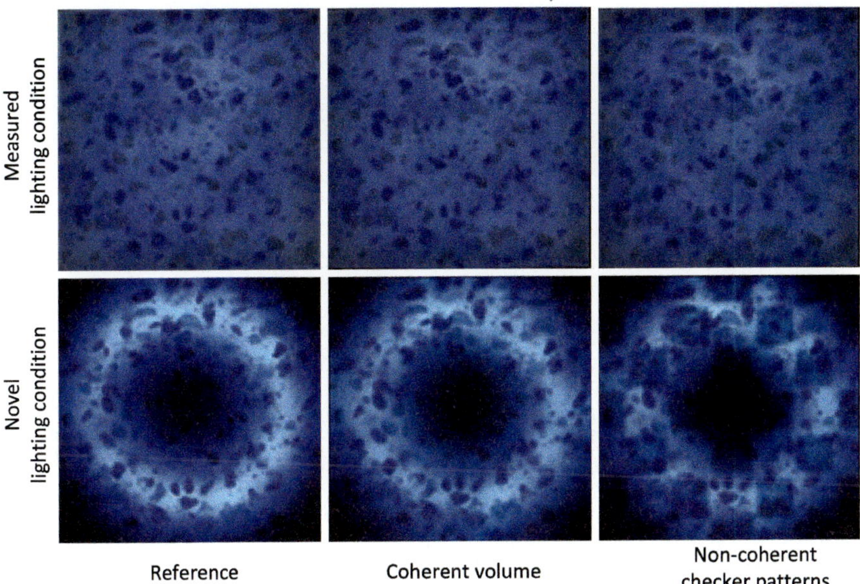

Fig. 7.12 Effect of coherence-based regularization on material relighting

Table 7.3 Rendering configuration and performance. For the rendering times, t_i indicates the time for the ith rendering pass. The final speed is measured both without frame coherence and with frame coherence (in parentheses)

Model	Polygrid resolution	Texture size (MB)	Rendering time $t_1/t_2/t_3$ (ms)	Final speed (fps)
Bunny	$253 \times 16 \times 16 \times 16$	24.9	3.9/23.2/11.5	25.9 (34.7)
Bust	$17 \times 32 \times 32 \times 32$	18.9	2.5/19.9/7.0	34.0 (52.7)
Bird	$108 \times 24 \times 24 \times 24$	39.6	4.0/48.3/13.0	15.3 (24.0)
Hole	$36 \times 12 \times 12 \times 12$	4.8	1.5/8.9/2.1	80.0 (160.4)
Snail	$81 \times 12 \times 12 \times 12$	18.9	1.6/14.0/3.1	53.4 (106.7)

ity of local lighting. A three-level polygrid with the adaptive scheme is used in the measurements for this table.

Figure 7.13 charts the convergence speed of the different rendering methods on the hole model of Fig. 7.15. Here, the error of a result L is computed as $\sum_{x \in A}(L(x) - L_0(x))^2 / \sum_{x \in A} L_0(x)^2$, where L_0 is the converged result precomputed without hierarchical and adaptive acceleration. A multi-resolution polygrid with three levels is used in the hierarchical schemes. The polycube for the hole model contains 36 cubes, and the grid resolution in each cube at the finest level is $12 \times 12 \times 12$. For the hierarchical method without the adaptive scheme, we use all grid nodes in the light diffusion computation. In the adaptive scheme, we manually specify the depth of nodes that are involved in computing each resolution such that

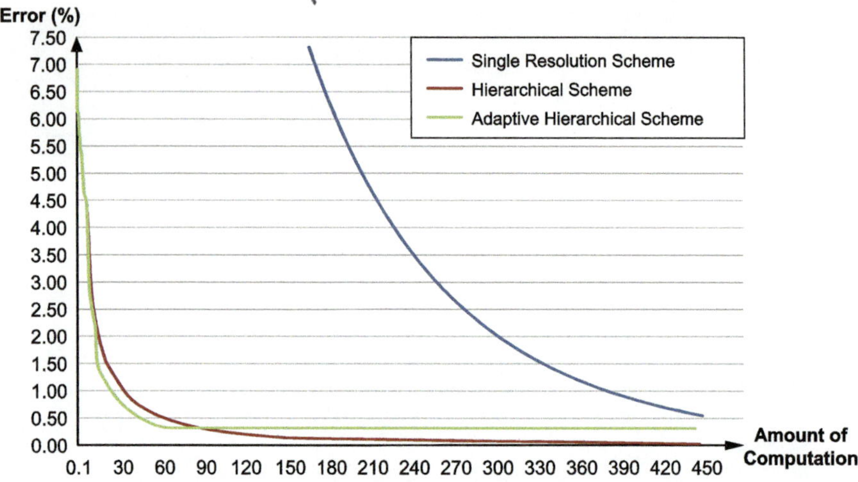

Fig. 7.13 Convergence speed of the three schemes. The X axis represents convergence speed in terms of 100k's of nodes that are processed

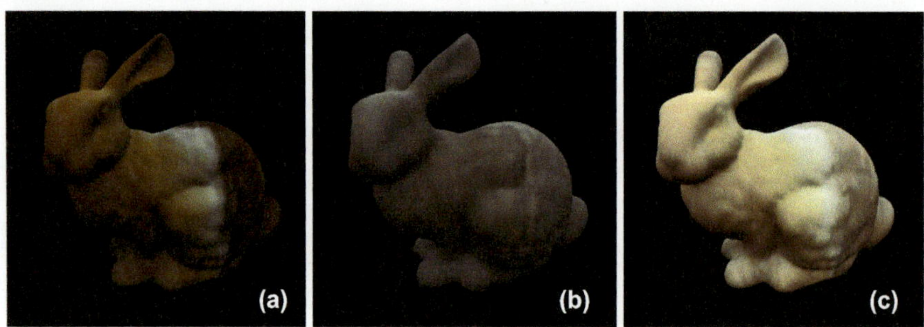

Fig. 7.14 Illustration of scattering components. (**a**) Approximated single scattering term. (**b**) Multiple scattering term. (**c**) Overall rendering result

the final error is less than 0.5 %. It can be seen that the hierarchical scheme can substantially improve light diffusion performance on the polygrid. With the adaptive scheme, the computation is further accelerated (a two-fold speedup in this case) to generate a result with an error below a user-specified threshold.

A rendering result for a bunny model under environment lighting is shown in Fig. 7.14. The different scattering components and the overall rendering result are exhibited. The overall result is the sum of the two components.

Figure 7.15(a, b) shows rendering results with global illumination for a bust model, whose volumetric material properties are acquired from a marble sample. In Fig. 7.15(c, d), a hole model is generated with acquired wax material. Complex surface appearances from subsurface scattering and volumetric material variations are well preserved with our volumetric appearance model.

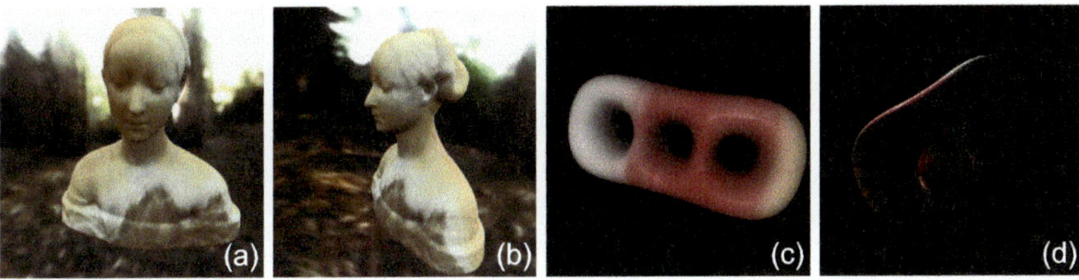

Fig. 7.15 Rendering results of bust and hole model with material acquired from real samples. (**a**, **b**) Bust model rendered with environment lighting. (**c**, **d**) Hole model rendered with local lighting

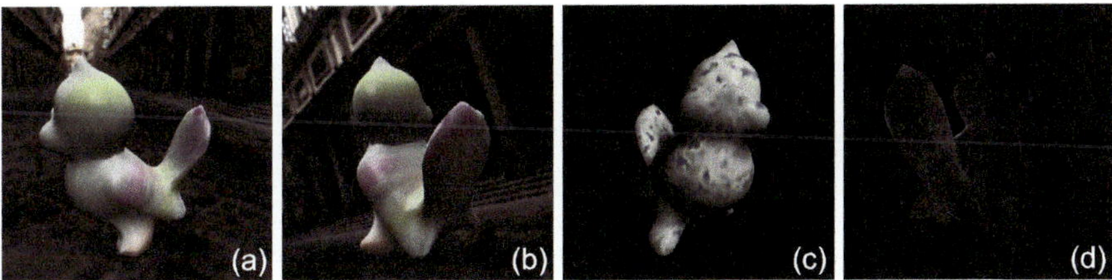

Fig. 7.16 Rendering results of bird with different materials. (**a**, **b**) With wax material. (**c**, **d**) With artificial stone material

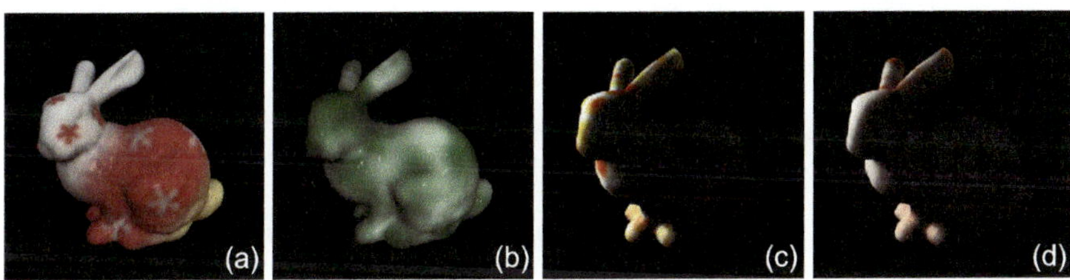

Fig. 7.17 Rendering results of a bunny model with different materials edited by a user. (**a**) Edited from an acquired wax material. (**b–d**) Edited from various homogeneous materials

In Fig. 7.16, a bird model is rendered with a reconstructed wax material and an artificial stone material. Results are shown from different viewing directions. The heterogeneity beneath the surface is well handled in our modeling and rendering technique.

Rendering results of a bunny with different translucent materials edited by the user are shown in Fig. 7.17. Both the local scattering properties of the material and their distributions are modified in these cases. With the volumetric material model, editing of physical attributes can be done in an intuitive manner. Additional editing results are exhibited in Fig. 7.18.

Finally, we display the rendering result of a snail in Fig. 7.19. The volumetric material properties of the snail body are designed by an artist using our editing tool. The artist also painted the surface texture and opaque snail shell.

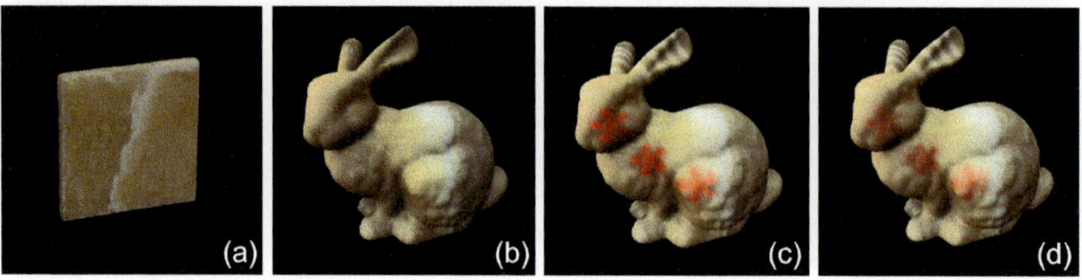

Fig. 7.18 Synthesis of a bunny with marble material. (**a**) Physical sample. (**b**) Bunny rendered with the acquired material model. (**c**) After interactive editing to add patterns. (**d**) After placing the flower pattern at the same location but at a different depth

Fig. 7.19 The rendering result of a snail with environment lighting. The translucent material of the snail body was designed using our editing tool, while the snail shell was modeled and rendered as an opaque surface

7.6 Conclusion

In this chapter, we proposed efficient techniques based on the diffusion equation for modeling and rendering heterogeneous translucent materials. A practical scheme is presented for acquiring volumetric appearance models from real material samples, and for rendering the appearance effects of multiple scattering in real time. With this method, a user can easily edit translucent materials and their volumetric variations with real-time feedback.

Although our approach effectively acquires a detailed appearance model of subsurface scattering, it cannot determine the actual material properties and their variations in the volume, especially deep within the volume. This results from object appearance being relatively insensitive to the material composition far beneath the surface. So while the acquired model is useful for rendering surface appearance, it lacks the precision needed in applications such as solid texture mapping, where deep volumes may become exposed on the surface.

In rendering, the polygrid representation used in this chapter leads to an approximate FDM solution for arbitrary-shaped object volumes. With this approximation, we obtain realistic rendering results and real-time performance. For objects with fine geometric detail or complex topology, however, the presented polygrid construction scheme may produce large distortions in some regions, which can lead to rendering artifacts. We intend to address this issue in future work by examining better methods for mesh and volume parameterization.

Another problem we plan to investigate is acquisition of the single scattering effects and phase functions of heterogeneous translucent materials. In addition, we would like to extend our rendering algorithm to real-time animation of translucent objects.

References

1. Goesele, M., Lensch, H.P.A., Lang, J., Fuchs, C., Seidel, H.-P.: DISCO: acquisition of translucent objects. ACM Trans. Graph. **23**(3), 835–844 (2004)
2. Tong, X., Wang, J., Lin, S., Guo, B., Shum, H.-Y.: Modeling and rendering of quasi-homogeneous materials. ACM Trans. Graph. **24**(3), 1054–1061 (2005)
3. Peers, P., vom Berge, K., Matusik, W., Ramamoorthi, R., Lawrence, J., Rusinkiewicz, S., Dutré, P.: A compact factored representation of heterogeneous subsurface scattering. ACM Trans. Graph. **25**(3), 746–753 (2006)
4. Ishimaru, A.: Wave Propagation and Scattering in Random Media. IEEE Press Series on Electromagnetic Wave Theory (1999)
5. Schweiger, M., Arridge, S., Hiraoka, M., Delpy, D.: The finite element method for the propagation of light in scattering media: boundary and source conditions. Med. Phys. **22**, 1779–1792 (1995)
6. Boas, D., Brooks, D., DiMarzio, C., Kilmer, M., Gauette, R., Zhang, Q.: Imaging the body with diffuse optical tomography. IEEE Signal Process. Mag. **18**(6), 57–75 (2001)
7. Stam, J.: Multiple scattering as a diffusion process. In: Eur. Rendering Workshop, June 1995, pp. 41–50 (1995)
8. Jensen, H.W., Marschner, S.R., Levoy, M., Hanrahan, P.: A practical model for subsurface light transport. In: SIGGRAPH pp. 511–518 (2001)
9. Arridge, S., Lionheart, B.: Non-uniqueness in diffusion-based optical tomography. Opt. Lett. **23**, 882–884 (1998)
10. Lions, J.-L.: Optimal Control Systems Governed by Partial Differential Equations. Springer, Berlin (1971)
11. Gibson, A., Hebden, J., Arridge, S.: Recent advances in diffuse optical imaging. Phys. Med. Biol. **50**, R1–R43 (2005)
12. Jensen, H.W., Buhler, J.: A rapid hierarchical rendering technique for translucent materials. ACM Trans. Graph. **21**(3), 576–581 (2002)
13. Carr, N.A., Hall, J.D., Hart, J.C.: GPU algorithms for radiosity and subsurface scattering. In: Proc. Graphics Hardware, pp. 51–59 (2003)
14. Mertens, T., Kautz, J., Bekaert, P., Seidel, H.-P., Reeth, F.V.: Interactive rendering of translucent deformable objects. In: The Eurographics Symposium on Rendering, pp. 130–140 (2003)
15. Lensch, H.P.A., Goesele, M., Bekaert, P., Magnor, J.K.M.A., Lang, J., Seidel, H.-P.: Interactive rendering of translucent objects. ACM Trans. Graph. **22**(2), 195–205 (2003)
16. Haber, T., Mertens, T., Bekaert, P., Van Reeth, F.: A computational approach to simulate light diffusion in arbitrarily shaped objects. In: Proc. Graphics Interface, pp. 79–85 (2005)
17. Debevec, P., Hawkins, T., Tchou, C., Duiker, H.-P., Sarokin, W., Sagar, M.: Acquiring the reflectance field of a human face. In: Proc. SIGGRAPH 2000, pp. 145–156 (2000)
18. Debevec, P.E., Malik, J.: Recovering high dynamic range radiance maps from photographs. In: ACM SIGGRAPH, pp. 369–378 (1997)
19. Zhang, R., Tsai, P.-S., Cryer, J.E., Shah, M.: Shape from shading: a survey. IEEE Trans. Pattern Anal. Mach. Intell. **21**, 690–706 (1999)
20. Press, W.H., et al.: Numerical Recipes in C, 2nd edn. (1992)

21. Giles, M.B., Pierce, N.A.: An introduction to the adjoint approach to design. In: ERCOFTAC Workshop on Adjoint Methods, Touluse, France (1999)
22. McNamara, A., Treuille, A., Popović, Z., Stam, J.: Fluid control using the adjoint method. ACM Trans. Graph. **23**(3), 449–456 (2004)
23. Chen, Y., Tong, X., Wang, J., Lin, S., Guo, B., Shum, H.-Y.: Shell texture functions. ACM Trans. Graph. **23**(3), 343–353 (2004)
24. Porumbescu, S.D., Budge, B., Feng, L., Joy, K.I.: Shell maps. ACM Trans. Graph. **24**(3), 626–633 (2005)
25. Ju, T., Schaefer, S., Warren, J.: Mean value coordinates for closed triangular meshes. ACM Trans. Graph. **24**(3), 561–566 (2005)
26. Sloan, P.-P., Kautz, J., Snyder, J.: Precomputed radiance transfer for real-time rendering in dynamic, low-frequency lighting environments. In: SIGGRAPH '02: Proceedings of the 29th Annual Conference on Computer Graphics and Interactive Techniques, pp. 527–536. ACM, New York (2002)
27. Ng, R., Ramamoorthi, R., Hanrahan, P.: All-frequency shadows using non-linear wavelet lighting approximation. ACM Trans. Graph. **22**(3), 376–381 (2003)
28. Tarini, M., Hormann, K., Cignoni, P., Montani, C.: PolyCube-maps. ACM Trans. Graph. **23**(3), 853–860 (2004)
29. Kraevoy, V., Sheffer, A.: Cross-parameterization and compatible remeshing of 3d models. ACM Trans. Graph. **23**(3), 861–869 (2004)
30. Schreiner, J., Asirvatham, A., Praun, E., Hoppe, H.: Inter-surface mapping. ACM Trans. Graph. **23**(3), 870–877 (2004)
31. Turk, G.: Re-tiling polygonal surfaces, SIGGRAPH **26**(2), 55–64 (1992)
32. Gu, X., Yau, S.-T.: Global conformal surface parameterization. In: Proc. Symp. Geometry Processing, pp. 127–137 (2003)
33. Krüger, J., Westermann, R.: Linear algebra operators for GPU implementation of numerical algorithms. ACM Trans. Graph. **22**(3), 908–916 (2003)
34. Bolz, J., Farmer, I., Grinspun, E., Schröder, P.: Sparse matrix solvers on the GPU: conjugate gradients and multigrid. ACM Trans. Graph. **22**(3), 917–924 (2003)

Chapter 8
Modeling Textured Translucent Materials with Lazy Solid Texture Synthesis

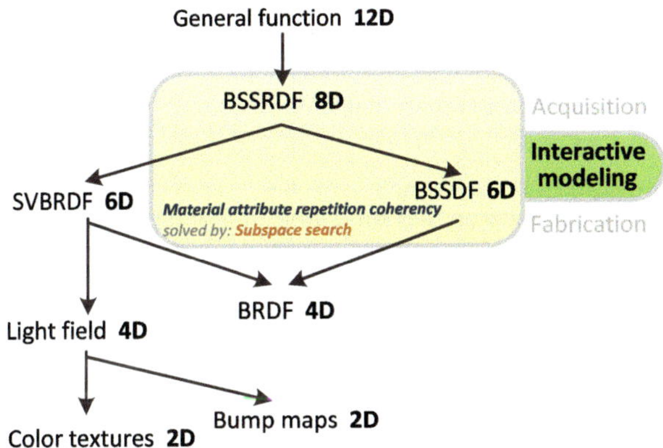

In the previous chapter, we presented a method for spatially varying subsurface scattering based on the diffusion model with a volumetric representation. The optical properties defined within a three-dimensional volume generally follow a coherent spatial distribution in materials and can be modeled as *solid textures*. With a solid texture, the translucent appearance of a material can be reproduced for objects of arbitrary shapes.

Direct acquisition methods cannot recover material volumes with very high resolution, due to the high computation cost and memory requirements. However, the coherent and repetitive spatial patterns in real-world material volumes allow a material to be modeled by relatively little data as shown in existing research on texture synthesis based on the Markov Random Field (MRF) model. Several works generate a 3D texture volume from 2D example images of a material [1–3]. Such methods typically solve a *global* problem, where the entire volume is synthesized because the color of each voxel directly or indirectly depends on *all* of the other voxels.

For modeling translucent appearance, however, texture synthesis generally is not needed throughout the entire volume. While material properties on or near the sur-

Y. Dong et al., *Material Appearance Modeling: A Data-Coherent Approach*,
DOI 10.1007/978-3-642-35777-0_8,

face need to synthesized at a high resolution, voxels deep beneath the surface contribute only low frequency lighting effects to the overall appearance, and thus can be modeled more simply with little or no variation in optical values. Taking advantage of this property by performing synthesis only *locally* along the surface can reduce storage and computation by orders of magnitude in comparison to global texture synthesis of a 3D volume.

Local evaluation for texture synthesis cannot be done by existing example-based methods, but is possible with classical solid texturing methods such as procedural texturing [4]. In this approach, the texture values at a point in the volume are generated by a simple procedure that does not depend on surrounding values. Little memory is consumed since only the procedural algorithm is stored. Unfortunately though, only a limited set of materials—such as marble, wood and cellular patterns—can be effectively generated by procedures.

In this chapter, we utilize the *material attribute repetition* coherence of textures in material volumes to bridge the gap between procedural texturing, which can evaluate textures locally at run time but is limited to few materials, and solid texture synthesis, which requires pre-computation and storage of an entire volume. Our approach starts from 2D images and synthesizes a solid texture on a surface, as if it were carved out of a volume of matter. However, only the parts of the volume needed for accurate rendering are synthesized. To determine the texture value of a voxel, our method relies only on the colors of a small number of surrounding voxels. The result for an entire surface is computed at once, usually in a few seconds, and stored for later display. Our GPU implementation is fast enough to synthesize textures on demand, in a few milliseconds, for surfaces appearing when interactively cutting or breaking objects.

The key idea that makes this possible is to pre-compute a small number of carefully selected *3D candidates* which are later used in our solid synthesis algorithm. Each candidate is formed by interleaving three well-chosen 2D neighborhoods from the example images. Synthesis is performed by *subspace search* within this limited space of pre-computed 3D candidates, which improves efficiency and significantly reduces the dependency chain required to compute voxel colors. This allows us to develop our new parallel, spatially deterministic solid texture synthesis algorithm.

The result is a *lazy* solid synthesis scheme, only computing colors in voxels actually being used, as demonstrated in Fig. 8.1. High resolution solid textures are applied to objects in seconds, at low memory cost. Our GPU implementation is fast enough to synthesize textures on demand, enabling interactive cutting and breaking of objects. Our synthesis scheme is spatially deterministic, in that the same value is always generated at the same location in space. Hence, the textures synthesized for surfaces that appear will remain consistent.

The generated solid textures are rendered with an advanced diffusion based rendering method, which enables real-time rendering of high-resolution translucent material volumes with interactive cutting. As an object is cut, full resolution textures are synthesized only along the newly appearing surface, and this greatly reduces the computation and memory cost of modeling textured translucent materials.

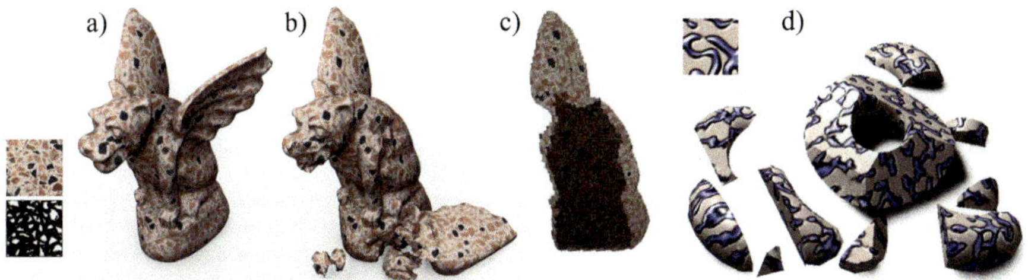

Fig. 8.1 Lazy solid synthesis starts from 2D images and synthesizes a solid texture on a surface. Only the required parts of the volume are effectively synthesized. (**a**) A gargoyle textured by a 1024^3 volume. (**b**) Thanks to spatial determinism, the object may be broken and the interior textured in a consistent manner. (**c**) 0.42 % of the voxels are synthesized by our algorithm, requiring only 5.4 seconds for synthesis and 17.9 MB of storage, instead of 3 GB for the full volume. (**d**) Our approach enables interactive cutting of objects with on demand synthesis for the appearing surfaces. New textures are synthesized in about 8 milliseconds

8.1 Previous Work

Various techniques have been presented for synthesizing planar textures from an example image (or *exemplar*). Often this is performed by pasting together small pixel neighborhoods [5–7] or entire patches of texture content [8, 9]. A different class of algorithms instead synthesizes textures in a parallel per-pixel manner [10, 11]. This approach is of particular interest to us for solid synthesis, since it enables efficient synthesis of subsets of an image while enforcing spatial determinism. However, an extension to 3D is not straightforward, because a full volume is typically not available as input. Even if such a volume were available, its cubic size would imply both a large increase in computation and memory consumption.

Methods for per-pixel synthesis generally operate in the following way. For each pixel, a small neighborhood representing its current surrounding is extracted. The exemplar is then searched to find the pixel with the most similar neighborhood, and the pixel color is copied to the output. To expedite the search process, a set of candidates, referred to as *k-coherent candidates* [12, 13], can be pre-computed for each exemplar pixel. These candidates consist of coordinates of the k pixels having the most similar neighborhood. Then during synthesis, the search for a best matching neighborhood is limited to candidates in the pre-computed sets of already synthesized pixels.

The synthesis of solid 3D textures from examples was introduced in the pyramid histogram matching of Heeger and Bergen [14] and the spectral analysis methods of Ghazanfarpour and Dischler [15, 16]. The former reproduces global statistics of the 2D example images in the volume, while the latter two create a procedural solid texture from the spectral analysis of multiple images. Among later techniques, Qin and Yang [2] synthesizes a volume by capturing the co-occurrences of grayscale levels in the neighborhoods of 2D images. Jagnow et al. [17] proposed a solid synthesis method targeted at aggregates of particles, whose distribution and shape is analyzed from an input image. Owada et al. [18] adapted constrained 2D synthesis [19] to

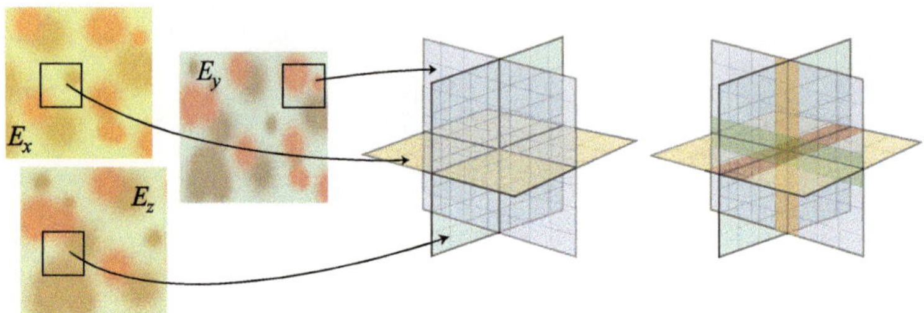

Fig. 8.2 *Left*: three exemplars E_x, E_y, E_z and a corresponding 3-neighborhood. *Right*: crossbar defined by the 3-neighborhood

illustrate object interiors. These approaches share the drawback that spatial determinism is not enforced and seams appear at transitions between different cuts.

Wei [1] first adapted 2D neighborhood matching synthesis schemes to 3D volumes. The key idea is to consider three 2D exemplars, one in each direction. In each pixel of the output volume (*voxel*), three interleaved 2D neighborhoods are extracted (see Fig. 8.2). The best matches are found independently in each of the three exemplars, and a local optimization step then attempts to converge toward the best color for all three directions. Kopf et al. [3] relies on similar interleaved neighborhoods, but uses a global optimization approach [7]. A histogram matching step is also introduced, further improving the result. Both these approaches search for best matching neighborhoods independently in each direction. Consequently, a large number of iterations are required before the algorithm reaches a satisfactory result.

While these approaches produce impressive results, none is appropriate for fast synthesis of subsets of the volume. They either rely on sequential generation or global optimization. In both cases, the dependency chain in the computations implies that a complete volume has to be computed, even if the user is only interested in a small subset of the voxels.

8.2 Overview and Terminology

Our goal is to generate high-quality, high-resolution solid textures given three 2D exemplars—often the same image repeated thrice. Since we target texturing of surfaces, we want our approach to allow very fast synthesis of subsets of the volume.

A first idea would be to revisit the solid synthesis approach of [1], adapt it to be parallel and use the 2D k-coherent candidates mechanism to achieve a significant speed-up. However, it is important to realize that 2D candidates are not likely to be meaningful for 3D synthesis: Each candidate will represent a correct 2D neighborhood in its image, but once put together they are likely to introduce color inconsistencies. This will both reduce synthesis quality, and require a long time for the iterative synthesis process to produce good results. As many iterations of neighborhood matching will be required, the dependency chain to compute the color of a voxel will involve a large number of other voxels, making subset synthesis impractical. For a detailed comparison between this approach and ours, please refer to Sect. 8.5.5.

Instead, our novel scheme pre-computes 3D candidates given three 2D example images. Each candidate is made of three interleaved 2D neighborhoods, and is carefully selected to provide both quality and speed during synthesis (Sect. 8.3). This is done as a pre-computation, and only once for a given set of three 2D exemplars. The candidates are later used during the neighborhood matching step of our parallel solid synthesis scheme (Sect. 8.4). Our algorithm performs multi-resolution synthesis in a sparse volume pyramid, only synthesizing the small subset of the voxels necessary to texture the surface. Synthesis is performed within seconds, and the result is stored for display. Our GPU implementation generates textures on demand, in a few milliseconds, for instance for new surfaces appearing when interactively cutting or breaking objects (Sect. 8.5).

Terminology We now introduce some terminology. We refer to *pixels* in 2D images, while the term *voxel* is used for pixels located in a volume. In this work we consider neighborhoods made of three interleaved 2D neighborhoods: Three $N \times N$ 2D neighborhoods embedded in three orthogonal planes and meeting at their center (see Fig. 8.2 (middle)). In our implementation we choose $N = 5$, which provides both good quality and performance. We refer to these triples of 2D neighborhoods as *3-neighborhoods*, and name them *3D candidates* after selection. We define the *crossbar* to be the set of pixels which are contained in more than one 2D neighborhood (Fig. 8.2 (right)).

E_x, E_y, E_z are the three 2D exemplars corresponding to each one of the three orthogonal planes (Fig. 8.2 (left)). The term *triple* indicates a triple of 2D coordinates, defining a 3-neighborhood: Each coordinate is the center of a 2D neighborhood in the corresponding exemplar.

Our algorithm performs multi-resolution synthesis in a volume pyramid, denoted as V. Each level is designated by V^l where $l \in [O \ldots L]$ and L is the maximum (finest) resolution.

8.3 3D Candidates Selection

For each pixel of each exemplar we compute a small candidate set of 3-neighborhoods represented as coordinate triples. These sets are used during synthesis as candidates for best matching neighborhoods. Hence, they must capture the appearance of the 3D neighborhoods implicitly described by the input images.

Given the exemplars E_x, E_y, E_z, the search space for possible candidates is enormous, as it contains all possible triples of coordinates. The key novelty of our approach is to drastically prune the search space *prior* to synthesis. The major difficulty is that we cannot explicitly test whether a candidate triple forms a neighborhood representative of the not-yet-synthesized volume. This information is only *implicitly* given by the input images.

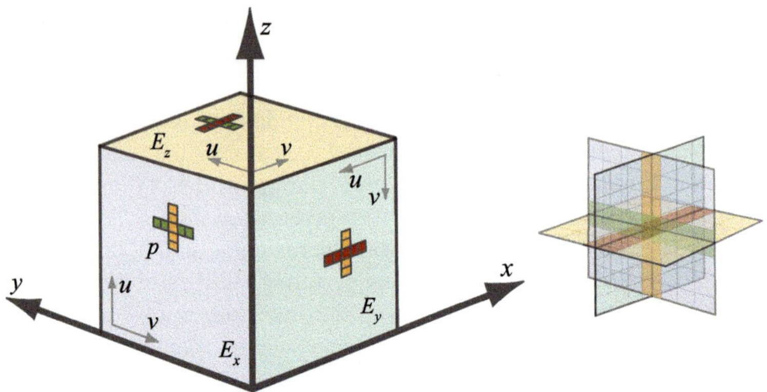

Fig. 8.3 Each candidate consists of three exemplar coordinates defining a 3-neighborhood. Consistent triples have low color differences along the crossbar. We seek to minimize the color differences along the three pairs of pixel strips, shown here with the same color

We hence propose to select candidate triples following two important properties. First, a good triple must have matching colors along the crossbar of the 3-neighborhood. This provides an easy way to select only triples with good *color consistency* (see Sect. 8.3.1). The second property is less obvious. A major step forward in 2D texture synthesis speed and quality was achieved by giving a higher priority to candidates likely to form coherent patches from the example image [12, 19]. This notion is however not trivial to extend to 3D, as three exemplars are interleaved. Candidates providing coherence in one exemplar are not likely to provide coherence in the other two. Here, our approach of forming candidates prior to synthesis gives us a crucial advantage: We are able to consider coherence across *all three exemplars*, keeping only those triples likely to form coherent patches with other neighboring candidates *in all three directions* (see Sect. 8.3.2).

Since our synthesis algorithm is multi-resolution, we first compute an image pyramid for each 2D exemplar and apply the candidate set construction independently on each level of the pyramid of each exemplar. For clarity, the following description is for a single level.

8.3.1 Color Consistency

Our first observation comes from the fact that a suitable candidate should be consistent across the crossbar. We use this observation to build first sets of potential candidates for each pixel of each exemplar.

As illustrated in Fig. 8.3, we seek to minimize the color disparity between the lines shared by interleaved 2D neighborhoods. We compute an L^2 color difference between pairs of 1-dimensional "strips" of pixels (i.e., an $N \times 1$ or $1 \times N$ vector) from the appropriate exemplars (E_x, E_y, or E_z). The sum of color differences for the three pairs of pixel strips defines our crossbar error *CB* for any candidate triple.

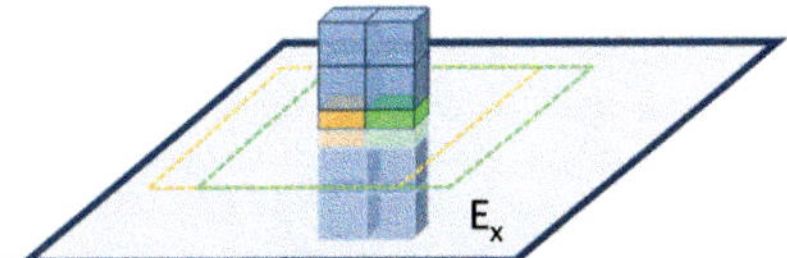

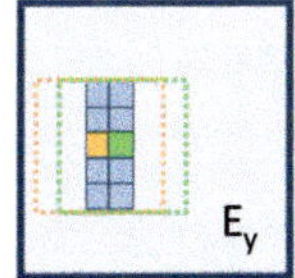

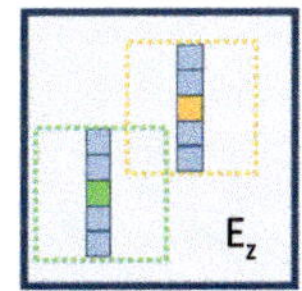

Fig. 8.4 Two candidates of neighboring pixels in E_x. Each candidate is a triple with coordinates in E_x, E_y and E_z. The first triple is shown in *orange*, the second in *green*. Notice how the coordinates of the candidates in E_y are contiguous: Along both vertical pixel strips, the candidates form a coherent patch from E_y. This is not the case in E_z. Note that the *orange* and *green triples* will only be kept if another neighboring triple with a contiguous coordinate in E_z is found

For each pixel of each exemplar, we form triples using the pixel itself and two neighborhoods from the other two exemplars. We select the triples producing the smallest crossbar error. For efficiency, we approximate this process first by separately extracting the S most similar pixel strips from each of the two other exemplars, using the ANN library [20]. For the example of Fig. 8.3, assuming that we are computing a candidate set for p in E_x, we would first find in E_y the S pixel strips that best match the orange line from E_x, and in E_z the S pixel strips that best match the green line from E_x. We then produce all possible S^2 triples—using the current pixel as the third coordinate—and order them according to the crossbar error CB. In our results, we keep the 100 best triples and typically use a value of $S = 65$, experimentally chosen to not miss any good triple.

8.3.2 Triples of Coherent Candidates

Color consistency is only a necessary condition and many uninteresting candidate triples may be selected. As a consequence, if we directly use these candidates our algorithm will be inefficient as many will always be rejected.

After constructing candidates based on color consistency, we obtain a set of candidate triples at each pixel of each exemplar. Our key idea is to check whether a candidate may form coherent patches in *all* directions with candidates from neighboring pixels. This is in fact a simple test. We consider each coordinate within a candidate triple and verify that at least one candidate from a neighboring pixel has a continuous coordinate. Figure 8.4 illustrates this idea for pixels in E_x. We only keep candidates with continuous coordinates for all three entries of the triple. Note that one is trivially true, i.e. by definition neighboring candidates in E_x have a continuous coordinate in E_x.

To formalize this notion, let us only consider exemplar E_x without loss of generality. We denote as ${}^xC$ (resp. ${}^yC$, ${}^zC$) the set of candidates for exemplar E_x (resp. E_y, E_z). ${}^xC^k[p]$ is the kth candidate triple for pixel p in E_x. We denote as ${}^xC^k[p]_y$ and ${}^xC^k[p]_z$ the coordinates in exemplar E_y and E_z, respectively, for the candidate triple.

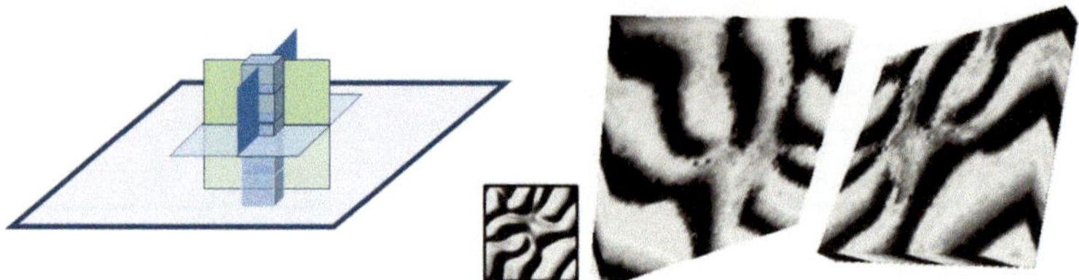

Fig. 8.5 *Left*: exemplar thickening. *Right*: candidate slab obtained from the first candidates. The slab is shown from top and bottom views. Notice how coherent structures appear around the exemplar. (This is not a synthesis result, but simply a visualization of the candidates)

In a given pixel p, we iteratively update the set of candidates as:

$$
{}^{x}C_{i+1}[p] = \left\{ \begin{array}{l} c \in^{x} C_i[p]\colon \exists k_1, k_2, |\delta_1| = 1, \\ |\delta_2| = 1 \text{ s.t. } \left[\begin{array}{l} |{}^{x}C_i^{k_1}[p+\delta_1]_y - c_y| = 1 \\ \text{and} \\ |{}^{x}C_i^{k_2}[p+\delta_2]_z - c_z| = 1 \end{array} \right. \end{array} \right\}
$$

where i is the iteration counter, k_1, k_2 are indices in the candidate sets, and δ_1, δ_2 are offsets to direct neighbors. We perform several iterations of this process, reducing the number of candidates with each pass. In our current implementation we iterate until having no more than 12 candidates per pixel, which typically requires two iterations. If more candidates remain, we keep the first 12 with the smallest crossbar matching error. While it is possible that no candidate coherency exists, this happens rarely in practice.

8.3.3 Candidate Slab

After candidate generation, we obtain a set of candidate triples at each pixel. These candidates are not only useful for neighborhood matching, but also provide a very good initialization for the synthesis process.

Let us consider a single exemplar. Recall that each candidate triple defines a 3-neighborhood, that is three interleaved $N \times N$ 2D neighborhoods. One 2D neighborhood is in the plane of the exemplar, while the two others are orthogonal to it (see Fig. 8.5, left) and intersect along a line of N voxels *above* and *below* the exemplar. This provides a way to *thicken* the exemplar and to form *candidate slabs*. To initialize synthesis we create such a slab using the best (first) candidate at each pixel (see Fig. 8.5, right).

Please note, however, that the slab is formed using a *single* candidate among the several available per exemplar pixel. Using the slab directly as a 3D exemplar would be very limiting, as this would ignore all other candidates. Instead, our algorithm exploits the full variety of the candidates for neighborhood matching and uses a slab only for initialization. This is very different from using a 3D exemplar as input, which would require a large example volume to offer a similar variety of candidates.

8.4 Lazy Solid Synthesis

For each pixel of each 2D exemplar, we now have a set of pre-computed 3D candidates, which we will use to perform efficient solid synthesis.

Our parallel deterministic synthesis is inspired by the 2D parallel algorithm of [11]. While it has the same overall structure, it adapts and extends it in several ways.

8.4.1 Parallel Solid Texture Synthesis

A first evident change to the original 2D algorithm is that our algorithm performs synthesis in a multi-resolution 3D volume pyramid, instead of operating on a 2D image pyramid. Only part of this volume pyramid may be visited by the algorithm, depending on the subset of desired voxels.

We perform two successive steps at every resolution level: *upsampling* which increases the resolution of the previous level result, and *correction* which applies several passes of neighborhood matching using our pre-computed 3D candidates. Contrary to the original scheme, we found it unnecessary to add variation at every level, and perturb the result through *jitter* only once, after initialization. If finer control is desired, jitter could be explicitly added after each upsampling step.

This is summarized below:

Synthesize(l_{start}, V_{init}, E_x, E_y, E_z, ${}^xC$, ${}^yC$, ${}^zC$, $DesiredVoxels$)

    $Mask^{l_{start}} \leftarrow$ ComputeMask($DesiredVoxels$, l_{start})

    $V^{l_{start}} \leftarrow$ tiling of V_{init}

    $V^{l_{start}} \leftarrow$ Jitter($V^{l_{start}}$)

    For $l = l_{start} \ldots L$

        If $l > l_{start}$ then $V^l, Mask^l \leftarrow$ Upsampling($V^{l-1}, Mask^{l-1}$)

        For p $= 1 \ldots 2$

            $V^l, Mask^l \leftarrow$ Correction($V^l, Mask^l, {}^xC, {}^yC, {}^zC$)

End

l_{start} is the level at which synthesis starts. `ComputeMask` computes the mask of voxels that have to be synthesized at level l_{start} (see Sect. 8.4.2). V_{init} is an initial result from which to begin synthesis, as explained below.

In every voxel of the synthesis pyramid we maintain a coordinate triple, representing a 3-neighborhood. For a voxel at coordinates v in the volume of level l, we

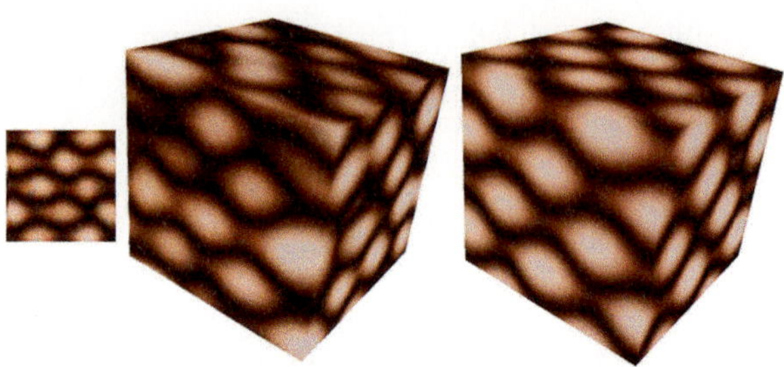

Fig. 8.6 Quality of solid texture synthesis is improved by using candidate slabs for initialization (*right*), compared to random initial values (*left*). This is especially the case on structured exemplars

note the stored triple coordinates $V[v]^l_x$, $V[v]^l_y$ and $V[v]^l_z$. The color of a voxel is obtained by averaging the three colors at coordinates $V[v]^l_x$, $V[v]^l_y$ and $V[v]^l_z$ in respectively E_x, E_y and E_z.

Initialization To reduce synthesis time, multi-resolution synthesis algorithms can start from an intermediate level of the image pyramid. The initial result given as input is then iteratively refined, with successive passes of neighborhood matching. A good initialization is key to achieve high-quality synthesis.

Since we do not have an example volume, we rely on the candidate slabs (Sect. 8.3.3) for initialization. They provide a good approximation of the 3D content to be synthesized. We simply choose one of the candidate slabs as V_{init} and tile it in the volume to initialize synthesis. In practice, we initialize the process three levels above the finest ($l_{start} = L - 3$) using the candidate slab from the corresponding level of the exemplar pyramid.

Figure 8.6 shows how our initialization improves quality compared to a typical random initialization. In particular, it preserves regularity present in the input images.

Jitter Since we initialize with a tiling, we have to explicitly introduce variations to generate variety in the result. We hence perturb the initial result by applying a continuous deformation, similar to a random warp. We compute the distorted volume J as

$$\forall v, \quad J[v] = V\left[v + \sum_{i=0\ldots G} A_i \vec{d}_i e^{-\frac{\|v-c_i\|^2}{2\sigma_i^2}}\right]$$

where v are voxel coordinates, A_i is a scalar, $\vec{d}_i$ a random normalized direction, c_i a random point in space and σ_i controls the influence of Gaussian i. G is typically around 200, with values of A_i ranging from 0.1 to 0.3 and σ_i from 0.01 to 0.05 in unit volume space. While exact values do not matter—the main purpose is to randomize—it is important for A_i to have larger magnitude with smaller σ_i, as this adds stronger perturbation at small scales, while adding subtle distortions to coarser scales. Small scale distortions are corrected by synthesis, introducing variety. The overall magnitude of the jitter is directly controllable by the user.

Upsampling Upsampling is a simple coordinate inheritance, in which each of the eight child volume cells inherits three coordinates from its parent, one for each direction. The new coordinates of the child at location ijk within the volume of level l are computed as

$$V[ijk]^l_x = 2 \cdot V\left[\left(\left\lfloor \frac{i}{2} \right\rfloor, \left\lfloor \frac{j}{2} \right\rfloor, \left\lfloor \frac{k}{2} \right\rfloor\right)\right]^{l-1}_x + (j \bmod 2, k \bmod 2),$$

$$V[ijk]^l_y = 2 \cdot V\left[\left(\left\lfloor \frac{i}{2} \right\rfloor, \left\lfloor \frac{j}{2} \right\rfloor, \left\lfloor \frac{k}{2} \right\rfloor\right)\right]^{l-1}_y + (i \bmod 2, k \bmod 2),$$

$$V[ijk]^l_z = 2 \cdot V\left[\left(\left\lfloor \frac{i}{2} \right\rfloor, \left\lfloor \frac{j}{2} \right\rfloor, \left\lfloor \frac{k}{2} \right\rfloor\right)\right]^{l-1}_z + (i \bmod 2, j \bmod 2).$$

Correction The correction step relies on our candidate sets to perform fast neighborhood matching. It is performed on all synthesized voxels simultaneously, in parallel. Input data is read from the previous step result so that neighboring voxels do not influence each other during correction.

The result from the previous step gives us a coordinate triple in each voxel, from which we compute a color by averaging the corresponding three colors from the exemplars. In each synthesized voxel, we start by gathering its *current* 3-neighborhood, that is the one that can be observed in the colored version of the result. We will use this 3-neighborhood to search for a best matching candidate.

Next, we gather a set of potential candidates for the voxel. We visit each of its direct neighbors, and use the stored coordinate triples to gather the candidate sets. This relies on the coherent candidate idea introduced by [12] and [13]. The final candidate set $\mathscr{C}(v)$ for voxel v is computed as

$$\begin{aligned}
\mathscr{C}(v) &= \mathscr{C}_x(v) \cup \mathscr{C}_y(v) \cup \mathscr{C}_z(v) \quad \text{where} \\
\mathscr{C}_x(v) &= \left\{{}^xC^k\left[V[v + P_x\delta]_x - \delta\right] : k = 1 \ldots K, \delta \in \{-1, 0, 1\}^2\right\} \\
\mathscr{C}_y(v) &= \left\{{}^yC^k\left[V[v + P_y\delta]_y - \delta\right] : k = 1 \ldots K, \delta \in \{-1, 0, 1\}^2\right\} \\
\mathscr{C}_z(v) &= \left\{{}^zC^k\left[V[v + P_z\delta]_z - \delta\right] : k = 1 \ldots K, \delta \in \{-1, 0, 1\}^2\right\}
\end{aligned}$$

${}^xC^k[p]$ is the k-th candidate at location p in E_x. P_x, P_y and P_z are 3×2 matrices transforming a 2D offset from exemplar to volume space (see Fig. 8.3).

Each candidate is itself a triple of coordinates forming a 3-neighborhood. We search for the best matching candidate by considering the distance between the candidate 3-neighborhood and the 3-neighborhood we extracted for the current voxel. The distance is a simple L^2 norm on color differences. In practice, we speed up these comparisons using PCA-projected neighborhoods.

We finally replace the coordinate triple in the current voxel by the coordinate triple of the best matching candidate. Note that because the candidate triples have been precomputed and optimized, we are guaranteed that the color disparity between the three colors in each voxel is kept low.

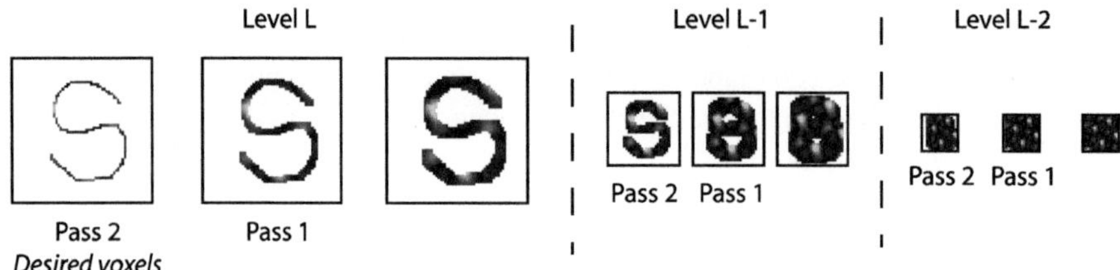

Fig. 8.7 From a set of desired voxels at the finest resolution, we have to determine the entire dependency chain throughout the volume pyramid. The neighborhood matching passes performed at every level imply the dilation of the set of voxels to synthesize

We perform two correction passes at every level of the pyramid, and improve convergence of the correction process by adapting the sub-pass mechanism of [11]. We simply perform 8 sub-passes instead of 4 in 2D, while processing interleaved subsets of voxels one after the other.

Separation of the First Candidate Coordinate While our candidate selection is very efficient, we still end up with many candidate comparisons. We gather 12 candidates from the $3^3 = 27$ direct neighbors (including the center), for a total of 324 candidates per voxel. We further reduce the search space by performing a two-step search.

During synthesis, the first step is to search for the best matching 2D candidates in each of the three directions. The second step is to gather the 3D candidates only from these three best matching pixels. This greatly reduces the size of the candidate set to consider, but still allows for a large number of candidate combinations. In practice we keep 4 2D and 12 3D candidates per exemplar pixel at coarse levels, while we reduce to 2 2D and 4 3D candidates at the finest level for maximum performance. At most, we thus perform a search within $27 \times 4 = 108$ 2D candidates and $3 \times 12 = 36$ 3D candidates.

8.4.2 *Lazy Subset Synthesis*

In order to synthesize the smallest number of voxels, we determine, from a requested set of voxels at the finest resolution, the entire dependency chain throughout the volume pyramid. This guarantees that all necessary information is available to ensure spatial determinism. Figure 8.7 illustrates this idea on a simple 2D example.

To restrict synthesis to only the necessary voxels, we compute a synthesis mask. When $Mask^l_p[v]$ is true, it indicates that voxel v at pass p and level l has to be synthesized. Note that we only need to compute the mask for level l_{start}, since during synthesis the mask for the next level or next pass is trivially obtained through upsampling and correction (see Sect. 8.4.1).

We compute the mask from the last to the first pass, and from fine to coarse levels. The number of required voxels depends on the size and shape of the neighborhoods used during synthesis. In the following pseudo-code, we denote as $Mask^l_p \otimes NeighborhoodShape$ the dilation of the mask by the shape of the neighborhoods. Function *Downsample* reduces the resolution of the mask and flags a parent voxel as required if any of its children are required. *DesiredVoxels* contains the set of voxels requested by the user.

To compute a single voxel, with $N = 5$, two passes and synthesis of the three last levels, our scheme requires a dependency chain of 6778 voxels. Note that in a volume the size of the dependency chain grows quadratically with the number of passes.

1. ComputeMask (*DesiredVoxels*)
2. $\quad Mask^{finest\ level}_{last\ pass} \leftarrow DesiredVoxels$
3. $\quad$ Foreach level l from finest to l_{start}
4. $\quad\quad$ Foreach pass p from last to first
5. $\quad\quad\quad Mask^l_{p-1} = Mask^l_p \otimes NeighborhoodShape$
6. $\quad\quad$ end foreach
7. $\quad\quad$ If $l > l_{start}$ then $Mask^{l-1}_{last\ pass} = Downsample(Mask^l_{first\ pass})$
8. $\quad$ end foreach
9. $\quad$ return $Mask^{l_{start}}$

8.5 Implementation and Results

We implemented our solid texture synthesis approach both entirely in software and using the GPU to accelerate the actual synthesis. All our results are created on an Intel Core™2 6400 (2.13 GHz) CPU and an NVIDIA GeForce 8800 Ultra.

Note that we sometimes add feature distance [3] to the RGB exemplars. Whenever this is the case, the feature distance is shown along with the original image.

8.5.1 Candidate Pre-computation

Apart from Fig. 8.10, all results in this chapter are computed from a single example image repeated three times. Depending on the orientation chosen for the image in E_x, E_y and E_z, the pre-computed candidates may be shared. This incurs savings in computation and data structures since we can perform the pre-computation only once. All reported sizes and timings are for a single example image sharing a same candidate data structure, using the orientation depicted in Fig. 8.3. The entire pre-computation is fast, typically 7 seconds for 64^2 exemplars, and 25 to 35 seconds for 128^2 exemplars. This includes building the exemplar pyramids, computing the PCA bases and building the candidate sets. A typical memory requirement for our pre-computation data structure is 231 KB for a 64^2 exemplar.

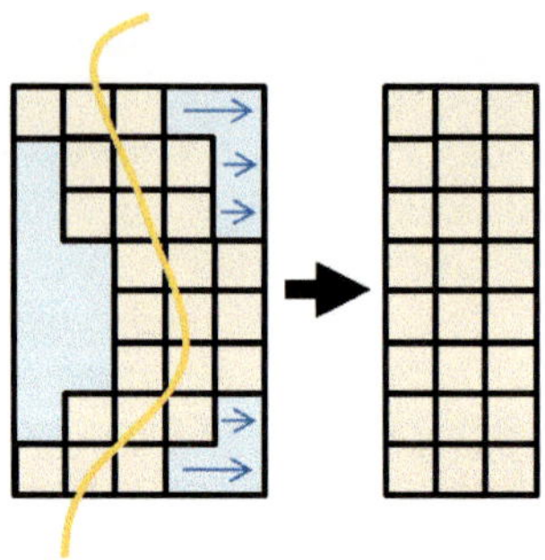

Fig. 8.8 Pushing the voxel columns to the side of the tile

After pre-computation we can quickly perform synthesis on any surface, and generate many variations of a given texture as illustrated in the supplemental material. This affords a very convenient tool to decorate objects from a database of pre-computed exemplars.

8.5.2 GPU Implementation

The synthesis algorithm is implemented in fragment shaders, using the OpenGL Shading Language. We unfold volumes in tiled 2D textures, using three 2-channel 16 bit render targets to store the synthesized triples. We pre-compute and reduce the dimensionality of all candidate 3-neighborhoods using PCA, keeping between 12 and 8 dimensions. We typically keep more terms at coarser levels since less variance is captured by the first dimensions. We finally quantize the neighborhoods to 8-bits to reduce bandwidth. Hence, candidate sets are stored in RGBA 8 bit textures.

Synthesizing Around Surfaces When texturing objects, our goal is to focus computations only around the voxels intersecting the surface. In order to minimize memory consumption, we perform synthesis into a TileTree data structure [21], but other approaches such as octree textures [22] could be used. After synthesis, rendering is performed directly using the TileTree, or the texture can be unfolded in a standard UV map.

The TileTree subdivides the surface into a set of square tiles. Each tile is in fact a height-field and corresponds to the set of voxels intersecting the surface. We enlarge the voxel set as described in Sect. 8.4.2, and perform synthesis independently in each tile. In order to reduce the size of the 3D texture used for synthesis, we 'push' the voxel columns to the side of the tile, as illustrated in Fig. 8.8. This slightly complicates addressing, but greatly reduces memory consumption on the GPU.

Synthesizing tiles independently implies that many voxels at coarse resolution are computed several times. This is especially unfortunate since these voxels only represent 10 percent of the total number of voxels. We reduce this overhead by emulating a very simple cache mechanism for coarse level voxels. We first synthesize a small 32^3 volume up to level $L-1$, and store this intermediate result. When synthesizing the surface, we restart synthesis at level $l_{start} = L-1$ using a tiling of the intermediate result. Variety is added as usual by perturbing the tiling with warping.

When interactively cutting an object, synthesis occurs only once for the newly appearing surfaces. Since the TileTree cannot be updated interactively, we store the result in a 2D texture map for display. For simplicity our implementation only allows planar cuts, where the new surfaces are planar and are trivially parameterized onto the 2D texture synthesized when the cut occurs.

8.5.3 Rendering

To efficiently render synthesized translucent volumes, we combine the advantages of lazy solid synthesis and the multi-resolution algorithm of TransCut [23], which employs a fast solver of the diffusion equation that adapts to changes in topological structure during object cutting. TransCut obtains its efficiency by computing discrete divergences of the diffusion equation and constructing the diffusion equation matrix using analytic formulas derived for linear finite elements. For synthesis, only those voxels on or near the object surface are synthesized at full resolution, while deeper volumes are assigned low resolution texture, since they contribute only low frequency effects to the final rendering result.

8.5.4 Full Volume Synthesis and Comparisons

While our scheme is designed for fast surface synthesis, we can also use it to quickly generate full volumes of color content. Here we discuss this possibility and use it to compare our algorithm with previous work.

Quality For comparison purposes, we reproduce in Fig. 8.9 solid textures similar to those presented in [3]. As can be seen, our new approach produces results which are at least of comparable quality and often slightly better. Figure 8.10 illustrates how complex structures are synthesized from different example images.

Timings In Fig. 8.9, for the 64^2 examples of the first row our method requires a total of 7.22 seconds for synthesizing the 64^3 volume (7 seconds for pre-computation and 220 milliseconds for synthesis). The memory requirement during synthesis is 3.5 MB. For the 128^2 image of the last row, our method requires a total of 28.7 seconds for synthesizing the 128^3 volume (27 seconds for pre-computation and 1.7 seconds for synthesis). In comparison, Kopf et al. [3] reported timings between 10 and 90 minutes.

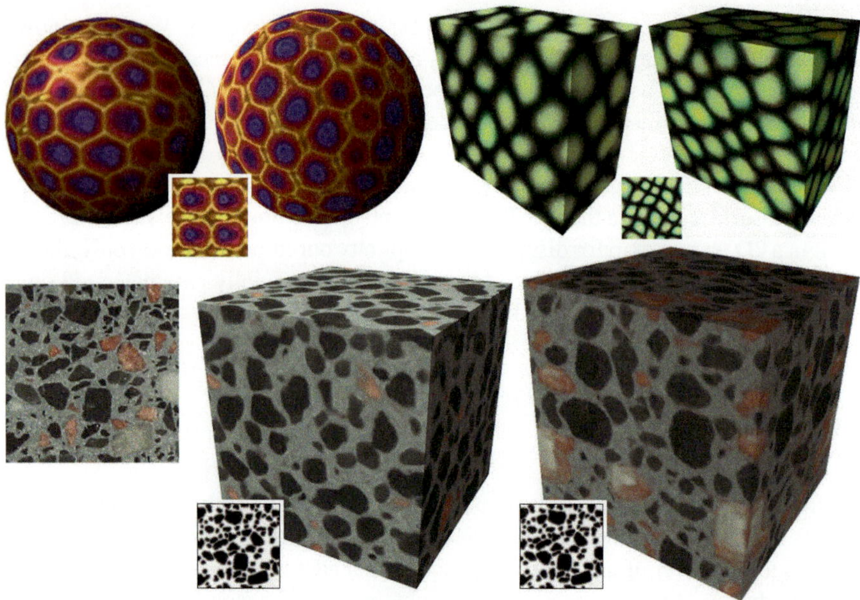

Fig. 8.9 Comparisons to some of the result textures in [3]. For each comparison, our result is shown on the *right*

Fig. 8.10 *Left*: A volume generated from two different images. *Right*: Transparency reveals shape distribution. Background gray voxels are transparent for the stones, green voxels for the spheres. For clarity we removed shapes crossing the volume boundary

8.5.5 Solid Synthesis for Translucent Objects

Figure 8.11 shows results of synthesizing solid textures for translucent material volumes. Performing synthesis using our lazy scheme results in very low memory consumption compared to the equivalent volume resolution.

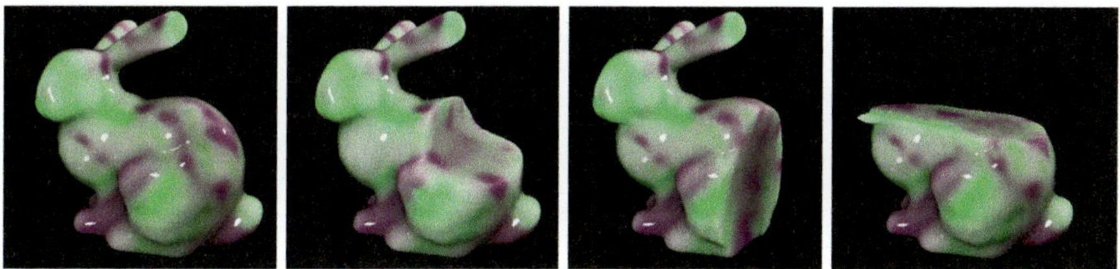

Fig. 8.11 Results on modeling translucent materials. The bunny model is textured with the equivalent of a 512^3 volume. Three frames of real-time cutting are shown. The interior surfaces are synthesized on demand, in 8 milliseconds on average, while the user cuts the object. Notice the coherent structures across cut boundaries

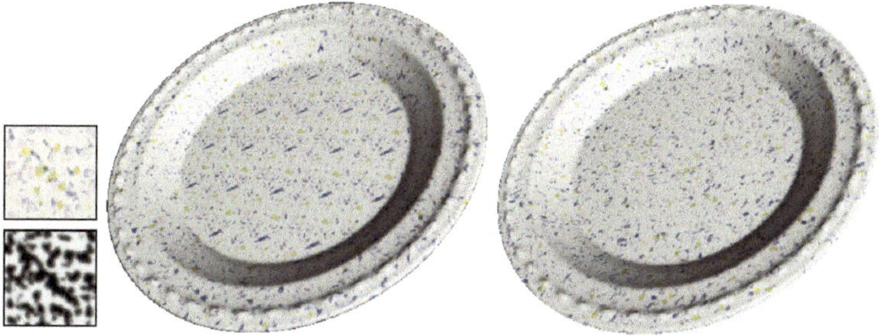

Fig. 8.12 *Left*: Result of tiling a 128^3 volume to texture a surface. Obvious repetitions are visible along some particular directions. *Right*: Our approach does not exhibit visible repetitions thanks to synthesis

Synthesis speed for the initial bunny surface is 2.5 seconds, excluding precomputation, while storage of the texture data requires only 7.1 MB, compared to the 375 MB for full volume storage.

While being slower than state-of-the-art pure surface texture synthesis approaches, our scheme inherits all the properties of solid texturing: no distortions due to planar parameterization, a unique feeling of a coherent block of matter, and consistent texturing when the object is cut, broken or edited. None of the pure 2D synthesis approaches can enforce these properties easily.

Our timings nonetheless allow for on-demand synthesis when cutting or breaking objects. Figure 8.11 shows three frames of real-time cutting. The average time for synthesizing textures for a new cut is 10 ms. In terms of memory, synthesizing a 256^2 slice of texture content requires 14.4 MB. The overhead is due to the necessary padding to ensure spatial determinism (see Sect. 8.4.2).

Comparison with a Simple Tiling A typical approach for solid texturing is to pre-compute a full cyclic volume and to tile it in space for texturing objects. As shown Fig. 8.12, our scheme offers richer textures than a simple volume tiling and avoids the appearance of repetitive patterns along some particular directions. Recall that synthesis occurs only once, and there is no overhead for displaying the object.

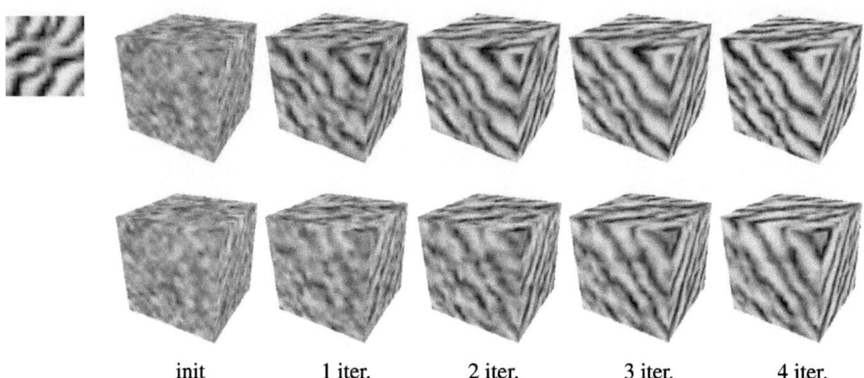

Fig. 8.13 Comparison of 3D candidates (*top*) versus 2D candidates (*bottom*). Using our 3D candidates, a visually pleasing result is reached in two iterations. After four iterations, the 2D candidates barely reached the same quality

Comparison with a Method Using Standard 2D Candidates In order to experimentally verify that our 3D candidates provide good quality results with fewer iterations, we also implemented our synthesis algorithm using only standard 2D candidates. As seen in Fig. 8.13, it takes roughly twice the number of iterations to obtain a result of equivalent visual quality (we obtain similar numbers on different textures). Due to the increased number of iterations, the size of the dependency chain for computing a single voxel grows from 6778 voxels with 3D candidates to 76812 voxels with 2D candidates, hence a factor of 11.3 in *both* memory usage and speed. This makes local evaluation impractical, and would not be useful for synthesis on surfaces.

8.6 Discussion and Conclusions

Our method is of course not without limitations. In particular, if the exemplars E_x, E_y, E_z do not define a coherent 3D volume, the quality of the result will be poor, as shown Fig. 8.14 (left). An interesting direction of future research is to exploit our pre-computation to determine whether three exemplars are likely to generate a consistent 3D volume.

A related limitation is that it may be impossible to find coherent candidates during our candidate selection process for some parts of the image. As shown in Fig. 8.14 (right) this will introduce a bias in the algorithm, removing some features.

Conclusion We presented a new algorithm for 3D synthesis of translucent materials, creating a consistent volume of matter from 2D example images. Our algorithm has the unique ability to synthesize colors for a subset of the voxels, while enforcing spatial determinism. This affords efficient surface synthesis as the complexity in both space and time only depends on the area to be textured.

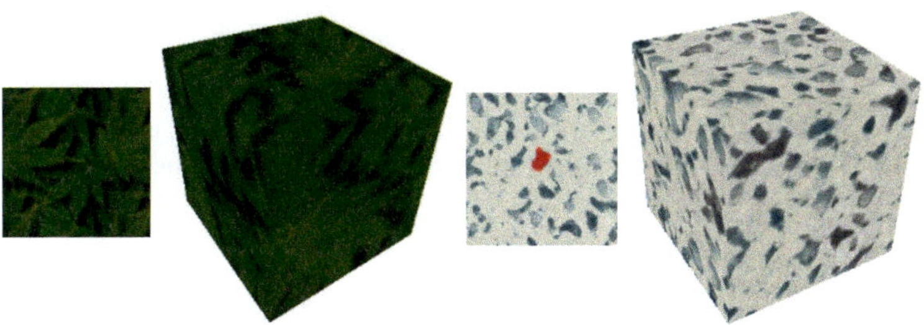

Fig. 8.14 *Left*: A case where the 2D example is incompatible with a good solid texture definition. *Right*: A case where a part of the exemplar has no coherent candidates. The red feature is lost through synthesis

Our key idea is to pre-compute 3D candidates in a pre-process, by interleaving three 2D neighborhoods from the input images. Thanks to a careful selection, our pre-computed candidates significantly improve synthesis efficiency and reduce the number of iterations required to produce good results. This is essential in reducing the size of the dependency chain when evaluating subsets.

Our GPU implementation is fast enough to provide on-demand synthesis when interactively cutting or breaking objects, enabling realistic texturing effects in real-time applications and physical simulations.

References

1. Wei, L.-Y.: Texture synthesis by fixed neighborhood searching. PhD thesis, Stanford University, Palo Alto, CA, USA (2002)
2. Qin, X., Yang, Y.-H.: Aura 3d textures. IEEE Trans. Vis. Comput. Graph. **13**(2), 379–389 (2007)
3. Kopf, J., Fu, C.-W., Cohen-Or, D., Deussen, O., Lischinski, D., Wong, T.-T.: Solid texture synthesis from 2d exemplars. In: ACM SIGGRAPH (2007)
4. Ebert, D., Musgrave, K., Peachey, D., Perlin, K., Worley: Texturing and Modeling: A Procedural Approach. Academic Press, New York (1994). ISBN: 0-12-228760-6
5. Efros, A.A., Leung, T.K.: Texture synthesis by non-parametric sampling. In: Proceedings of the IEEE International Conference on Computer Vision, Corfu, Greece, September 1999, pp. 1033–1038 (1999)
6. Wei, L.-Y., Levoy, M.: Fast texture synthesis using tree-structured vector quantization. In: ACM SIGGRAPH, pp. 479–488 (2000)
7. Kwatra, V., Essa, I., Bobick, A., Kwatra, N.: Texture optimization for example-based synthesis. In: SIGGRAPH '05: ACM SIGGRAPH 2005 Papers, pp. 795–802. ACM, New York (2005)
8. Efros, A.A., Freeman, W.T.: Image quilting for texture synthesis and transfer. In: ACM SIGGRAPH, pp. 341–346 (2001)
9. Kwatra, V., Schödl, A., Essa, I., Turk, G., Bobick, A.: Graphcut textures: image and video synthesis using graph cuts. In: ACM SIGGRAPH, pp. 277–286 (2003)
10. Wei, L.-Y., Levoy, M.: Order-independent texture synthesis. Technical Report TR-2002-01, Computer Science Department, Stanford University (2003)
11. Lefebvre, S., Hoppe, H.: Parallel controllable texture synthesis. ACM Trans. Graph. **24**(3), 777–786 (2005)

12. Ashikhmin, M.: Synthesizing natural textures. In: ACM Symposium on Interactive 3D Graphics, pp. 217–226 (2001)
13. Tong, X., Zhang, J., Liu, L., Wang, X., Guo, B., Shum, H.-Y.: Synthesis of bidirectional texture functions on arbitrary surfaces. ACM Trans. Graph. **21**(3), 665–672 (2002)
14. Heeger, D.J., Bergen, J.R.: Pyramid-based texture analysis/synthesis. In: ACM SIGGRAPH, pp. 229–238 (1995)
15. Ghazanfarpour, D., Dischler, J.-M.: Spectral analysis for automatic 3d texture generation. Comput. Graph. **19**(3) (1995)
16. Ghazanfarpour, D., Dischler, J.-M.: Generation of 3d texture using multiple 2d models analysis. Comput. Graph. **15**(3) (1996)
17. Jagnow, R., Dorsey, J., Rushmeier, H.: Stereological techniques for solid textures. In: ACM SIGGRAPH, 329–335 (2004)
18. Owada, S., Nielsen, F., Okabe, M., Igarashi, T.: Volumetric illustration: designing 3d models with internal textures. In: ACM SIGGRAPH, 322–328 (2004)
19. Hertzmann, A., Jacobs, C.E., Oliver, N., Curless, B., Salesin, D.H.: Image analogies. In: ACM SIGGRAPH, pp. 327–340 (2001)
20. Mount, D., Arya, S.: Ann: a library for approximate nearest neighbor searching. In: 2nd CGC Workshop on Computational Geometry (1997)
21. Lefebvre, S., Dachsbacher, C.: Tiletrees. In: Proceedings of the ACM SIGGRAPH Symposium on Interactive 3D Graphics and Games (2007)
22. Benson, D., Davis, J.: Octree textures. In: ACM SIGGRAPH, pp. 785–790 (2002)
23. Li, D., Sun, X., Ren, Z., Lin, S., Guo, B., Zhou, K.: Transcut: interactive rendering of translucent cutouts. Technical Report (2011)

Part III
Material Fabrication

The techniques described up to this point have focused on how to transfer real-world material appearance into the virtual world. In fact, the vast majority of computer graphics algorithms are designed to render appearance on display systems such as video monitors. Though the appearance of materials can be faithfully represented by computer models, it has not been well studied how to reproduce them in the physical world.

With the recent advent of 3D printing, it has become possible for geometric models in computer graphics to be physically constructed. Real objects can be scanned as 3D meshes, manipulated with computer-aided design tools, and then fabricated as an actual object in the real world. This closed loop from the physical to the virtual and then back to the physical may lead to greater relevance of computer graphics in our daily lives, and has already made an impact in areas such as industrial design, where this closed loop system has been used to accelerate the rapid-prototyping work cycle.

Though a closed loop for object geometry has been established, closing the loop for material appearance is much less straightforward. While a 3D printer is designed to output a broad range of volumetric shapes, the materials from which such shapes can be manufactured are quite limited. The fabrication of different material appearances is nevertheless an important pursuit, as it could drive new applications and expand the scope of existing ones such as in industrial design. Effective production of material appearance may moreover lead to a new appearance modeling paradigm, one that incorporates the ability to go back and forth between the real and virtual worlds.

In the final part of this book, we address the problem of how to fabricate different material appearances from a limited set of basis materials that can be controlled within a milling machine or 3D printer. Though new materials cannot be created by a printer, we show how it is possible to volumetrically arrange its material elements to produce a physical sample whose spatially varying subsurface scattering effects closely match that of a given translucent material [1]. Our solutions are obtained both efficiently and stably by accounting for *inter-attribute correlation* coherence among scattering profiles and element arrangements within the given material, with reconstruction by *subspace search*. Adding this fabrication technique for subsurface scattering to existing methods for manufacturing surface reflectance closes the gap in the appearance modeling loop.

References

1. Dong, Y., Wang, J., Pellacini, F., Tong, X., Guo, B.: Fabricating spatially-varying subsurface scattering. ACM Trans. Graph. **29**(4) (2010)

Chapter 9
Overview of Material Fabrication

We review in this chapter common hardware and previous algorithms for material fabrication in computer graphics.

9.1 Hardware

In describing the hardware used in the fabrication of materials, we introduce the basic mechanism of each solution and discuss the common practices and practical constraints of using these devices. Before describing specific fabrication solutions, we first discuss a few basic considerations in deciding on a fabrication scheme.

9.1.1 Basic Considerations

Basis Materials The raw materials, typically referred to as *basis materials*, that can be processed by a particular fabrication device for object construction are an important factor in selecting an appearance fabrication method. In a subtractive process such as milling or drilling, the basis materials comprise the base material block to be milled; while for an additive process such as printing, the basis materials are the inks used by the printer as well as the base media that they are printed on. Different fabrication hardware are designed to process different materials, and thus a basis material is bounded to a specific hardware solution. Later when presenting the various fabrication hardware, we will also discuss the basis materials that are used with them.

Basis materials are critical for appearance fabrication, since the final appearance of generated objects is constrained by the appearance of the basis materials. Taking traditional printing as an example, the color of basis inks determines the range of color that a printer can reproduce. If only yellow ink can be used, then cyan or magenta prints cannot be produced. Although the relationship between basis materials

Y. Dong et al., *Material Appearance Modeling: A Data-Coherent Approach*,
DOI 10.1007/978-3-642-35777-0_9, © Springer-Verlag Berlin Heidelberg 2013

and the overall range of appearance that can be fabricated is often complicated, due to the non-linear behavior of material appearance, the link between them nevertheless is a major factor that affects the choice of fabrication hardware. Determining the range of appearance that can be well fabricated based on the basis materials has also become an important problem for appearance fabrication research.

Resolution vs. Minimal Feature Size The level of fabrication detail is also an important consideration, as it affects the appearance quality and reconstruction limits of a given device. There are two terms—resolution and minimal feature size—that are typically used in discussing fabrication detail. Though they both represent the same quantity when it comes to commercial printers, they are actually different in the context of fabrication devices, and this can be a source of confusion. Taking a 3D printer for example, the 3D Systems ZPrinter 850 has a spatial resolution of 600 DPI (dots per inch) in the XY directions, which results in a spatial precision of under 0.04 mm. However, its minimal feature size is 0.1 mm, more than two times larger than the spatial precision.

The difference is that the *resolution* refers to *positional precision* of fabricated features, while the *minimal feature size* describes the *size precision* of the features. In other words, with the ZPrinter 850, one can print a dot with 0.04 mm precision in its *position*, but the *size* of the dot cannot be smaller than 0.1 mm. The position and size precision may not be the same due to the particular fabrication method, so such differences are common in fabricating 3D shapes. One reason for this difference is that, due to the strength of the basis material, tiny structures smaller than a certain size may not strong enough to sustain themselves during the fabrication process, or may be too fragile after construction. As a result, the minimal feature size is often much larger than the spatial resolution for many 3D fabrication solutions.

9.1.2 Milling Machine

The milling machine, which shapes a material surface with a mill head, is one of the most commonly used industrial tools.

Basis Materials Compared to other fabrication tools, a milling machine can operate on a much broader range of materials, including metals, plastics, nylons, and woods. With this variety of basis materials comes a wide range of material appearances. However, it can mill only a single block at a time, which generally restricts the number of basis materials to one, in a single milling pass. Multiple basis material components can be milled separately in multiple milling passes, but assembly of these parts can be difficult. Moreover, complex combinations and arbitrary mixtures of basis materials cannot be achieved with this method.

Precision A milling machine has high precision in the milling drill position, which allows for precise cuts on a material block. A typical resolution of the stepper motor in a milling machine is about 0.002 to 0.01 mm. However, as previously discussed, the minimal feature size is much larger than this resolution. Also, it varies with respect to the basis material.

Besides structural strength of materials, the size of the mill head also affects the minimal feature size of milled samples. The smallest mill head has a diameter of about 0.5 mm to 1 mm, thus the smallest feature it can fabricate is restricted to that range.

Constraints and Limitations In contrast to conventional printing in which the spatial domain is divided into discrete pixels, a milling machine generates a surface in milling passes where the mill head moves in a continuous manner over the material surface. As a result, surfaces with smooth shape variations are more suitable for milling. Moreover, due to the finite size of the mill head and its round shape, sharp features cannot be accurately reproduced, especially for features near the minimal feature size. As a result, when working with a milling machine, spatial continuity and smoothness constraints are often incorporated into the solution method to favor a result that can be better fabricated.

During the fabrication process, a milling machine *subtracts* material from a block, rather than *adding* materials to a base as in other printing technologies. And in most milling machines, its mill head has a fixed direction, which can limit the complexity of the milled surface. In common practice, a milling machine is often used to produce flat objects. Objects with complex shapes, especially topologically complex shapes, are hard to reproduce in this way.

One limitation of the milling machine is that it needs to hold the base material while milling on one side of it. As a result, a milled sample will only have features on one side, with the other sides being planar. Another side could potentially be milled with a second milling pass. However, this requires complex holding devices, and the registration between the two sides may not be accurate.

9.1.3 3D Printer

A 3D printer can produce 3D shapes directly using a special resin as 'ink'. With a washable or powder-like support material, 3D printers can generate complicated 3D shapes. The flexibility of 3D printers make it an ideal choice for rapid prototyping and also a powerful tool for appearance fabrication.

Basis Materials Unlike for a milling machine, the basis material of a 3D printer is rather limited by the printing process. Typical basis materials for 3D printing are plastics and resins.

However, 3D printers provide greater control over the spatial distribution of the basis materials. Spatially mixing different basis materials within a given object is easily achievable by a 3D printer, while it is impractical with a milling machine.

Additionally, since a 3D printer prints an object layer by layer, an ink-jet printer could also be used to apply color inks to the basis material, which significantly broadens the color range. In fact, some commercial 3D printers already have the ability to print colors while producing the 3D shape.

Precision 3D printers generally have a spatial resolution of about 0.01 mm to 0.1 mm, similar to milling machines. The resolution varies among printers and is also determined by the basis material. The evolution of 3D printing technology has been rapid in recent years, and spatial resolutions are likely to improve in the near future.

In terms of minimal feature size, 3D printers have a clear advantage over milling machines. In the best cases, features of 0.1 mm in scale can be accurately reproduced. Moreover, 3D printers do not have other constraints in fabricating tiny features, which makes complex details easy to reproduce. However, the minimal feature size for certain basis materials can be relatively large, e.g. 1 mm for plastics which are more fragile. Much smaller sizes are possible with some high quality resins.

Constraints and Limitations As discussed previously, advanced 3D printers have very high precision and can easily produce complex geometry in a single printing pass. However, the minimal feature size is significant larger than the printing resolution, which might need to be considered in some applications.

The choice of basis materials is fairly limited. Besides the small range of printable materials, the number of materials that can be jointly printed into a single object is also rather limited. For most entry-level 3D printers, only one or two materials can be used at a time to print an object.

9.1.4 Conventional Printer

Conventional ink-jet printers also play an important role in the appearance fabrication field. Printing with inks is still the most convenient way to produce vivid colors and reproduce highly detailed textures.

Basis Materials Conventional printers use color inks as their fundamental basis material, and apply the inks onto paper or other media. Standard CMYK ink colors cover most visible colors. Inks generally have similar reflectance properties, and tend to preserve the reflectance properties of its media, e.g. printing on a diffuse white paper will yield diffuse reflectance, while printing on glossy photo paper will produce a more specular appearance.

However, there also exist many special inks designed to produce different reflectance effects. Specular inks and purely diffuse inks can adjust the surface reflectance of the prints, which allows for greater control over the final printed appearance.

Since the printing medium also affects the final appearance, it is also an important basis material that needs to be considered.

Thanks to the long history of the printing industry, there is a very broad range of basis inks and papers from which to choose. These choices of basis materials can lead to interesting effects using only conventional printers.

Precision Unlike geometry-based processes which often have very limited spatial resolution and precision, conventional printing can achieve very high resolution and spatial precision. In addition, printing is done at individual pixels, thus the precision is equivalent to the spatial resolution. Typical conventional printers can print at about a 600 DPI resolution and use ink mixtures to generate at least 256 grayscale levels. With such high precision, highly detailed textures can be well reproduced.

However, the printing resolution is also related to the basis materials. Even with traditional CMYK color inks, different kinds of paper can significantly differ in maximal printing resolution, with the highest DPI achievable only with specially designed photo paper. When printing with special inks, the resolution will heavily depend on what is being printed. As discussed in [1], exotic inks like metal foils can only be dithered at a relatively low spatial resolution, often 3 or 4 times lower than conventional inks. Since the mechanism with which metal foils attach to paper is very different from traditional inks, the amount of ink that can be successfully dithered and attached to the paper is different.

Nevertheless, traditional printers still offer high resolution and spatial precision, which makes them a good solution for reproducing complex spatial textures.

Constraints and Limitations Despite the advantages of having higher spatial precision and the ability to freely mix basis materials, conventional printers have an obvious limitation that they only print on planar surfaces, typically paper sheets. By the nature of conventional printing, it cannot produce 3D geometry from its basis materials.

9.2 Material Fabrication

Various techniques have been presented for fabricating different appearance effects. In the following, we describe previous works that address diffuse shading, surface reflectance, subsurface scattering, and deformations.

9.2.1 Diffuse Shading

Diffuse shading is the simplest appearance effect, solely determined by the surface normal direction. Production of desired shading with a relatively flat surface was developed in ancient times with a technique called bas-relief sculpturing.

Geometry-Based Approach Starting from a 3D model and a given camera view, the goal of bas-relief sculpturing is to find an optimal height map which gives shading effects similar to that of the input 3D model and the given camera view. The height map is constrained to a limited range of depths which can be fabricated with bas-relief sculpturing, essentially compressing the original depth map into a much smaller range.

The goal of compressing a signal into a limited range shares similarities to the tone mapping process, which compresses the dynamic range of luminance in an image. Similar to tone mapping, research on bas-relief generation can be classified into global mapping algorithms and locally adaptive mapping algorithms.

Cignoni et al. [2] first introduced semi-automatic bas-relief generation by compressing the depth map. The depth map is computed by projecting the 3D model to the viewing plane, and the compressed depth is generated in a global manner proportionally to the original depth. Regions with the same depth are mapped into the same target depth, with distant features undergoing greater compression.

Instead of casting the problem as a global depth mapping, other methods have compressed the depth in the gradient domain. Gradient domain depth compression will have effects similar to gradient-based tone mapping operators, which preserve local contrast and details while compressing the global component.

Song et al. [3] use a series of unsharp masking operations with Gaussian kernels to enhance detailed features while compressing the depth globally. They also examined view-dependent mesh saliency measurements in their fully automatic solution. However, as mentioned by the authors, the unsharp masking they use will generate distortion in the final results.

Weyrich et al. [4] proposed a gradient domain compression method that reconstructs the final height field in a final integration step. Special treatment is given to silhouettes where large gradients caused by depth discontinuities occur and may cause unwanted effects in the final depth field. Artistic control is allowed for better preserving salient geometry features.

Concurrently, Kerber et al. [5] also presented a gradient domain compression technique that applies thresholding to large gradients. Unsharp masking with a Gaussian kernel is also applied to enhance fine-scale details. Kerber provides a detailed analysis of this approach in his master thesis [6], where a comprehensive survey on relief generation from 3D meshes can also be found.

Image-Based Approach Most bas-relief generation methods focus on reproducing shading effects from 3D models. Alexa et al. [7] cast this problem in a very different way. Instead of using a 3D model as input, they reproduce a surface that has shading effects that match a set of input images and their lighting directions. Their formulation is that of a classical shape-from-shading problem. However, to address more complicated shading, they add more degrees of freedom such that each pixel in the depth map contains four triangles. Four normals can thus be packed into a single pixel instead of only one in traditional shape-from-shading problems. Since an arbitrary combination of images and their lighting directions may not necessarily form a valid relief surface, they also provide a detailed analysis on printable combinations, in terms of a gamut space of shading fabrications.

9.2.2 Surface Reflectance

Micro-Geometry Solution According to the microfacet reflectance model, many surface reflectance functions can be represented by a set of mirror-like microfacets with normal directions that follow a certain distribution function. Inspired by this, Weyrich et al. [8] pioneered the fabrication of surfaces with desired surface reflectance by generating specially designed micro-geometry. In this way, complex surface reflectance functions can be well reproduced.

In theory, with enough microfacets and a base material with sharp reflectance, the proposed method can reproduce almost any microfacet BRDF. However, in practice it sacrifices spatial resolution in order to produce enough angular samples to approximate the normal distribution function.

Basis Inks Solution Besides producing a desired surface reflectance by fabricating micro-geometry, another approach is to utilize basis inks. Matusik et al. [1] reproduce a given surface reflectance using multiple inks with different reflectance functions that are blended into the final reflectance function. High-frequency half-toning patterns cannot be well printed with specular inks, so they proposed a new half-toning algorithm that addresses this issue. Also, since the BRDFs that can be generated by mixing specular inks is limited, a gamut-mapping algorithm was introduced. This gamut mapping algorithm was improved by Pereira and Rusinkiewicz [9] with the use of a perceptual BRDF similarity metric that was validated through a user study. To better preserve texture details of an input SVBRDF, they also consider its spatial distribution and proposed a locally adaptive gamut mapping algorithm.

Similar to images encoded with shading effects [7], spatially varying surface reflectance can be used to encode multiple images under different lighting conditions. Following this idea, Dong et al. [10] printed spatially varying surface reflectance that reproduces the different exposures of an HDR image by changing the viewing or lighting direction. They find the optimal set of exposures for an input HDR image and find the best fitting reflectance functions within the printable BRDFs to reproduce them. The resulting print can preserve both global contrast and local details, providing an alternative way to represent HDR images.

Other than reproducing surface reflectance, a fixed-view reflectance field can also be fabricated. Malzbender et al. [11] utilized curve-shaped micro-mirrors as individual pixels of an input reflectance field, and used a printed mask to block the light reflected from certain illumination directions, thus producing the desired reflectance field. Due to certain properties of printed masks, a half-toning algorithm is used in producing it. They also studied the tradeoff between angular resolution and spatial resolution, since their half-toning can be performed in both the spatial domain among pixels and in the angular domain with an area light source.

9.2.3 Subsurface Scattering

To reproduce subsurface scattering effects, a translucent material volume is required to simulate light transmission behavior. To set the optical properties of voxels, the volume is produced by stacking layered materials.

Hasan et al. [12] carefully measured the scattering profiles of the printable materials for a 3D printer. A pruning algorithm is then used to search for an optimal layer ordering and thickness for each layer. To print heterogeneous scattering effects, they factorize the input BSSRDF into scattering profiles defined on each pixel, and search for an optimal layer layout for each pixel. However, the predicted scattering from this factorization may be inaccurate because a pixel is not homogeneous but rather a stack of layers.

Concurrently, Dong et al. [13] also proposed a system to fabricate desired subsurface scattering effects. Instead of factorizing the BSSRDF and treating each pixel as homogeneous, they only use the factorization result as an initialization and find the optimal volume via a global optimization process. By solving a constrained inverse diffusion problem, the scattering across pixel boundaries is better considered and the reconstruction error is reduced. They presented results not only with a 3D printer, but also with a milling machine, which provides a broader gamut of scattering properties because of the wider range of basis materials.

9.2.4 Deformation Behavior

Other than appearance, there are other material properties of interest in computer graphics. Deformation is a key element when animating or interacting with a material, so fabricating a desired deformation behavior of materials has also been studied in recent works.

Bickel et al. [14] is the first to consider material deformation in fabrication. They measured the deformation of basis materials, and modeled them as a non-linear stress-strain relationship in a finite element model. To achieve a desired deformation behavior, they stacked layers of basis materials such that the final deformation effects of the layered material volume fit the required deformation properties. To find the optimal layering, an optimization algorithm similar to subsurface scattering fabrication was proposed. They also considered different deformation effects caused by different forces.

Besides elastic deformations, rigid deformations such as that of articulated characters can also be fabricated as desired. Bacher et al. [15] start from a skinned mesh and produced joint designs for 3D printing. The printed joint parts can perform the same animation as the input skinned mesh character.

References

1. Matusik, W., Ajdin, B., Gu, J., Lawrence, J., Lensch, H.P.A., Pellacini, F., Rusinkiewicz, S.: Printing spatially-varying reflectance. ACM Trans. Graph. **28**(5), 128 (2009)
2. Cignoni, P., Montani, C., Scopigno, R.: Computer-assisted generation of bas- and high-reliefs. J. Graph. Tools **2**(3), 15–28 (1997)
3. Song, W., Belyaev, A., Seidel, H.-P.: Automatic generation of bas-reliefs from 3d shapes. In: Proceedings of the IEEE International Conference on Shape Modeling and Applications, SMI '07, pp. 211–214. IEEE Computer Society, Washington (2007)
4. Weyrich, T., Deng, J., Barnes, C., Rusinkiewicz, S., Finkelstein, A.: Digital bas-relief from 3d scenes. ACM Trans. Graph. **26**(3) (2007)
5. Kerber, J., Belyaev, A., Seidel, H.-P.: Feature preserving depth compression of range images. In: Sbert, M. (ed.) Proceedings of the 23rd Spring Conference on Computer Graphics, Budmerice, Slovakia, April 2007, pp. 110–114. Comenius University, Bratislava (2007)
6. Kerber, J.: Digital art of bas-relief sculpting. Masters thesis, Universität des Saarlandes (August 2007)
7. Alexa, M., Matusik, W.: Reliefs as images. ACM Trans. Graph. **29**(4), 60 (2010)
8. Weyrich, T., Peers, P., Matusik, W., Rusinkiewicz, S.: Fabricating microgeometry for custom surface reflectance. ACM Trans. Graph. **28**(3), 32 (2009)
9. Pereira, T., Rusinkiewicz, S.: Gamut mapping spatially varying reflectance with an improved brdf similarity metric. Comput. Graph. Forum **31**(4), 1557–1566 (2012)
10. Dong, Y., Tong, X., Pellacini, F., Guo, B.: Printing spatially-varying reflectance for reproducing hdr images. ACM Trans. Graph. **31**(4), 40 (2012)
11. Malzbender, T., Samadani, R., Scher, S., Crume, A., Dunn, D., Davis, J.: Printing reflectance functions. ACM Trans. Graph. **31**(3), 20 (2012)
12. Hašan, M., Fuchs, M., Matusik, W., Pfister, H., Rusinkiewicz, S.: Physical reproduction of materials with specified subsurface scattering. ACM Trans. Graph. **29**, 61 (2010)
13. Dong, Y., Wang, J., Pellacini, F., Tong, X., Guo, B.: Fabricating spatially-varying subsurface scattering. ACM Trans. Graph. **29**, 62 (2010)
14. Bickel, B., Kaufmann, P., Skouras, M., Thomaszewski, B., Bradley, D., Beeler, T., Jackson, P., Marschner, S., Matusik, W., Gross, M.: Physical face cloning. ACM Trans. Graph. **31**(4), 118 (2012)
15. Bächer, M., Bickel, B., James, D.L., Pfister, H.: Fabricating articulated characters from skinned meshes. ACM Trans. Graph. **31**(4), 47 (2012)

Chapter 10
Fabricating Spatially-Varying Subsurface Scattering

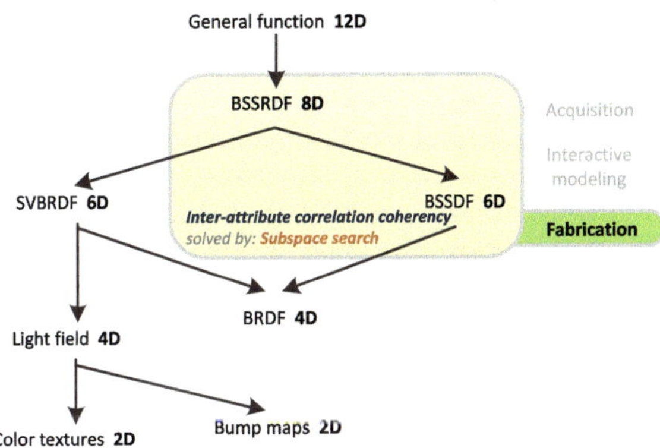

In Chap. 9, we described various methods for fabricating surfaces with different reflectance properties. For example, the system of Matusik et al. [1] combines several types of inks with different reflectance properties to reproduce the directionally dependent behavior of spatially-varying opaque materials. How to fabricate translucent objects that exhibit subsurface scattering effects, however, has remained an open problem.

Fabricating a material volume with desired subsurface scattering effects is useful in many applications. In the food industry, great effort is made to manufacture realistic-looking fake food for exhibition and advertisements. Artists need powerful techniques for mimicking realistic human skin in wax sculptures. Interior designers use faux painting to reproduce the appearance of marble and other materials for surface decoration. Although dedicated techniques have been developed for many of these applications, there does not exist a general and automatic solution for fabricating a desired translucent material volume. Considerable manual work and experience is generally needed to craft materials with a particular translucent appearance.

In this chapter, we present a method for automatically fabricating a material volume with a desired BSSRDF. As in Chap. 7, we focus on optically thick materials

Y. Dong et al., *Material Appearance Modeling: A Data-Coherent Approach*,
DOI 10.1007/978-3-642-35777-0_10, © Springer-Verlag Berlin Heidelberg 2013

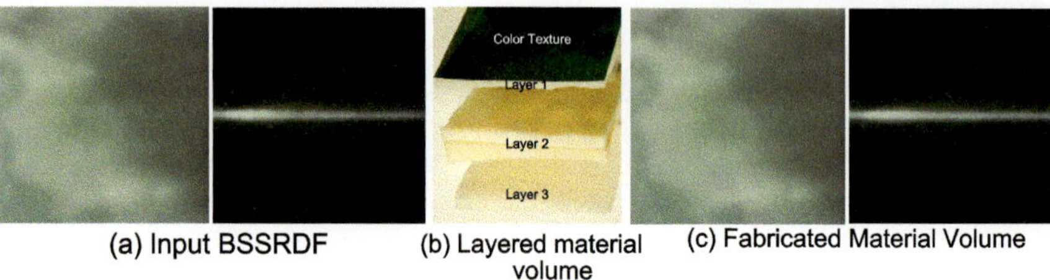

Fig. 10.1 Our system automatically generates a layered material volume for approximating a custom BSSRDF. (**a**) The appearance of a real material sample under diffuse lighting and a beam light. (**b**) A collection of layers generated by our system for assembling the output volume. (**c**) The appearance of the fabricated material volume under the same diffuse lighting and beam light

whose subsurface scattering behavior is well modeled by the diffusion approximation. For such materials, our key observation is that it is possible to reproduce the visual appearance of a given material by carefully combining other materials with different optical properties. Thus with a fixed set of basis manufacturing materials, we can reproduce a wide variety of heterogeneous BSSRDFs by stacking material layers whose thickness and composition vary spatially. The type of basis manufacturing materials and number of layers are constrained by the hardware setup. Given these constraints, our method computes the distribution of basis materials and spatially variant layer thicknesses so that the BSSRDF of the output volume is as close to the target BSSRDF as possible. A surface texture layer may be added to enrich the BSSRDF colors of the output volume when needed. Figure 10.1 shows an example volume manufactured with our system.

We compute the optimal layout of each layer of the output volume, i.e., the distribution of basis materials and thickness of each layer, by a *subspace search* of the possible layer layouts for the corresponding BSSRDF that is closest to the input BSSRDF. For a homogeneous material, the material and thickness is constant within each layer but may vary across layers. In this case, the computation is relatively easy and to further facilitate this computation we have developed an efficient method for quickly constructing the BSSRDFs of all layer layouts. The case of heterogeneous materials is much harder. The complex interactions between the optical properties and spatial distributions of the materials lead to a non-linear relationship between the BSSRDF over the surface and the underlying volumetric material properties. Deriving the optimal layer layout from the input BSSRDF is difficult as it amounts to solving a large non-linear optimization problem. Furthermore, manufacturing constraints impose limits on valid material distributions and thickness of layers, which makes this non-linear optimization even more challenging. We solve this problem in two steps. In the first step, we decouple the non-local BSSRDF into local scattering profiles and determine the material composition (i.e. the basis material in each layer) under each individual surface point based on *inter-attribute correlation* coherence, in which points with similar scattering profiles have similar material compositions beneath them. After that, we model the light transport between surface points using a diffusion process and optimize the thickness of the layers at each location by an adapted inverse diffusion optimization. For any given BSSRDF, our approach automatically computes the optimal material volume in dozens of minutes.

We have experimented with two hardware setups having different tradeoffs: a milling machine and a 3D printer. The milling machine allows us to choose manufacturing materials with a variety of scattering properties, but has limitations in the number and precision of the layers it can effectively produce. The 3D printer allows us to print quickly a larger number of layers with high precision, but has a very limited selection of manufacturing materials. With these hardware setups, our method can generate material volumes with a wide range of homogeneous and heterogeneous BSSRDFs.

10.1 Related Work

Few works have proposed fabrication methods for computer graphics. For surface appearance, a traditional color printing system can faithfully print the color of surfaces, but cannot reproduce the directional dependence aspect of appearance. Weyrich et al. [2] used a milling machine to fabricate a designed microfacet pattern on a physical surface for generating custom surface reflectance. Matusik et al. [1] developed a system for printing spatially varying BRDFs via a set of inks with known BRDFs. Although these systems can well reproduce a given surface reflectance, they cannot model the subsurface scattering effects caused by light transport inside the object volume.

Concurrent to our work, Hašan et al. [3] proposed a 3D printer based solution for reproducing material volumes with a specified BSSRDF. Although both approaches are based on the diffusion approximation and approximate the input BSSRDF with layers of basis materials, they are different in several ways. To find the layer layout for approximating homogeneous BSSRDFs, Hašan et al. developed efficient search heuristics by pruning the layer layouts that yield poor solutions, while our work presents a cluster based approach for computing the BSSRDFs of all valid layer layouts. This allows us to precompute the gamut of basis materials and then find the layer layout for a specified BSSRDF via nearest neighbor search. For heterogeneous BSSRDFs, Hašan et al. determined the layer layout for each surface point separately from the local scattering profiles that are factorized from the input BSSRDF as in [4]. In our method, the local scattering profiles are only used to initialize the layer layout in the volume. A volume optimization algorithm is proposed to further optimize the volume layer layout for approximating the input BSSRDF. Combined with a surface texture layer and two hardware solutions (3D printer and milling machine), our method can effectively reproduce a wide variety of heterogeneous BSSRDFs with a fixed set of basis manufacturing materials.

In object manufacturing, most traditional computer aided design and manufacturing systems represent 3D shape with B-rep geometry [5] and fabricate each separate part of a 3D shape with one homogeneous substrate. The material variation inside the object volume is ignored. 3D printers construct complex 3D objects by aggregating materials layer by layer. Despite their hardware capability to support voxel-based object and material variations in the object volume, most commercial systems available now can only print B-rep geometry with one or two proprietary materials inside [6]. Some printers such as the Z Corp Spectrum Z510 have the capability to print colors at any voxel in an object volume. However, the basis materials available for printing are very limited and almost opaque.

Our system models the output volume as a set of layers of basis materials, each of which can be well converted to a B-rep geometry and fabricated by traditional manufacturing hardware (such as milling machines or 3D printers). It also can be easily extended for future 3D printing systems that support more materials and flexible material variations in the object volume.

10.2 System Pipeline

The goal of this work is to approximate the appearance of a desired subsurface scattering material that is described by the BSSRDF $S(\mathbf{x}_i, \omega_i; \mathbf{x}_o, \omega_o)$, which relates the outgoing radiance $L(\mathbf{x}_o, \omega_o)$ at a point $\mathbf{x}_o$ in direction ω_o to the incoming radiance $L(\mathbf{x}_i, \omega_i)$ as

$$L(\mathbf{x}_o, \omega_o) = \int_A \int_\Omega S(\mathbf{x}_i, \omega_i; \mathbf{x}_o, \omega_o) L(\mathbf{x}_i, \omega_i) \big(\mathbf{n}(\mathbf{x}_i) \cdot \omega_i\big) \mathrm{d}\omega_i \mathrm{d}\mathbf{x}_i, \qquad (10.1)$$

where Ω is the hemisphere around $\mathbf{x}_i$; A is the area around the point $\mathbf{x}_o$, and $\mathbf{n}(\mathbf{x}_i)$ is the surface normal at $\mathbf{x}_i$. As in [4, 7, 8], we decompose the light transport into two components as $L(\mathbf{x}_o, \omega_o) = L_s(\mathbf{x}_o, \omega_o) + L_d(\mathbf{x}_o, \omega_o)$, where $L_s(\mathbf{x}_o, \omega_o)$ accounts for light immediately reflected from the surface and L_d accounts for light scattered in the material volume. We focus on the latter component L_d that is captured by the *diffuse BSSRDF* S_d, which we further decompose as

$$S_d(\mathbf{x}_i, \omega_i; \mathbf{x}_o, \omega_o) = \frac{1}{\pi} F_r\big(\eta(\mathbf{x}_i), \omega_i\big) R_d(\mathbf{x}_i, \mathbf{x}_o) F_r\big(\eta(\mathbf{x}_o), \omega_o\big), \qquad (10.2)$$

where F_r is the angular dependent Fresnel function that is determined by the refraction index η of the material, while R_d is a four dimensional function of two surface locations that encodes the spatial subsurface scattering of heterogeneous materials. Again following [4, 7, 8], we focus exclusively on a representation for the 4D spatial component of the diffuse BSSRDF R_d and ignore the angular dependencies.

We simulate the appearance of the input BSSRDF by printing an object volume V. Different manufacturing hardware can construct objects using a fixed set of basis materials (with given translucent properties) specific to that hardware. To approximate the BSSRDF on the surface, we construct the volume with layers of these basis materials, as shown in Fig. 10.2. The thickness of layers under each surface point is identical for homogeneous BSSRDFs, and varied appropriately for simulating heterogeneous BSSRDFs. To model a BSSRDF with sharp variations, the basis

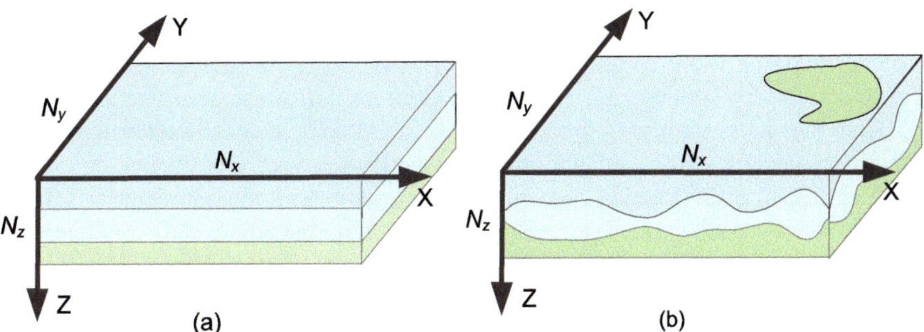

Fig. 10.2 The output volume V. Different colors indicate layers with different basis materials. (**a**) The layered volume for a homogeneous BSSRDF. (**b**) The layered volume for a heterogeneous BSSRDF

materials in the layer may also be varied under each surface point. In our experiments, we found that to ensure that the output volume is not too fragile, the minimal thickness of material layers needs to be limited. Furthermore, to save manufacturing time and cost, we also limit the total number of layers in the output volume. Essentially, 3D manufacturing methods impose *layout constraints* that we have to respect during printing.

As in standard printing methods, the output volume provides just an approximation of the input BSSRDF. Given the basis materials and layout constraints, our goal is to produce an output volume that is as close to the original input as possible. We call *material mapping* the process by which we determine the volume to print. More formally, while respecting layout constraints, we seek to minimize the L^2 difference E between the input BSSRDF R_d and output BSSRDF R'_d of the printed volume V, written as

$$E = \int_{\mathbf{x}_i} \int_{\mathbf{x}_j} \left\| R_d(\mathbf{x}_i, \mathbf{x}_j) - R'_d(\mathbf{x}_i, \mathbf{x}_j) \right\|^2 \mathrm{d}\mathbf{x}_i \, \mathrm{d}\mathbf{x}_j. \tag{10.3}$$

To print the volume, we need to determine the basis material and thickness of each layer, which we call the *layer layout*, under each surface point in the volume V. Since the surface BSSRDF depends on the volume distribution in a non-linear manner, determining the layer layouts for the volume V amounts to a non-linear optimization. This makes BSSRDF printing very different from color and reflectance printing, since in those cases determining what to print involves simpler operations.

To print homogeneous materials, we map the BSSRDF to a volume made by layering slabs of homogeneous basis materials that have the same thickness for points on the surface. Conceptually, to determine the basis material and the thickness of each layer, we compute the BSSRDF for all possible layer layouts generated by the basis materials, and pick the closest one. Since computing the BSSRDF for each layer layout by brute force is expensive, we develop an efficient method for quickly constructing the BSSRDFs of all layer layouts.

To print a BSSRDF generated from heterogeneous translucent materials, we vary the column layer layouts under different surface points in the output volume. The resulting light transport becomes more complex due to the heterogeneity, making material mapping more challenging. We make this process manageable by introducing a two-step process. First, in the *volume initialization step*, we factor the BSSRDF into local scattering profiles. We then approximate each scattering profile with a homogeneous BSSRDF and initialize the layer layout (i.e. the basis material and thickness of each layer) in each column separately with the homogeneous mapping method. At each surface point, this initialization determines the basis material for each layer and a starting layer thickness. We use this as the starting configuration for a second step, the *volume optimization step*, where we model the light transport in the volume using a diffusion process and optimize the thickness of the layers at each location using an adapted inverse diffusion optimization [9]. The details of our material mapping procedure are described in the next section.

Since we use only a small number of basis materials with limited color hues and saturations, it is possible that some of the rich chromatic variations in input BSSRDFs fall outside the color gamut of our basis. To further enrich the color of the BSSRDF generated by the output volume, a very thin color texture layer is placed on the top surface for modulating both incoming and outgoing radiance. We ignore the thickness of this color texture layer and represent it as an $N_x \times N_y$ 2D surface color texture T that represents the transmission for RGB channels, in which 1 indicates fully transparent and 0 is opaque. Given input BSSRDF R_d, we solve the optimal color texture and the output volume iteratively. Given the initial color texture T_0, we modulate the input BSSRDF $R_d(\mathbf{x}_i, \mathbf{x}_o)$ as $R_d^T(\mathbf{x}_i, \mathbf{x}_o) = R_d(\mathbf{x}_i, \mathbf{x}_o)/(T(\mathbf{x}_i)T(\mathbf{x}_o))$ and use the result R_d^T as the input for material mapping. After material mapping, we update the color texture by

$$T(\mathbf{x}) = \frac{\sum_{\mathbf{x}_o \in A} R_d(\mathbf{x}, \mathbf{x}_o)^2 R_d^{'}(\mathbf{x}, \mathbf{x}_o)}{\sum_{\mathbf{x}_o \in A} R_d(\mathbf{x}, \mathbf{x}_o)}, \tag{10.4}$$

where $R_d^{'}$ is the BSSRDF computed from the output volume obtained by material mapping. We repeat this process until the update of the color texture is small enough.

We tested our system with two manufacturing configurations. The first solution is based on a milling machine, where the basis material for each layer can be chosen from a set of substrates with different translucency and colors. We mill each material layer separately from a substrate block and assemble all layers together to generate the output volume. We use three basis materials and limit the number of layers to three for this hardware.

The second solution is based on a 3D printer, which can print complex geometric shapes with high precision. Our 3D printer provides one basis material used to print 3D shapes and one support material that is used during the printing process, but is normally removed after printing. In our system, we retain the support material after printing and use it as a second basis material. We use six layers for this hardware. Figure 10.3 illustrates all basis materials and their scattering properties in these two solutions.

Even with this small number of basis materials, the generated output volumes well approximate a wide range of BSSRDFs. We borrow the term "gamut" from traditional printing to indicate the space of homogeneous BSSRDFs reproducible by

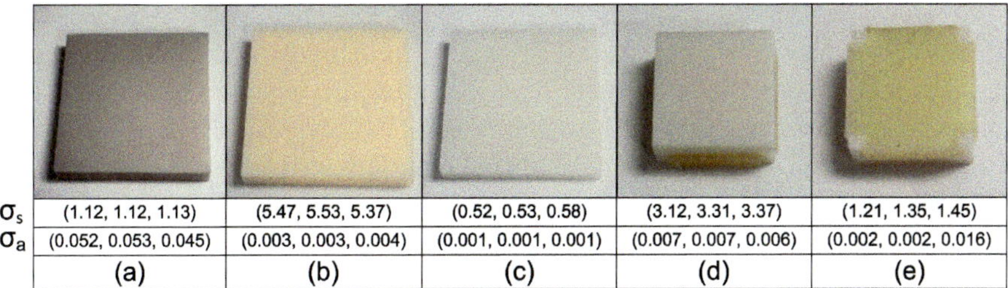

Fig. 10.3 Photographs and optical properties of basis materials used in our two manufacturing solutions. (**a–c**) Basis materials used for the milling machine solution. (**d–e**) Basis materials used for the 3D printer solution

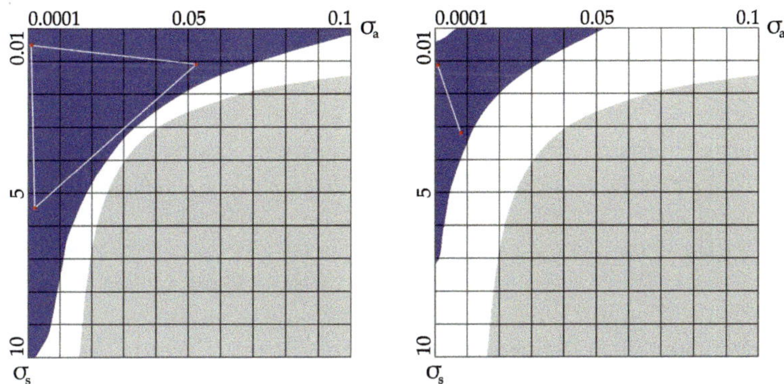

Fig. 10.4 The gamuts of our two manufacturing setups. The basis materials are indicated by *red points*. The *blue gamut regions* indicate homogeneous materials whose BSSRDFs can be reproduced by our setup. The *grey regions* mark homogeneous materials with little scattering (with BSSRDF radius smaller than 1.0 mm), which are not the main targets of our method. (**a**) The gamut of three basis materials used for the milling machine solution. (**b**) The gamut of two basis materials used for the 3D printer solution

our setup. Figure 10.4 shows the gamut of our two manufacturing setups, where σ_s and σ_a are the scattering coefficient and absorption coefficient of the homogeneous material, respectively. We compute this gamut by mapping each homogeneous BSSRDF to a layered volume of basis materials and include in the gamut all BSSRDFs with relative mapping errors smaller than 10^{-4}. We compute the relative error as

$$\frac{\int_{\mathbf{x}_i}\int_{\mathbf{x}_j} \|R_d(\mathbf{x}_i,\mathbf{x}_j) - R'_d(\mathbf{x}_i,\mathbf{x}_j)\|^2 \,\mathrm{d}\mathbf{x}_i \,\mathrm{d}\mathbf{x}_j}{\int_{\mathbf{x}_i}\int_{\mathbf{x}_j} \|R_d(\mathbf{x}_i,\mathbf{x}_j)\|^2 \,\mathrm{d}\mathbf{x}_i \,\mathrm{d}\mathbf{x}_j}. \tag{10.5}$$

Different from material and reflectance printing, the gamut of homogeneous materials we can simulate is larger than the convex hull of the basis materials. This is the result of the non-linear relationship between the BSSRDF and the volumetric material properties. From a intuitive standpoint, since an observer can only see the object surfaces, we are free to vary the volume as needed to reproduce that appearance.

Computing all the possible heterogeneous BSSRDFs that can be reproduced by our setup is prohibitively expensive. To gain an intuition of which heterogeneous variations we can reproduce, we make the observation that heterogeneous BSSRDFs can be factored into products of 1D scattering profiles independently defined at each surface location [4]. These scattering profiles represent well the local scattering effects at each surface location, effectively decoupling the pairwise correlations in the heterogeneous BSSRDF. Intuitively, at each surface location we can think of the scattering profile as approximately defining a homogeneous BSSRDF that describes scattering from a small homogeneous region around the point. If all these homogeneous BSSRDFs fit within our gamut, our material volume should approximate well the original heterogeneous BSSRDF.

10.3 Material Mapping

In this section we discuss the details of how we compute the output volume that best matches the input BSSRDF. In our algorithms, the volume V is represented as $N_x \times N_y \times N_z$ voxels on a regular 3D grid, where $N_x \times N_y$ indicates the surface resolution and N_z is determined by the thickness of the layered material volume (Fig. 10.2). The voxel size is set to the precision of the manufacturing hardware along three axes. The volume is composed of N_l layers, each made of one of the basis materials. We discretize each layer thickness by the voxel size and limit it to be larger than a minimal thickness determined by the manufacturing hardware. We denote by $M_{\mathbf{x}}$ the *layer layout* under a surface point $\mathbf{x}$, defined as the set of basis materials and thickness for each layer in the column under $\mathbf{x}$.

10.3.1 Homogeneous BSSRDFs

Let us first consider the BSSRDF generated from a semi-infinite homogeneous material slab, which is isotropic and can be represented as a function of distance $r = \|\mathbf{x}_i - \mathbf{x}_o\|$ between two surface points as $R(r) = R_d(\mathbf{x}_i, \mathbf{x}_o)$. To reproduce this BSSRDF, we layer N_l slabs of base materials that have equal thickness for all points on the surface. The resulting multi-layered volume is homogeneous along the X and Y directions but heterogeneous along Z.

To determine the basis material and thickness of each layer (i.e. the number of voxels it occupies along Z), we solve Eq. (10.3) by computing the BSSRDFs for all possible layer layouts of the basis materials, and pick the closest one to the input BSSRDF.

For each configuration, we compute the BSSRDF $R_{N_l}(r)$ generated by the volume according to Kubelka-Munk theory [10]:

$$\hat{R}_{N_l} = \hat{R}_1 + \frac{\hat{T}_1 \hat{R}_1 \hat{T}_1}{1 - \hat{R}_1 \hat{R}_{N_l - 1}} \tag{10.6}$$

where $\hat{R}$ and $\hat{T}$ refer to the Fourier transformed functions $R(r)$ and $T(r)$. $R_1(r)$ and $T_1(r)$ are the BSSRDF and transmission functions of the top layer computed using the multipole model [10]. $R_{N_l-1}(r)$ is the BSSRDF of the remaining $N_l - 1$ layers beneath the top layer, which can be recursively computed using Eq. (10.6). After computation, we transfer the result back to the spatial domain via the inverse FFT.

Performing this computation for each layer layout separately would be impractical given the very large number of possible configurations. We reduce the number of needed BSSRDF evaluations by observing that many layer layouts of basis materials generate similar BSSRDFs. This is because small variations of layer thickness generally have little effect on a BSSRDF. Therefore, for layer layouts that have the same top layer and similar $R_{N_l-1}(r)$, we can compute their BSSRDF once.

Based on this observation, our algorithm starts by constructing the set $M^1 = \{m^1\}$ of all layouts m^1 that include a single basis material whose thickness is varied from the minimal layer thickness to the output volume thickness in voxel sized steps along Z. We compute the BSSRDFs and transmission functions of each slab using the multipole model [10]. We then cluster these layouts using k-means clustering such that the distance of BSSRDFs in each cluster is less than a small threshold. For each cluster, we compute the representative BSSRDF and transmission function as the average of BSSRDFs and transmission functions of layer layouts in the cluster.

After that, we iteratively construct all layer layouts from bottom to top in N_l steps. In each step, we generate the set M^{i+1} of candidate layouts constructed by adding a basis material layer m_l^1 from M^1 to a layer layout m_l^i from M^i. Formally, $M^{i+1} = \{m_l^1 \cup m_l^i \mid m_l^1 \in M^1, m_l^i \in M^i\}$, where the $\cup$ operator adds a layer on top of a layout. We discard all layouts with thickness larger than the output volume. The BSSRDF of each layout in M^{i+1} is computed with the representative of M_l^1 and M_l^i using Eq. (10.6). Thus the total number of BSSRDF computations is $N_{M^1} \times N_{M^i} \ll |M^1| \times |M^i|$, where N_{M^1} and N_{M^i} are the number of clusters in M^1 and M^i and $|\cdot|$ is the size of a set. We then cluster M^{i+1} based on the layout BSSRDFs and pick representatives.

After N_l steps, we remove all layer layouts whose thickness is not equal to the volume thickness and compute the BSSRDF for layouts in the final set. Given an input BSSRDF, we first search for the best matched representative BSSRDF. We then compute the BSSRDF of each layer layout in this cluster and search for the best match. The approximate nearest neighbor acceleration scheme is used to speed up this search process [11].

10.3.2 Heterogeneous BSSRDFs

To print a BSSRDF generated from heterogeneous translucent materials, we vary the column layer layouts (i.e. the basis material and thickness in each layer) under different surface points, resulting in a heterogeneous output volume. Computing the layer layouts for each column amounts to solving the non-linear optimization problem defined in Eq. (10.3). This optimization is much more challenging than homogeneous mapping since the BSSRDF of a heterogeneous output volume is determined

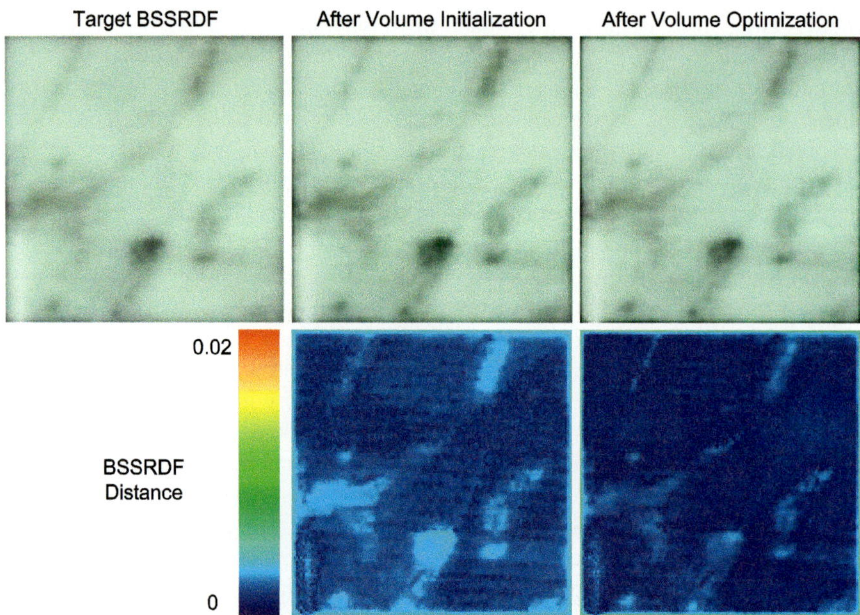

Fig. 10.5 Rendering results of BSSRDFs after volume initialization and volume optimization under diffuse lighting are shown in the *top row*. The errors of BSSRDFs after the initialization and optimization processes are presented in the *bottom row*

by the couplings of different layer layouts in all columns. We do so with a two-step process. First, in the *volume initialization step*, we decouple the BSSRDF into local scattering profiles and use the homogeneous algorithm in the preceding section to assign basis materials and initial layer thicknesses to each column separately. Second, in the *volume optimization step*, we then optimize all layer thicknesses for all columns concurrently by using an inverse diffusion optimization. Figure 10.5 shows the best fit volume after each step compared to the original BSSRDF. After initialization, the layered material volume roughly approximates the input BSSRDF. Further improvements to the approximation are achieved with volume optimization.

To determine the material layout in each column, we first decouple the input diffuse BSSRDF R_d into a product of 1D scattering profiles $P_{\mathbf{x}}(r)$ defined at each surface location $\mathbf{x}$, and parameterized over the local distance $r = \|\mathbf{x}_o - \mathbf{x}_i\|$ as in [4]: $R_d(\mathbf{x}_i, \mathbf{x}_o) \approx \sqrt{P_{\mathbf{x}_i}(r)P_{\mathbf{x}_o}(r)}$.

For a heterogeneous BSSRDF, this factorization effectively decouples the nonlocal light transport between pairs of surface points into a set of local scattering profiles, each of which is defined at a single point and mainly determined by the scattering properties of the material volume under such a surface point.

Based on this observation, we consider the homogeneous BSSRDF determined by the scattering profile at each location $\mathbf{x}$, defined as $R_{\mathbf{x}}(r) = \operatorname{argmin}_R \int_0^\infty [P_x(r) - R(r)]^2 r\,\mathrm{d}r$, and use the algorithm for homogeneous BSSRDFs to assign a layer layout for the material column at $\mathbf{x}$. More specifically, we first precompute the BSS-

RDFs of all valid homogeneous layer layouts. For each surface location, we then search for the best matching representative BSSRDF in the precomputed dataset. We then choose the layer layout in this cluster that is most similar to the ones assigned to the neighboring points, proceeding in scanline order. To assign a layer layout to the point, the similarity of layer layouts is measured by $\sum_z \delta(b_x(z), b_y(z))$ where $b_x(z)$ and $b_y(z)$ are the basis materials at depth z for the layer layouts at x and y. This assignment scheme favors smoothly varying layer layouts for regions with similar local scattering profiles.

The initialized volume only provides a rough approximation for the input BSSRDF because the light transport between columns is not considered in the last step. To obtain a better match, we fix the basis materials used in all layers and further optimize all layer thicknesses concurrently to better approximate the input BSSRDF by minimizing the objective function in Eq. (10.3). Here the BSSRDF of the output volume R'_d is computed by simulating the light transport in the volume with a diffusion process, which is described by the following equations for points $\mathbf{v}$ in the volume V and points $\mathbf{x}$ on the surface A [12, 13]:

$$\nabla \cdot \big(\kappa(\mathbf{v})\nabla\phi(\mathbf{v})\big) - \sigma_a(\mathbf{v})\phi(\mathbf{v}) = 0, \quad \mathbf{v} \in V, \tag{10.7}$$

$$\phi(\mathbf{x}) + 2\mathbf{C}\kappa(\mathbf{x})\frac{\partial\phi(\mathbf{x})}{\partial\mathbf{n}(\mathbf{x})} = \frac{4}{1 - F_{dr}}L_i(\mathbf{x}), \quad \mathbf{x} \in A \tag{10.8}$$

where $\sigma_a(\mathbf{v})$ and $\kappa(\mathbf{v}) = 1/[3(\sigma_a(\mathbf{v}) + \sigma_s(\mathbf{v}))]$ denote the absorption and diffusion coefficients at $\mathbf{v}$, $\phi(\mathbf{v})$ is the radiant flux, F_{dr} is the diffuse Fresnel reflectance (determined by the refraction index η of the material [14]) and $\mathbf{C} = (1 + F_{dr})/(1 - F_{dr})$. Here we assume that the phase function of the material is isotropic. The diffuse incoming lighting $L_i(\mathbf{x})$ at a surface point $\mathbf{x}$ is given by $L_i(\mathbf{x}) = \int_\Omega L(\mathbf{x}, \omega_i)(\mathbf{n} \cdot \omega_i)F_r(\eta(\mathbf{x}), \omega_i)d\omega_i$. Once the radiant flux is determined for a given incoming lighting by the diffusion process, the multiple scattering component of the outgoing radiance at $\mathbf{x}$ is computed as

$$L_d(\mathbf{x}, \omega_o) = \frac{F_r(\eta(\mathbf{x}), \omega_o)}{4\pi}\left[\left(1 + \frac{1}{\mathbf{C}}\right)\phi(\mathbf{x}) - \frac{4}{1 + F_{dr}}L_i(\mathbf{x})\right]. \tag{10.9}$$

We can then compute the diffuse BSSRDF between two surface points, by considering a unit incoming lighting $L_i(\mathbf{x}) = 1$ at $\mathbf{x}$ and ignoring the angular Fresnel terms for both incoming and outgoing lighting, as

$$R'_d(\mathbf{x}_i, \mathbf{x}_o) = \begin{cases} \frac{1}{4\pi}[(1 + \frac{1}{\mathbf{C}})\phi(\mathbf{x}_o)], & \mathbf{x}_i \neq \mathbf{x}_o, \\ \frac{1}{4\pi}[(1 + \frac{1}{\mathbf{C}})\phi(\mathbf{x}_o) - \frac{4}{1+F_{dr}}], & \mathbf{x}_i = \mathbf{x}_o. \end{cases} \tag{10.10}$$

We determine the thickness of each layer by minimizing the objective function in Eq. (10.3) where the volume BSSRDF is computed using the diffusion process above. This can be solved by inverse diffusion optimization, such as in Chap. 7.

Table 10.1 Conjugate gradient based algorithm for minimizing E_h

Set basis materials for each layer using the *volume initialization step*
Set initial thicknesses $\mathbf{h}_0$ using the *volume initialization step*
Set initial search direction: $\mathbf{d}_0 = -\nabla E_h(\mathbf{h}_0)$ and $\mathbf{p}_0 = \mathbf{d}_0$
Repeat following steps until $E_h < \varepsilon$
Compute gradient: $\nabla E_h(\mathbf{h}_t) = \left(\frac{\mathrm{d}E_h}{\mathrm{d}h(\mathbf{x},l)}\right)$
Set $\mathbf{p}_t = -\nabla E_h(\mathbf{h}_t)$
Update search direction: $\mathbf{d}_t = \mathbf{p}_t + \beta \cdot \mathbf{d}_{t-1}$,
$\beta = \max\left(\frac{\mathbf{p}_t^T(\mathbf{p}_t - \mathbf{p}_{t-1})}{\mathbf{p}_{t-1}^T \mathbf{p}_{t-1}}, 0\right)$
Compute λ: Golden section search by $\min_\lambda [E_h(\mathbf{h}_t + \lambda \mathbf{d}_t)]$
Update solution $\mathbf{h}_{t+1} = \mathbf{h}_t + \lambda' \mathbf{d}_t$

Since the basis materials in all layers are determined during initialization, the objective function E_h is a function of only the set of spatially varying layer thicknesses $\mathbf{h} = \{h(\mathbf{x}, l)\}$, where $h(\mathbf{x}, l)$ is the starting depth of layer l at $\mathbf{x}$.

To minimize E_h, we apply the conjugate gradient algorithm, summarized in Table 10.1. We begin by initializing basis materials and layer thicknesses using the homogeneous method. At each step, we determine the gradient ∇E_h of E_h with respect to $\mathbf{h}$. To guarantee that the thickness is larger than the minimal layer thickness defined by the material configuration, we set the gradient to 0 when the thickness reaches the minimal thickness constraint. The search direction is then updated with the Polak-Ribiere method [15]. The optimal step size λ along the search direction is found by a golden section search. We then update $\mathbf{h}$ using the computed gradient ∇E_h and λ. We continue iterating until the layer thickness converges.

The most expensive step of this algorithm is the computation of the E_h gradient relative to the thicknesses $h(\mathbf{x}, l)$. A straightforward method is to perturb each layer boundary at each location, update the material properties in the volume, and compute the resulting change in objective function value. This would require $N_x \times N_y \times N_l$ diffusion simulations, becoming prohibitively expensive. We speed up this procedure by using an adjoint method similar to that in Chap. 7.

We represent the error $E_h(\{\kappa\}, \{\sigma_a\})$ as a function of the material properties κ and σ_a of all voxels in the volume. Since these are in turn defined by the layer thickness (and the basis materials fixed during optimization), we can use the chain rule to derive the gradient of the objective function relative to layer thickness as

$$\frac{\mathrm{d}E_h}{\mathrm{d}h(\mathbf{x}, l)} = \frac{\mathrm{d}E_h}{\mathrm{d}\kappa(\mathbf{x}, z_l - 1)} \frac{\mathrm{d}\kappa(\mathbf{x}, z_l - 1)}{\mathrm{d}h(\mathbf{x}, l)} + \frac{\mathrm{d}E_h}{\mathrm{d}\sigma_a(\mathbf{x}, z_l - 1)} \frac{\mathrm{d}\sigma_a(\mathbf{x}, z_l - 1)}{\mathrm{d}h(\mathbf{x}, l)} \tag{10.11}$$

where $(\mathbf{x}, z_l)$ refers to the first voxel in the l-th layer at $\mathbf{x}$, and $(\mathbf{x}, z_l - 1)$ is the last voxel of the upper $l - 1$ layers. Note that this computation only involves voxels at the layer boundaries because the change of the layer boundary only modifies the material properties in the boundary voxels. We compute $\mathrm{d}E_h/\mathrm{d}\kappa(\mathbf{x}, z_l - 1)$ and $\mathrm{d}E_h/\mathrm{d}\sigma_a(\mathbf{x}, z_l - 1)$ using the adjoint method as done in

Chap. 7, while $\mathrm{d}\kappa(\mathbf{x}, z_l - 1)/\mathrm{d}h(\mathbf{x}, l)$ and $\mathrm{d}\sigma_a(\mathbf{x}, z_l - 1)/\mathrm{d}h(\mathbf{x}, l)$ are directly computed by

$$\begin{aligned} \frac{\mathrm{d}\kappa(\mathbf{x}, z_l - 1)}{\mathrm{d}h(\mathbf{x}, l)} &= \kappa(\mathbf{x}, z_l) - \kappa(\mathbf{x}, z_l - 1), \\ \frac{\mathrm{d}\sigma_a(\mathbf{x}, z_l - 1)}{\mathrm{d}h(\mathbf{x}, l)} &= \sigma_a(\mathbf{x}, z_l) - \sigma_a(\mathbf{x}, z_l - 1). \end{aligned} \tag{10.12}$$

Using this scheme, we only need two diffusion simulations for computing the gradient, which is much more efficient than the straightforward method.

In inverse diffusion optimization, the diffusion simulation is used in both gradient computation and golden search. To solve the diffusion equation on a 3D regular grid of a layered material volume, we discretize the diffusion equation as a set of linear equations over the voxels using the finite difference method (FDM) scheme in [16]. We implemented a multigrid method [15] for solving this sparse linear system on the GPU using CUDA. The adjoint diffusion equation is discretized and computed in the same way.

10.4 Hardware Manufacturing Setup

We fabricate the output volume determined during material mapping using two different hardware solutions: a milling machine and a 3D printer.

The milling machine solution is based on an Atrump M218 CNC machining center. The maximum operating range is 660 mm, 460 mm, and 610 mm in the X, Y and Z directions respectively. The stepper motor resolution is 0.005 mm. The machining center has an automated tool changer with 16 drill bits. The size of drill bits ranges from 6 mm to 0.5 mm. Based on these hardware properties, we set the output volume size to be 130 mm along each dimension, and the voxel size is 1.0 mm × 1.0 mm × 0.1 mm so one pixel of the measured BSSRDF corresponds to one voxel of the output volume. The number of layers in the volume is three and the minimal layer thickness is 1.0 mm.

Given the output volume, we convert each layer into a B-rep and fabricate it with the milling machine. If both sides of a layer are not flat, our system splits it into two or more pieces, each of which has one flat side. For all results shown in this chapter, we only need to split the middle layer into two pieces for manufacturing. Given the B-rep of each layer piece, the machining center mills a basis material block into our desired layer shape. A typical output of the milling machine is shown in Fig. 10.1. After the milling process, we use UV sensitive glass glue to assemble those layers into the final volume and ignore the light refraction between the layer boundaries. The milling time varies with the complexity of the layer surface. For the homogeneous cases, the average total milling time for all three layers is about 30 minutes. For the heterogeneous cases, the total milling time ranges from one hour to six hours.

In our implementation, we use the Mastercam software to execute GCode to control the milling process. We do not optimize the smoothness of the layer thickness of neighboring columns as in [2] because the voxel size along the X and Y directions in our setup is larger than the drill bit diameters. Moreover, our solution is not sensitive to the layer surface orientation. In practice, we found that the milling machine can reproduce well our desired layer shapes without visual artifacts in the final results.

The 3D printer solution is based on an Object Eden250 3D printing system. The net build size is 250 mm $\times$ 250 mm $\times$ 200 mm, and the precision of the resulting volume is 0.1 mm along each dimension. Thus we set the output volume size to be 100 mm $\times$ 100 mm $\times$ 30 mm and 0.1 mm as the voxel size. The minimal layer thickness is 0.1 mm in this setup. Since the printer can control the material distribution in a more flexible way, we set the number of layers to six in the output volume. For this solution, one pixel of the measured BSSRDF corresponds to 10 $\times$ 10 voxels of the fabricated volume. We obtain the BSSRDF for each voxel by upsampling the original BSSRDF.

The printer manufactures objects with a single resin. It prints the 3D shapes with the resin material, while the support substrate automatically fills the vertical gaps between the resins and the vertical gaps between the resin and the build tray. Therefore, we convert the layers consisting of resin materials as B-rep shapes and send them together to the 3D printer. To print the volume with the support material in the top layer, we add an extra thin resin layer on top of the volume for printing and then remove it after printing. Both materials in the output volume are kept. Depending on the complexity of material distribution and output volume size, the printing time varies from 1.5 hours to 3 hours.

For each basis material, we measure the optical properties from a thick homogeneous block of size of 100 mm $\times$ 100 mm $\times$ 64 mm, where the light transport in the volume is well modeled by the dipole approximation. We then shoot red (635 nm), green (532 nm) and blue laser beams (473 nm) at a point on the top surface and capture HDR images of the scattering profiles around the lighting point for each color channel. We then follow the method in [14] to fit the material properties from the captured scattering profiles. Since the basis material blocks are not perfectly homogeneous, we randomly sampled scattering profiles at ten points on the top surface and averaged them to get the final scattering profile for fitting. Figure 10.3 lists the material properties of all basis materials used in our two hardware solutions. All the basis materials we used have a similar refractive index of 1.5. Thus in our implementation we ignore the mismatch of refractive index between layers.

We printed our color texture with a Canon PIXMA iP8500 ink jet printer on a transparent film. To calibrate the color, we printed out a color pattern and captured a photo under uniform back lighting with a calibrated camera. Then we compute the transmission rate of the inks.

10.5 Experimental Results

We implemented our system on an Intel Xeon E5400 machine with an NVidia GeForce 9800GT graphics card. The material mapping algorithm is implemented

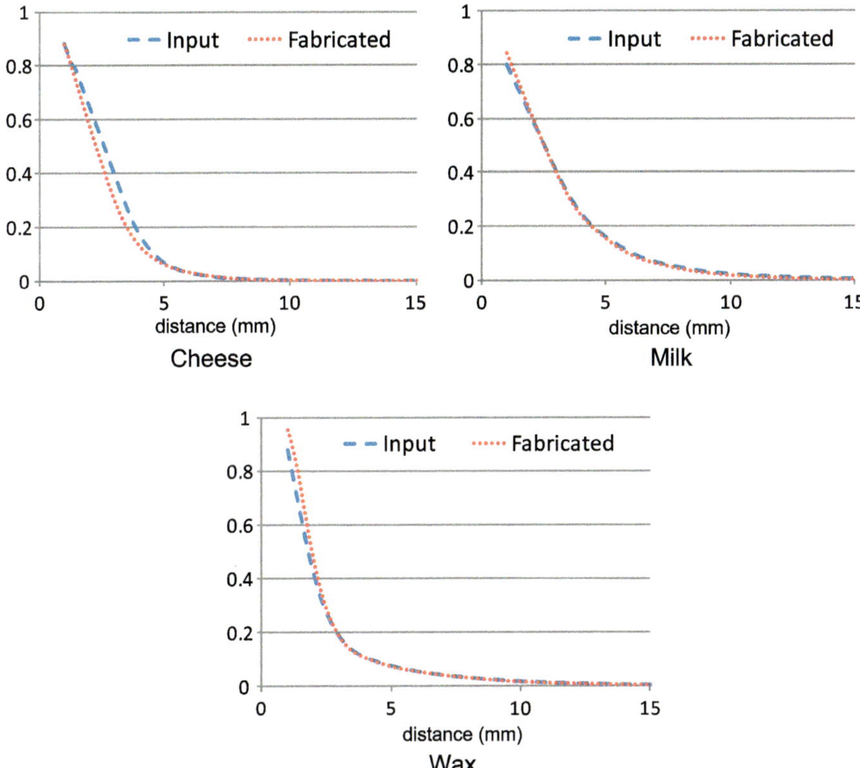

Fig. 10.6 Comparisons of the red channel scattering profiles measured from real homogeneous material samples (in *blue*) and ones measured from the fabricated volumes (in *red*)

in C++ on the CPU, while the diffusion simulation is implemented using CUDA on the GPU. The computation time for solving the volume layout of a homogeneous input BSSRDF is about 10 minutes. For all the heterogeneous BSSRDF results shown, our system takes about 10 minutes for computing the printing gamut and doing volume initialization. Depending on the volume size and the number of layers in the output volume, it then takes 15 to 45 minutes for volume optimization (Table 10.2), in which 80 % of the time is spent for golden section search, 16 % for gradient computation, and 4 % for other computations. The number of conjugate gradient steps in the volume optimization depends on the spatial complexity of the input BSSRDF and varies across samples, ranging from 5 to 50.

We evaluated our method with three homogeneous BSSRDFs measured from real material samples. For this purpose, we chose three materials (cheese, milk and wax) with various degrees of translucency and simulated their homogeneous BSSRDFs with layered volumes fabricated by the milling machine. One pixel of the measured BSSRDF corresponds to 1 mm of the actual size, thus the fabricated sample has a 1 : 1 scale with the real sample. No surface textures are applied to the resulting

Table 10.2 Computation times for all the heterogeneous BSSRDF results

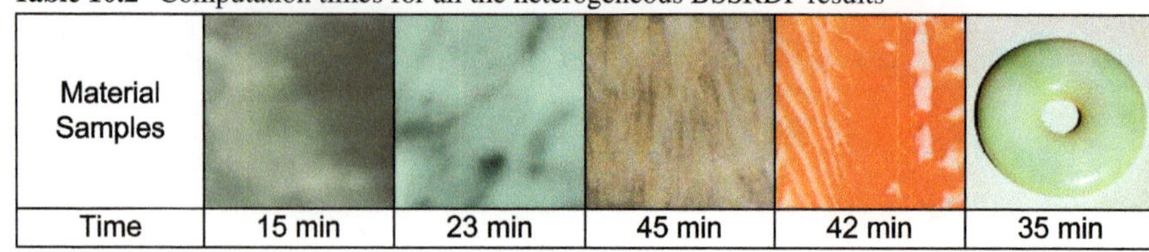

Material Samples					
Time	15 min	23 min	45 min	42 min	35 min

Fig. 10.7 Comparison of scattering effects of real material samples and fabricated volumes under circular lighting

volumes. Figure 10.7 illustrates the scattering effects of real homogeneous material samples and the fabricated material volumes under circular lighting. We measure the BSSRDF from the fabricated volume and compute its relative error by Eq. (10.5). Figure 10.6 compares the scattering profiles measured from real samples to the ones measured from the fabricated results. With three basis material slabs, the fabricated volumes faithfully reproduce the homogeneous BSSRDFs with different scattering ranges.

We also tested our method on three measured BSSRDFs with different kinds of heterogeneity. Figure 10.8 shows the rendering results of the input heterogeneous BSSRDFs with images of our output volumes under different lightings. The two marble data sets are from [8], and the jade data set is from [4]. We used the milling machine to fabricate the layered volumes for approximating the two marble data sets and used the 3D printer for generating the volume for simulating the jade BSSRDF. Surface textures are used for modulating the BSSRDFs of all three volumes. We ignored the physical size of the original sample and followed the pixel to voxel correspondence to determine the output scale (e.g. for the milling machine solution, one pixel of the measured BSSRDF corresponds to one voxel, and for the 3D printer solution, one pixel of the measured BSSRDF corresponds to 10×10 voxels of the fabricated volume). We calibrated the projector and camera used in our capturing setup and used the same lighting for rendering. As shown in Fig. 10.8, our method effectively simulates the heterogeneous scattering effects of different materials. We scanned the volume with a linear light projection and computed the relative errors by $E_r = \sum_i (I_i - I_i')^2 / \sum_i (I_i)^2$, where I_i' is the im-

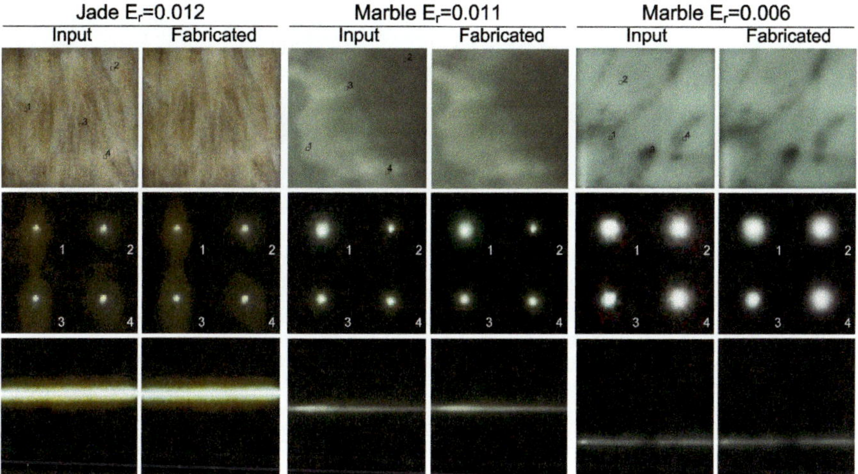

Fig. 10.8 Comparison of the rendering results of input heterogeneous BSSRDFs and the photographs of fabricated volumes under different lightings

Fig. 10.9 Fabricated salmon with BSSRDF measured from a real salmon slice. (**a**) Photograph of real salmon slice under diffuse lighting. The BSSRDF measured in the blue box is used as input to our system. (**b**) Photograph of the fabricated volume under diffuse lighting. (**c**) Rendering results of the input BSSRDF under linear light projection. (**d**) Photograph of fabricated volume taken under the same line lighting

age captured from the fabricated volume, while I is the rendering result of the input BSSRDF.

Figure 10.9 shows a fabricated material volume for simulating the heterogeneous BSSRDF of a real salmon slice. We followed the method in [8] to capture the BSSRDF from a real salmon slice (i.e. the blue box in Fig. 10.9(a)) and then used the measured BSSRDF as input to our system. We printed the output volume using the 3D printer and applied a color texture on its top surface. The size of the output volume is scaled to 100 mm $\times$ 100 mm $\times$ 12 mm, while the size of the actual salmon slice is 60 mm $\times$ 60 mm. As shown in Fig. 10.9(c), the sharp variations of scattering effects caused by different tissues are well captured by our fabricated volume. Combined with surface texture, the resulting volume generates convincing scattering effects under different lighting.

Using our method, the user can also fabricate arbitrary objects with convincing translucent appearance. To this end, our system first generates the layered ma-

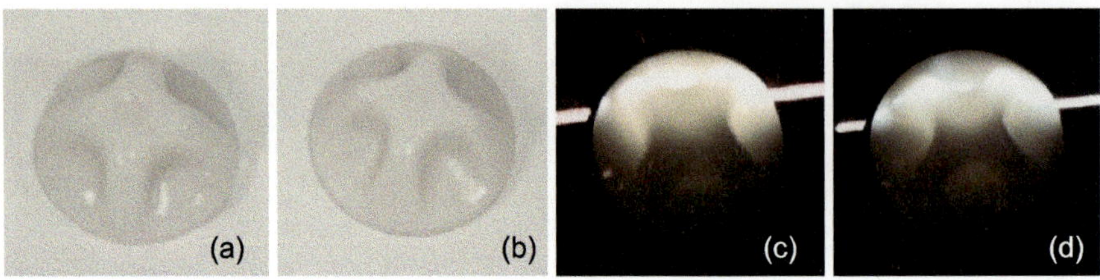

Fig. 10.10 Fabricated jelly. (**a**) A real piece of jelly, the homogeneous BSSRDF of which is used as input to our system. (**b**) A fabricated piece of jelly generated by 3D printer. (**c**) Photograph of the real piece of jelly under linear light projection. (**d**) Photograph of the piece of fabricated jelly under the same line lighting. The real jelly and the fabricated one have the same size of 50 mm × 50 mm × 27 mm

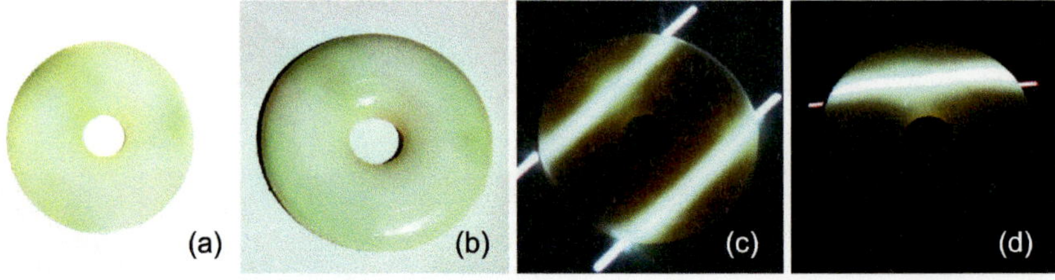

Fig. 10.11 Fabricated disk with designed jade-like subsurface scattering. (**a**) The input BSSRDF rendered with diffuse light. (**b**) Photograph of the fabricated disk under diffuse light. (**c, d**) Appearance of the fabricated disk captured under different illuminations. The object size is 82 mm × 82 mm × 9 mm

terial volume from the input BSSRDF and then maps the layered material volume to a 3D object volume via shell mapping [17]. After that, we print the 3D object volume via the 3D printer. Figure 10.10 displays a fabricated jelly piece with translucent appearance captured from a real piece of jelly. Figure 10.11 shows a fabricated disk with a jade BSSRDF designed by an artist. Under different lightings, the fabricated objects exhibit compelling subsurface scattering effects.

Since our method only focuses on diffuse BSSRDFs, it cannot well model subsurface scattering of very translucent materials. Surface reflectance as well as single scattering are also ignored in our approach. Moreover, due to the small number of basis materials used in our method, our method will fail to reproduce BSSRDFs with rich chromatic variations that are out of the color gamut. The surface texture used in our method alleviates this limitation but cannot totally compensate for it. Limited by the thickness of the output volume, our method cannot be applied for 3D objects with sharp geometric features.

10.6 Conclusion

In this chapter, we presented a complete and efficient solution for modeling and fabricating desired spatially varying subsurface scattering effects with a limited number of basis materials. In our system, the input BSSRDF is represented by a layered volume of basis materials, which can be separated into homogeneous components and easily manufactured by existing hardware. A material mapping algorithm is proposed for efficiently computing an optimal layered volume for an input BSSRDF. A surface texture is used to further enhance the color of the BSSRDF of the output volume. Experimental results show that our system can well reproduce a wide range of heterogeneous subsurface scattering effects.

References

1. Matusik, W., Ajdin, B., Gu, J., Lawrence, J., Lensch, H.P.A., Pellacini, F., Rusinkiewicz, S.: Printing spatially-varying reflectance. ACM Trans. Graph. **28**(3), 128 (2009)
2. Weyrich, T., Peers, P., Matusik, W., Rusinkiewicz, S.: Fabricating microgeometry for custom surface reflectance. ACM Trans. Graph. **28**(3), 1 (2009)
3. Hašan, M., Fuchs, M., Matusik, W., Pfister, H., Rusinkiewicz, S.M.: Physical reproduction of materials with specified subsurface scattering. ACM Trans. Graph. **29**(3) (2010)
4. Song, Y., Tong, X., Pellacini, F., Peers, P.: SubEdit: a representation for editing measured heterogeneous subsurface scattering. ACM Trans. Graph. **28**(3), 31 (2009)
5. Baumgart, B.G.: Winged edge polyhedron representation. Technical report, Stanford, CA, USA (1972)
6. Vilbrandt, T., Malone, E.H.L., Pasko, A.: Universal desktop fabrication. In: Heterogeneous Objects Modelling and Applications, pp. 259–284 (2008)
7. Goesele, M., Lensch, H.P.A., Lang, J., Fuchs, C., Seidel, H.-P.: DISCO: acquisition of translucent objects. ACM Trans. Graph. **23**(3), 835–844 (2004)
8. Peers, P., vom Berge, K., Matusik, W., Ramamoorthi, R., Lawrence, J., Rusinkiewicz, S., Dutré, P.: A compact factored representation of heterogeneous subsurface scattering. ACM Trans. Graph. **25**(3), 746–753 (2006)
9. Wang, J., Zhao, S., Tong, X., Lin, S., Lin, Z., Dong, Y., Guo, B., Shum, H.-Y.: Modeling and rendering of heterogeneous translucent materials using the diffusion equation. ACM Trans. Graph. **27**, 9 (2008)
10. Donner, C., Jensen, H.W.: Light diffusion in multi-layered translucent materials. ACM Trans. Graph. **24**(3), 1032–1039 (2005)
11. Mount, D., Arya, S.: Ann: A library for approximate nearest neighbor searching. In: 2nd CGC Workshop on Computational Geometry (1997)
12. Ishimaru, A.: Wave Propagation and Scattering in Random Media. IEEE Press Series on Electromagnetic Wave Theory (1999)
13. Arbree, A.: Scalable and heterogeneous rendering of subsurface scattering materials. PhD thesis, Cornell University, Ithaca, New York (2009). http://hdl.handle.net/1813/13986
14. Jensen, H.W., Marschner, S.R., Levoy, M., Hanrahan, P.: A practical model for subsurface light transport. In: SIGGRAPH, pp. 511–518 (2001)
15. Press, W.H., et al.: Numerical Recipes in C, 2nd edn. (1992)
16. Stam, J.: Multiple scattering as a diffusion process. In: Eur. Rendering Workshop, June 1995, pp. 41–50 (1995)
17. Porumbescu, S.D., Budge, B., Feng, L., Joy, K.I.: Shell maps. ACM Trans. Graph. **24**(3), 626–633 (2005)

Chapter 11
Conclusion

People have long pursued techniques for creating highly realistic visual content, initially in artistic forms such as paintings and sculptures, and more recently in modern media such as photography and advanced computer graphics. The commercial impact of realistic computer graphics has taken off in the past several years, as high definition rendering results and special effects have became a major selling point in many box office hits such as The Matrix, Transformers and Avatar. To support such magnificent effects, an important pillar is accurate reproduction of material appearance. Complex physical factors and countless details contribute to how a material appears, and every detail counts in generating a high quality reproduction. Throughout this book, numerous high quality appearance examples are exhibited, with the many detailed and subtle variations playing a pivotal role in imparting a realistic look. However, achieving a high level of quality is a challenging task, since extensive appearance data has generally been needed for modeling those details. This has made efficient appearance modeling a critical issue in the field of computer graphics.

Easy and efficient appearance modeling techniques can not only benefit professional graphics studios, but also be used by amateur artists who cannot afford expensive dedicated appearance acquisition devices. The techniques presented in this book require only off-the-shelf consumer electronics such as DSLR cameras and DLP projectors, and the interactive modeling method in Chap. 4 does not need an acquisition device at all, as appealing results can be generated just from images found on the Internet. We believe that with these advanced techniques, computer graphics appearance modeling will become accessible to a much wider audience, and allow more users to enjoy creating high quality appearance content.

Beyond classical appearance modeling tasks such as acquisition, interactive modeling and editing, the recent direction of appearance fabrication brings new applications and even more fun to appearance modeling. Unlike the past where people could only appreciate the beautiful materials they modeled in a virtual environment, now with appearance fabrication techniques we can reproduce these creations in the real world.

To realize these aims, this book developed several techniques based on the fundamental observation that coherence is an inherent property in the appearance of most

Y. Dong et al., *Material Appearance Modeling: A Data-Coherent Approach*,
DOI 10.1007/978-3-642-35777-0_11, © Springer-Verlag Berlin Heidelberg 2013

materials in our daily lives. Through close examination of material appearance—observing patterns, redundancies and subtle relationships—the various ways that materials are coherent emerged. The main challenges in appearance acquisition and modeling are caused by complex details which cannot be represented by simple formulas, and the solution advanced in this book is to explore and take advantage of the coherency that exists. With this approach, we account for the relationships among such details to simplify the modeling process, with compact appearance representations and efficient solutions for acquiring them. The techniques derived in this coherency-based framework span appearance acquisition, interactive modeling and fabrication. This underlying idea and the proposed techniques are applicable to both opaque surfaces with complex reflectance properties and translucent objects with subsurface scattering effects. The major technical contributions are reviewed in the following.

Acquisition and Modeling of Opaque Surfaces An efficient SVBRDF capturing system, called manifold bootstrapping, was introduced in Chap. 3. Based on the idea that reflectance over a given material sample forms a low-dimensional manifold, it reconstructs this manifold by decomposing reflectance measurement into two phases. The first measures reflectance at a high angular resolution, but only for sparse samples over the surface, while the second acquires low angular resolution samples densely over the surface. With this data, obtained with a novel and simple capturing scheme, high resolution SVBRDFs are acquired efficiently with relatively few measurements.

An interactive material modeling pipeline, called AppGen, that creates high quality spatially-varying reflectance from a single image was presented in Chap. 4. Given just a single image of a surface, AppGen recovers its SVBRDF with the help of simple user annotations that indicate global reflectance and shading information. This data is propagated over the surface in a manner guided by observed coherence in the material, and together with further image analysis the image is decomposed into different appearance components and fine scale geometry, from which the SVBRDF is constructed. With just minutes of interaction, convincing results are generated. A large variety of materials have successfully been generated from images with different reflectance and normal variations in this way.

Modeling and Rendering of Subsurface Light Transport A non-linear coherence-based framework for analysis and capture of subsurface light transport was presented in Chap. 6. The non-linear coherence of light transport is exploited to reconstruct the subsurface scattering of light within an object from a relatively small number of images. These images are captured using an adaptive scheme that minimizes the number needed for reconstruction. With this technique, the appearance of an object can be regenerated under a variety of lighting conditions different from those recorded in the images.

A diffusion model for translucent material acquisition and editing was described in Chap. 7. With a volume based representation, this model allows for capturing, editing and rendering of translucent materials with heterogeneous optical properties. With the diffusion equation and a volumetric model, our method solves for the most coherent material volume whose appearance is consistent with a sparse number of image observations. The use of material coherency significantly simplifies the acquisition of optical properties in a real material sample. The captured volumetric model can be easily edited and rendered in real time on the GPU, with accurate reproduction under novel lighting conditions and viewpoints.

An efficient solid texture synthesis system for modeling texture-like translucent material volumes was introduced in Chap. 8. Based on the coherence of textures in three dimensions, a high-resolution translucent material volume is efficiently generated from small 2D slices. The efficiency of this approach greatly facilitates modeling of translucent materials, allowing for interactive texture design and real-time synthesis when cutting or breaking translucent objects.

Material Fabrication A complete solution based on the diffusion model for fabricating spatially-varying subsurface scattering was presented in Chap. 10. Given the optical properties of material elements used in a 3D printing system, a volumetric arrangement of these elements that reproduces the appearance of a given translucent material is solved. By accounting for the coherence among the scattering profiles within the given material, this technique fabricates accurate results both efficiently and stably.

11.1 Future Work

This book focused on coherency properties in material appearance, which commonly exist in some form. A related approach may be to account for sparsity properties of the appearance data. An example of this is the recent work on compressive light transport sensing [1], which incorporates a sparsity-based algorithm into light transport modeling. Similar techniques could potentially be applied for modeling high resolution SVBRDFs and BSSRDFs. Moreover, coherency-based methods and sparsity-based approaches both have their inherent advantages and drawbacks, and how to combine them into a theoretically common framework would be an important direction for future work, one that could yield significant improvements in modeling efficiency.

In appearance modeling, an important topic for future work is device development for capturing material appearance. While our methods aim to use easy-to-build hardware constructed mostly from off-the-shelf consumer electronics, another direction is to develop easy-to-use gadgets designed with special components to further accelerate or simplify the appearance acquisition process. For example, based on the manifold bootstrapping idea, Ren et al. [2] designed a novel BRDF chart containing a carefully selected BRDF basis, which combined with a hand-held linear light source allows reflectance capture to be easily performed using a mobile phone camera. With portable and easy-to-use devices, the appearance modeling process can become more practical for ordinary users, enabling them to use self-measured appearance data in applications such as gaming with an environment or object they created.

Appearance analysis often requires a tremendous amount of data that is impractical to acquire when the measurement process is tedious and cumbersome. The efficient systems proposed in this book can greatly reduce the cost of obtaining high quality appearance data sets, and can potentially facilitate future work in data-driven appearance analysis. One direction is to explore the structure of the appearance space to possibly uncover coherence and other relationships among different materials, rather than only within a single specific sample as done in this book. An in-depth study of appearance space structure may lead to further technical advances in appearance capture, editing, and rendering.

Advanced computer graphics is having an impact commercially and in our daily lives like never before. This is reflected by a multitude of compelling applications such as creating digital avatars of ourselves with the Microsoft Kinect camera, and 3D visual displays supported by stereo rendering. We believe that with advances in appearance modeling, the time that anyone can digitize anything they want with accurate geometry and appearance information is coming soon, and the technologies introduced in this book will be an important step towards realizing this goal.

References

1. Peers, P., Mahajan, D.K., Lamond, B., Ghosh, A., Matusik, W., Ramamoorthi, R., Debevec, P.: Compressive light transport sensing. ACM Trans. Graph. **28**(1), 3–1318 (2009)
2. Ren, P., Wang, J., Snyder, J., Tong, X., Guo, B.: Pocket reflectometry. In: ACM SIGGRAPH 2011 Papers, SIGGRAPH '11, p. 45. ACM, New York (2011)

ERRATUM

Erratum

Erratum to: Y. Dong et al., ***Material Appearance Modeling: A Data-Coherent Approach,***
DOI 10.1007/978-3-642-35777-0,
© Springer-Verlag Berlin Heidelberg 2013

The acknowledgement was missing in the original text.

We would like to thank colleagues and collaborators who have worked with us on data-driven appearance modeling, including Xin Tong, Jiaping Wang, Fabio Pellacini, Sylvain Lefebvre, George Drettakis, John Snyder, Moshe Ben-Ezra, Zhouchen Lin, Shuang Zhao and Yanxiang Lan.

During the course of this research, both Yue Dong and Baining Guo were affiliated with the Institute for Advanced Study at Tsinghua University (IASTU). Yue Dong was a PhD student under the supervision of Prof. Heung-Yeung Shum, whereas Baining Guo was an adjunct professor. Yue Dong would like to thank Prof. Shum for his guidance and encouragement. Yue Dong also thanks Dr. Xin Tong for research guidance and mentoring during his internship at Microsoft Research. This work was made possible by the wonderful academic environment in IASTU, and the authors highly appreciate the guidance and unwavering support from Prof. Hwa-Tung Nieh, Prof. NianLe Wu, Prof. Zhan Xu, Prof. Binling Gu, and Prof. Zhengyu Weng.

Finally, we wish to thank our book editors, Lanlan Chang and Jane Li at Springer, for their kind guidance throughout the course of publication. Their friendly support and helpful suggestions made this challenging process smooth and enjoyable.

The online version of the original chapter can be found at doi: 10.1007/978-3-642-35777-0.

DOI 10.1007/978-3-642-35777-0_12,

The affiliations in the copyright page are incomplete. Yue Dong and Baining Guo have joint affiliations with Microsoft Research Asia (MSRA) and Institute for Advanced Study, Tsinghua University (IASTU). The copyright of this book is shared by both MSRA and IASTU.